TABLE OF CONTENTS

DLC CASES & COLLECTIBLES

Go to bradygames.com or
rockstargames.com to download
our free e-guide to the
DLC Cases & Collectibles.

BASICS

MOVEMENT
ON FOOT

ACTION(S)	XBOX 360	PS3
MOVEMENT/MANIPULATE CLUE	LEFT STICK	LEFT STICK
ROTATE CAMERA	RIGHT STICK	RIGHT STICK
ENTER-EXIT VEHICLE/PARTNER DRIVES (HOLD)	Y	△
LEAVE CLUES ANALYSIS/RELOAD	B	○
INTERACT/INVESTIGATE CLUE	A	✗
TALK/INTERROGATE/ASK PARTNER FOR HELP	X	□
ENTER-EXIT COVER	RIGHT BUMPER	R1
RUN/SHOOT (WITH WEAPON DRAWN)	RIGHT TRIGGER	R2
LOOK BEHIND	RIGHT SICK BUTTON	R3
DISCARD FOUND WEAPON	LEFT BUMPER	L1
AIM WEAPON	LEFT TRIGGER	L2
BRING UP NOTEBOOK/EXIT NOTEBOOK	BACK	SELECT
NAVIGATE NOTEBOOK OPTIONS	D-PAD	DIR. BUTTONS
CALL PARTNER	D-PAD RIGHT	RIGHT
ZOOM OUT MINI-MAP	D-PAD DOWN	DOWN
PAUSE GAME	START	START

SPRINTING

All directional movement is performed by using the Left Control Stick. You can run away from crime scenes. Sprinting is also possible when on foot during chase sequences. At these times, tap the "Tackle" button—this only works when "Tackle" is displayed onscreen, once you get close to the suspect.

CLAMBERING

Leap over small fences and clamber over taller ones. You can scale pipes, ladders, and get over just about any object that's waist-high. Here's the beauty of it: There are no extra buttons to press! Just tilt the Left Control Stick where you want to go and Cole takes care of the rest. Climbing multiple levels of fire escapes has never been easier.

ROCKSTAR GAMES PRESENTS

L.A. NOIRE

DRIVING

ACTION(S)	XBOX	PS3
STEERING	LEFT STICK	LEFT STICK
ROTATE CAMERA	RIGHT STICK	RIGHT STICK
CHANGE CAMERA	D-PAD UP	D-PAD UP
RESPOND TO DISPATCH CALL	Ⓐ	✖
HANDBRAKE	RIGHT BUMPER	R1
ACCELERATE	RIGHT TRIGGER	R2
LOOK BEHIND	RIGHT STICK BUTTON	R3
BRAKE	LEFT TRIGGER	L2
SIREN/HORN	LEFT STICK BUTTON	L3

Using the Siren

To reduce the amount of damage to your vehicle, injuries to policemen or civilians, and city damage, use your siren when driving quickly through the city. You will notice traffic pulling out of your way and intersection traffic stopping to allow clear passage.

Partner Drive-bys

You cannot shoot out the window of your vehicle, but your partner can. To improve his aim, drive as closely to the side of the suspect's vehicle so your partner can easily aim out the window and shoot either driver's side tire. After hitting both tires, the suspect usually wrecks.

FIGHTING

ACTION(S)	XBOX 360	PS3
PUNCH	Ⓐ	✖
DODGE/HOLD TO BLOCK	Ⓧ	◻
GRAPPLE MOVES	Ⓨ	△
LOCK ONTO TARGET	LEFT TRIGGER	L2
FINISHING MOVE	Ⓑ	◯

HEALTH

As you take damage from fists, bullets, or fire, the color in the game begins to fade to black and white. The more color that's drained, the closer you are to death. To reverse these effects, escape the danger and wait until color returns before putting yourself in harm's way again.

WEAPONS

There are a total of nine useable weapons in LA Noire. You are automatically given a service gun with unlimited ammo. Other weapons can be found during a gun battle or in the trunks of police cars during raids and other skirmishes.

SHOOTING & WARNING SHOTS

Weapons can be fired only during gun battles. Otherwise, Cole keeps them holstered. You are occasionally presented with the option of using warning shots on some fleeing suspects. This occurs only if they have not yet fired on you. As soon as the suspect fires their weapon, warning shots are a thing of the past.

COLT 45
Your service weapon. It has unlimited ammo.

COLT 38
Available in "Armed and Dangerous." You must drop your shotgun to use it.

ITHACA FULL STOCK SHOTGUN
Given to you automatically during "Armed and Dangerous." This shotgun is available (alongside the drummed Thompson) in police vehicle trunks that carry weapons.

M1 GARAND RIFLE
This .30 caliber rifle was standard issue for the US Armed Forces from 1936 to 1957.

M1 THOMPSON
A more common weapon that can be found during several cases, including Street Crime missions like "The Fallen Idol."

CHICAGO PIANO
Get this weapon as free DLC on May 31. Check your favorite platform store for availability. Once you have this, you can find the Chicago Piano in the trunk of any police vehicle that yields weapons.

BROWNING AUTOMATIC RIFLE
Claim the BAR in "Manifest Destiny," "A Polite Invitation," and "A Different Kind of War." This powerful, long-range, assault rifle packs an enormous punch per round.

FN BROWNING
Jack Kelso's default pistol; used in "A Polite Invitation." It's his default weapon, so it has unlimited ammo.

FLAMETHROWER
Find this in a weapons cache in the sewer tunnels during "A Different Kind Of War."

DETECTIVE WORK

Attention to detail is mandatory to climb the ranks of the police department. This includes being thorough at crime scene investigations, observantly collecting clues and statements, and most importantly, being sharp and firm during interrogations.

CRIME SCENE

You must thoroughly search crime scenes to find all the clues that can undeniably solve the case. The important ones enter your notebook automatically. You can review these clues at any time by accessing the notebook. If you're ever confused about what to do next, ask your partner for a tip by pressing ⬛ (PS3) or ✖ (Xbox 360). He may suggest where to go next or even tell you to find a phone to call R&I. Of course, you can also read this guide whenever you need a nudge in the right direction.

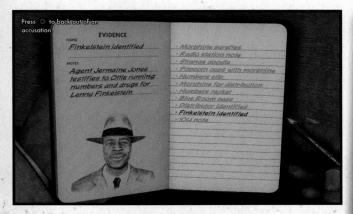

COLLECTING EVIDENCE

A distinctive melody plays while investigating the crime scene. When that music stops, you've either walked away from the relevant zone or you have found all the clues.

If the music stops abruptly, then you've wandered off the crime scene, maybe unwittingly. If the music ends with a crescendo and chiming, then you've found all the clues.

To find clues, thoroughly explore the entire crime scene and stop near anything that produces a chime from the soundtrack or a vibration from the controller. Press the Investigate button to pick up the possible clue.

EXAMINING OBJECTS

Manipulate the lifted object in Phelps' hand by moving the Left Stick. Look for writing or other marks to determine if it's important to the case. If so, the controller may vibrate for even closer examination. Hone in on the vibration to make it strong enough to trigger a new spot of interest.

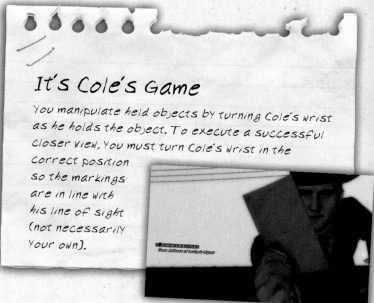

It's Cole's Game

You manipulate held objects by turning Cole's wrist as he holds the object. To execute a successful closer view, you must turn Cole's wrist in the correct position so the markings are in line with his line of sight (not necessarily your own).

This often triggers a zoomed view or prompts you to perform another number of actions, like flip a page or lift a secret compartment. When you find something interesting by fingering through book pages, confirm the point position to unlock even more clues from text or illustrations.

THE NOTEBOOK

The notebook is automatically updated with Person(s) of Interest (P.O.I.), Clues, and Locations instantly as they are discovered. Some clues are given automatically at the beginning of a case after your commander explains the case to you. The notebook also keeps track of the commander's case objectives and contains the questions to ask suspects during interrogations.

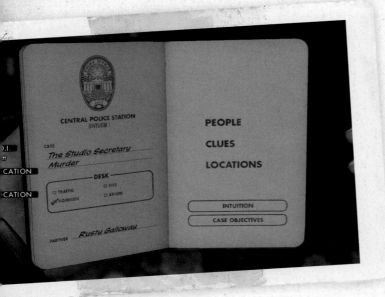

QUESTION ORDER
The order in which the questions line up in your notebook is often determined by when you discovered the clues linked to those questions. So your question sequence may not exactly match the lists featured in this guide.

PEOPLE

A Person of Interest (P.O.I.) is usually any name learned during the course of an investigation. They're all new people to you. Everyone is suspect. As you learn more information about a P.O.I., the notebook automatically updates their file.

CLUES

Clues become evidence when entered into the notebook, but not all clues make it in there—only those pertinent to the case get inked. Sometimes you uncover more information and a clue is simply updated. This evidence is essential when accusing someone of lying during an interrogation.

LOCATIONS

Locations are added when one of these events occurs: crime happens, you discover actual addresses, suspect names another establishment or residence. Once these locations are written in your notebook, you can select them to set a destination. This allows you to follow a flag blip on your mini-map to that location. You can also take advantage of trip skips by letting your partner drive.

Some locations may have a "?" behind them. You cannot select these locations as destinations. You must first find the address. Getting on the nearest phone or gamewell and calling R&I usually solves this problem.

Waypoint

You can place a waypoint (small gray circle) at any location on the map. A directional blip will then appear on the mini-map to guide you there. You can also trip skip to waypoints. This is how we suggest using our maps to quickly find hidden goodies.

INTERROGATION

ACTION(S)	XBOX	PS3
TRUTH	Ⓐ	✕
DOUBT	Ⓧ	⬜
LIE	Ⓨ	△
VIEW NOTEBOOK	BACK	SELECT
USE INTUITION POINT	LEFT BUMPER	L1

Your notebook opens automatically at the beginning of an interrogation and reveals the questions that arise from the clues you've discovered. You can ask the questions in any sequence; there's no "correct" order.

TRUTH, DOUBT, LIE

After the suspect answers a question, it's up to you to read facial expressions, body movements, and ticks, as well as listen to the tone of the suspect's voice, to decide if he or she is telling the "Truth" or if you "Doubt" it. Answering Truth and Doubt correctly usually leads to the witness sharing a little more information somewhat cooperatively.

If you think the suspect is not being truthful and you actually have evidence to back it up, select "Lie." After the accusation, the suspect will somehow challenge you to prove it. Do this by selecting the correct evidence from your notebook. If you cannot prove your accusation with evidence, you lose your control of the conversation and will not get a positive response that could lead to another clue.

Backing Out of Questions

You can always back out of a situation when you called someone a liar, but haven't yet selected bad evidence. Do this by simply asking another question. Just press ◉ (PS3) or Ⓑ (Xbox 360).

INTUITION & RANK

"Intuition" is a selectable option in your notebook. Selecting this takes you to the Rank page. As you progress through the game, you earn experience for performing certain tasks like collecting Film Reels, acing interrogations, or discovering Landmarks. All these things give you varying amounts of experience, which in turn contributes to Rank.

There are a maximum of 20 Ranks. Each level is achieved by filling the Rank gauge with the requisite amount of experience points. Reaching key Rank stages unlocks Outfits and Hidden Vehicle locations on the map. You also earn one Intuition point each time you increase your Rank.

USING INTUITION

You can hold up to five Intuition points during a case. One point can be used for these purposes: "Remove An Answer" during an interrogation, "Show All Clues" when on the crime scene, or "Ask The Community" to view the answers in order of popularity. On the next page, we provide details on each of these options.

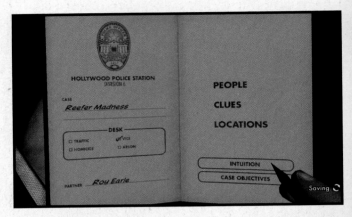
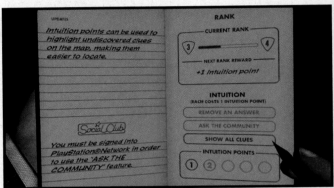

EXPERIENCE EARNINGS

TASK AWARDED	EXPERIENCE AWARDED
ANSWER ONE QUESTION CORRECTLY	5
ACQUIRE A SINGLE FILM REEL	5
DISCOVER A LANDMARK	5
COMPLETE A STREET CRIME CASE	15
COLLECT A DLC HIDDEN SHIELD	5

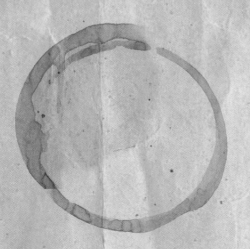

RANK AWARDS

RANK	REQ. XP	ACCUM. XP	UNLOCKS
1	STARTING RANK	N/A	–
2	15	N/A	–
3	20	(35)	SWORD OF JUSTICE OUTFIT
4	25	(60)	–
5	30	(90)	5 HIDDEN VEHICLES REVEALED
6	35	(125)	–
7	40	(165)	–
8	45	(210)	SUNSET STRIP OUTFIT
9	50	(260)	–
10	55	(315)	5 HIDDEN VEHICLES REVEALED
11	60	(375)	–
12	65	(440)	–
13	70	(510)	THE OUTSIDER OUTFIT
14	75	(585)	–
15	80	(665)	5 HIDDEN VEHICLES REVEALED
16	85	(750)	–
17	90	(940)	–
18	95	(1035)	HAWKSHAW OUTFIT
19	100	(1135)	–
20	105	(1140)	–

REMOVE AN ANSWER

One Intuition point can be used to "Remove An Answer" during an interrogation with a suspect. You have three answer choices: Lie, Doubt, or Truth. Taking away one of these improves your odds of choosing correctly.

ASK THE COMMUNITY

You can also use a point to "Ask The Community," which allows you to view the answers in order of popularity as chosen by those players logged into the Rockstar Social Club. You don't need to be logged in or even registered with Social Club to view these stats, but you must be signed into PlayStation Network or Xbox Live.

SHOW ALL CLUES

While at the crime scene, you can open the notebook and choose this option to reveal the remaining clues at the scene, indicated by magnifying glass icons on the mini-map. Note that some of them may not necessarily be key clues that end up in your notebook.

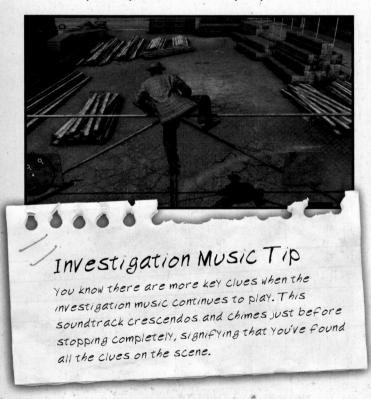

Investigation Music Tip

You know there are more key clues when the investigation music continues to play. This soundtrack crescendos and chimes just before stopping completely, signifying that you've found all the clues on the scene.

THE CASE REPORT

At the end of a case, you receive a Case Report that provides an overall grade (one to five stars) of your accomplishment. This score is determined by the number of clues you found, questions you got correct, and your conduct during the case.

CLUES FOUND & QUESTIONS CORRECT

Finding all the clues and answering all the interrogation questions correctly is the best way to achieve a good score at the end of a case. However, performing badly in the Conduct category could hurt all the flawless sleuthing you've done.

CONDUCT

Damaging your vehicle, wrecking city and civilian property, and running over pedestrians or police officers are damages that negatively reflect on your final case score. There are three categories of conduct tallied on the final score screen, they are: **Vehicle Damage, Injuries,** and **City Damage**. The higher the dollar amount in these categories, the more likely your final score will be negatively affected.

VEHICLE SHOWROOM

There are 95 total vehicles in LA Noire, 15 of these are rare hidden vehicles, which we cover in another section of the guide. However, once you have located a hidden vehicle, it does appear in the Showroom under the **Bonus** category.

All vehicles are locked in the Showroom from the beginning of the game. To unlock a vehicle, simply enter the vehicle during gameplay and start the engine. We suggest jumping into new vehicles at all of your destinations while working through the story. Look around for nearby parking lots when you stop at a crime scene or a suspect's home or workplace. If you do this devotedly throughout the story, you should only have a handful of vehicles left to unlock.

For those vehicles that are difficult to find, check out the "location" field in the vehicle stats in this chapter. If you see one of these elusive rides driving down the road, chase it down and use your authority to commandeer that vehicle. Good luck on your vehicle hunt!

```
100% COMPLETION
There are a total of 95 vehicles in the game. The 15 hidden bonus vehicles
are part of this total. Collecting all 95 vehicles adds 15% toward 100%
completion of the game.
```

2-DOOR (25)

BUICK COUPE

Showroom Number	2/25
Year	1941
Power	125 HP
Top Speed	95 MPH

LOCATION: DOWNTOWN, CENTRAL. Found in the parking lot directly adjacent to Eagleson's Gun Store in "Buyer Beware." You can also find it in the Hall of Records parking lot during "A Polite Invitation." It's the presented escape vehicle in "House of Sticks," as well.

BUICK BUSINESS COUPE

Showroom Number	1/25
Year	1936
Power	93 HP
Top Speed	86 MPH

LOCATION: WESTLAKE. You can find one of these parked in the parking lot to the east of the bloodstained door in "Upon Reflection."

BUICK EIGHT CONVERTIBLE

Showroom Number	3/25
Year	1939
Power	141 HP
Top Speed	105 MPH

LOCATION: WILSHIRE. You can find one parked to the right of the Central Gun Shop visited during "Upon Reflection," or in "A Polite Invitation" next to Kelso's Apartment in Hollywood on De Longpre Ave. There's another one in a parking lot across from the shootout alley where you also find the newspaper in "Manifest Destiny."

BUICK EIGHT COUPE

Showroom Number	4/25
Year	1939
Power	141 HP
Top Speed	105 MPH

LOCATION: DOWNTOWN, CENTRAL. Look for one parked in the motel parking lot where you find Film Reel #4.

CHRYSLER TOWN AND COUNTRY

Showroom Number	8/25
Year	1946
Power	135 HP
Top Speed	110 MPH

LOCATION: DOWNTOWN, HOLLYWOOD. You can also find one in Kelso's Apartment parking lot during "A Polite Invitation."

BUICK 2DR SEDANETTE

Showroom Number	5/25
Year	1947
Power	110 HP
Top Speed	100 MPH

LOCATION: WILSHIRE. Find one of these parked beside the corner apartment with green trim, cattycorner and southeast from the Sawyer House Fire.

CORD HARDTOP

Showroom Number	9/25
Year	1936
Power	115 HP
Top Speed	92 MPH

LOCATION: HOLLYWOOD. Outside the Hollywood Police Station at the beginning of "The Naked City."

CHEVROLET FLEETMASTER 2DR

Showroom Number	6/25
Year	1947
Power	90 HP
Top Speed	86 MPH

LOCATION: DOWNTOWN, CENTRAL. Also found in a fenced parking lot west and across the street from Cavanagh's Bar in "The Driver's Seat."

BUICK CUSTOM

Showroom Number	10/25
Year	1941
Power	125 HP
Top Speed	110 MPH

LOCATION: HOLLYWOOD. In the Boxing Stadium parking lot on Gower St near Selma Ave. A great time to get it is when you leave this location during "The Set Up."

CHEVROLET STYLELINE

Showroom Number	7/25
Year	1949
Power	90 HP
Top Speed	87 MPH

LOCATION: DOWNTOWN, CENTRAL. Parked in the parking lot across the street from the front of the Central Police Station during "A Marriage Made in Heaven." There's also one in the parking lot behind the pawn shop in the Unassigned Case "Pawn Shop Holdup."

FORD CONVERTIBLE

Showroom Number	11/25
Year	1936
Power	85 HP
Top Speed	80 MPH

LOCATION: HOLLYWOOD. In a parking lot behind the Numbers Operation building in "The Black Caesar."

FORD CUSTOM

Showroom Number	12/25
Year	1940
Power	90 HP
Top Speed	87 MPH

LOCATION: CENTRAL. This vehicle is practically dropped in your lap in "The White Shoe Slaying" when you begin chasing Richard Bates from Baron's Bar. It's the car that stops in the street so you can chase after Bates as he enters the pickup truck.

PACKARD CUSTOM

Showroom Number	13/25
Year	1940
Power	160 HP
Top Speed	132 MPH

LOCATION: WILSHIRE. In the InstaHeat Factory parking lot during "The Gas Man."

DESOTO 2DR CUSTOM

Showroom Number	14/25
Year	1946
Power	109 HP
Top Speed	96 MPH

LOCATION: WESTLAKE. Also parked in the lot beside The Bamba Club during "The Red Lipstick Murder."

FORD 2DR

Showroom Number	15/25
Year	1947
Power	90 HP
Top Speed	90 MPH

LOCATION: WESTLAKE. Also find one in the parking lot behind the Bamba Club during "The Red Lipstick Murder."

FORD BUSINESS COUPE

Showroom Number	16/25
Year	1940
Power	60 HP
Top Speed	80 MPH

LOCATION: WESTLAKE. Parked in the raised parking lot behind the Maldonado Residence in Central LA during "The Silk Stocking Murder." Also in the lot across from Central Station during "The Red Lipstick Murder."

FORD TUDOR CONVERTIBLE

Showroom Number	17/25
Year	1947
Power	100 HP
Top Speed	95 MPH

LOCATION: WILSHIRE. Also in the Hall of Records parking lot during "A Polite Invitation."

FORD V8 SEDAN

Showroom Number	18/25
Year	1940
Power	90 HP
Top Speed	85 MPH

LOCATION: DOWNTOWN, CENTRAL. Also used as a chase vehicle option at the beginning of the Street Crime, "The Badger Game."

LASALLE V8 SEDAN

Showroom Number	19/25
Year	1939
Power	125 HP
Top Speed	88 MPH

LOCATION: MOST COMMON IN WESTLAKE. In Central, one of these vehicles is often parked in the first lot on the left as you exit east out of the tunnel at the north end of Union Station (Landmark 18).

LINCOLN CONTINENTAL COUPE

Showroom Number	20/25
Year	1942
Power	130 HP
Top Speed	118 MPH

LOCATION: WILSHIRE. Parked at the curb as you leave the Bookmaker's Office during "The Set Up." Also often seen driving by the murder scene on 7th Street during "Buyer Beware."

NASH SUPER 600

Showroom Number	21/25
Year	1948
Power	112 HP
Top Speed	104 MPH

LOCATION: DOWNTOWN, CENTRAL. Look for these driving through the streets of Downtown.

PACKARD CLIPPER EIGHT

Showroom Number	22/25
Year	1946
Power	165 HP
Top Speed	120 MPH

LOCATION: DOWNTOWN, CENTRAL. Also, the fleeing suspects drive one of these in "Manifest Destiny." Follow them to the shootout alley at Haskell's Men's Wear. Enter their wrecked car to unlock this vehicle.

PONTIAC TORPEDO SIX

Showroom Number	24/25
Year	1941
Power	90 HP
Top Speed	84 MPH

LOCATION: WESTLAKE, HOLLYWOOD. Find one during "The Silk Stocking Murder" in the parking lot behind the Maldonado Residence. Also found in the Boxing Stadium parking lot on Gower St, near Selma Ave in Hollywood. A great time to get it is when you leave this location during "The Set Up."

PACKARD CLIPPER SIX

Showroom Number	23/25
Year	1948
Power	130 HP
Top Speed	104 MPH

LOCATION: WILSHIRE. Also found in the L.A. Public Library parking lot during "The Quarter Moon Murders," as well as in the parking lot beside Eagleson's Gun Store during "Buyer Beware."

STUDEBAKER COMMANDER

Showroom Number	25/25
Year	1947
Power	94 HP
Top Speed	86 MPH

LOCATION: WESTLAKE. The non-police vehicle version of this vehicle can be found parked near the miniature golf course (Film Reel #7 location).

4-DOOR (18/19)

PONTIAC
SEDAN SIX

YEAR
1937

POWER
105 HP

TOP SPEED
9 MPH

CADILLAC SERIES 75 LIMOUSINE

Showroom Number	4/19
Year	1942
Power	150 HP
Top Speed	90 MPH

LOCATION: HOLLYWOOD. Found in the parking lot across the street from Black Caesar Food Hut on Ivar Ave during "The Black Caesar."

CADILLAC LASALLE SERIES 50

Showroom Number	1/19
Year	1935
Power	105 HP
Top Speed	92 MPH

LOCATION: WESTLAKE AND EAST DOWNTOWN (Central Division 1) around Santa Fe Ave and 4th Street. You can usually find one parked in the parking lot across the street from the Central Police Station during "The Driver's Seat."

CHEVROLET SEDAN

Showroom Number	5/19
Year	1940
Power	85 HP
Top Speed	78 MPH

LOCATION: EAST DOWNTOWN. In the Belmont High School parking lot during "The Golden Butterfly."

CADILLAC SERIES 61 TOURING SEDAN

Showroom Number	2/19
Year	1947
Power	150 HP
Top Speed	95 MPH

LOCATION: WILSHIRE. You can find this car in the alley parking lot behind the building you circle around to sneak up behind the rooftop sniper in "Manifest Destiny."

PLYMOUTH P5

Showroom Number	6/19
Year	1938
Power	95 HP
Top Speed	85 MPH

LOCATION: EAST DOWNTOWN. You can also find this vehicle in the parking lot where you begin the case, "A Different Kind of War." This is in Wilshire off of Mariposa Ave between Rosewood and Melrose.

CADILLAC SERIES 61

Showroom Number	3/19
Year	1942
Power	150 HP
Top Speed	95 MPH

LOCATION: COMMON IN WESTLAKE. There's also one in the same motel parking lot with Film Reel #4.

CHRYSLER AIRFLOW

Showroom Number	7/19
Year	1934
Power	115 HP
Top Speed	90 MPH

LOCATION: DOWNTOWN, CENTRAL. There's one parked just outside the crime scene barricade in "The Golden Butterfly." They are also seen driving around Film Reel #35.

DESOTO CUSTOM SUBURBAN

Showroom Number	8/19
Year	1946
Power	109 HP
Top Speed	92 MPH

LOCATION: DOWNTOWN, CENTRAL. In the lot across the street from the Central Police Station in "The Red Lipstick Murder."

HUDSON SUPER SIX

Showroom Number	9/19
Year	1947
Power	92 HP
Top Speed	88 MPH

LOCATION: DOWNTOWN, CENTRAL. In the Scott's Garage parking lot on the corner of 4th and Los Angeles St.

INTERNATIONAL D SERIES SEDAN

Showroom Number	10/19
Year	1939
Power	82 HP
Top Speed	75 MPH

LOCATION: EAST DOWNTOWN. Often seen driving around Broadway and 8th. You can also find one of these parked in the lot to the east of the bloodstained door in "Upon Reflection."

FRAZER MANHATTAN

Showroom Number	11/19
Year	1947
Power	112 HP
Top Speed	106 MPH

LOCATION: DOWNTOWN, CENTRAL. In a parking lot on the corner of Hill St and 4th St.

LINCOLN ZEPHYR TOURING

Showroom Number	12/19
Year	1939
Power	110 HP
Top Speed	95 MPH

LOCATION: WESTLAKE. Also in a parking lot on the corner of Hill St and 4th St in the Central division.

OLDSMOBILE HYDRAMATIC 88

Showroom Number	13/19
Year	1948
Power	110 HP
Top Speed	100 MPH

LOCATION: DOWNTOWN, CENTRAL. You can find one during "The Silk Stocking Murder" in the parking lot beside Just Picked Fruit Market. There's also one in the Hall of Records parking lot during "The Quarter Moon Murders."

OLDSMOBILE SEDAN

Showroom Number	14/19
Year	1940
Power	110 HP
Top Speed	92 MPH

LOCATION: HOLLYWOOD. Also found in the parking lot directly behind Eagleson's Gun Store in "Buyer Beware." Parked at the curb at the Steffens house fire in "The Gas Man."

PACKARD CLIPPER EIGHT

Showroom Number	15/19
Year	1947
Power	130 HP
Top Speed	102 MPH

LOCATION: DOWNTOWN, CENTRAL. You find this four-door Clipper at Dewey Bros Dealership.

PLYMOUTH SEDAN

Showroom Number	16/19
Year	1939
Power	82 HP
Top Speed	76 MPH

LOCATION: EAST DOWNTOWN. You can also find one during "The Silk Stocking Murder" in the parking lot behind the Maldonado Residence. There's another parked near the crime scene in the "The White Shoe Slaying."

PONTIAC SEDAN SIX

Showroom Number	18/19
Year	1937
Power	105 HP
Top Speed	92 MPH

LOCATION: DOWNTOWN, CENTRAL. This vehicle can be found ambiently downtown.

PLYMOUTH SPECIAL DELUXE SIX

Showroom Number	17/19
Year	1947
Power	95 HP
Top Speed	89 MPH

LOCATION: WILSHIRE. Parked in the lot to the east of the bloodstained door in "Upon Reflection."

WILLYS OVERLAND

Showroom Number	19/19
Year	1939
Power	61 HP
Top Speed	55 MPH

LOCATION: DOWNTOWN, CENTRAL. You can often find these driving around the streets of Downtown.

SPORTS (8)

SPORTS (8/8)

OLDSMOBILE
S98 CONVERTIBLE

YEAR	1947
POWER	110 HP
TOP SPEED	100 MPH

CHEVROLET FLEETMASTER CONVERTIBLE

Showroom Number	2/8
Year	1947
Power	90 HP
Top Speed	86 MPH

LOCATION: HOLLYWOOD. This vehicle can be found ambiently in Hollywood.

CADILLAC V16 CONVERTIBLE

Showroom Number	1/8
Year	1934
Power	185 HP
Top Speed	90 MPH

LOCATION: HOLLYWOOD. Also found in the L.A. Public Library parking lot during "The Quarter Moon Murders." There's another in Curtis Benson's apartment parking lot in "A Polite Invitation." Find a third parked in the lot across the street from the Central Police Station during "The Driver's Seat."

MERCURY CUSTOM

Showroom Number	3/8
Year	1941
Power	110 HP
Top Speed	105 MPH

LOCATION: EAST DOWNTOWN. Parked behind the Maldonado Residence in "The Silk Stocking Murder."

FORD DELUXE CONVERTIBLE

Showroom Number	4/8
Year	1939
Power	85 HP
Top Speed	80 MPH

LOCATION: WESTLAKE. Also found in the parking lot beside Ray's Café during "A Marriage Made in Heaven."

NASH LA FAYETTE CONVERTIBLE

Showroom Number	7/8
Year	1939
Power	105 HP
Top Speed	94 MPH

LOCATION: HOLLYWOOD. You can find a couple of these parked in a lot across the street from the Black Caesar Food Hut in "The Black Caesar Murders." You can also find them driving in front of the Pawnbroker on Main St in "The Studio Secretary Murder."

LINCOLN CONTINENTAL CONVERTIBLE

Showroom Number	5/8
Year	1946
Power	120 HP
Top Speed	118 MPH

LOCATION: HOLLYWOOD. There's usually one parked in Central in a parking lot adjacent (north) to the worksite where Film Reel #29 is hidden.

OLDSMOBILE S98 CONVERTIBLE

Showroom Number	8/8
Year	1947
Power	110 HP
Top Speed	100 MPH

LOCATION: WILSHIRE. Often seen driving around the Wilshire district.

LINCOLN MODEL K CONVERTIBLE ROADSTER

Showroom Number	6/8
Year	1937
Power	150 HP
Top Speed	122 MPH

LOCATION: WILSHIRE. You can also find one in the parking lot behind the Bamba Club in "The Red Lipstick Murder."

SERVICE (20)

SERVICE (11/19)

DESOTO
CUSTOM SUBURBAN TAXI

INTERNATIONAL KB8

Showroom Number	1/19
Year	1946
Power	96 HP
Top Speed	76 MPH

LOCATION: EAST DOWNTOWN. This is an individual unique unlock from the regular KB8. It can be found in a parking lot on the west end of Hawthorn Ave in west Hollywood on La Brea Ave (near the first Film Reel).

CHEVROLET PICKUP

Showroom Number	2/19
Year	1947
Power	90 HP
Top Speed	72 MPH

LOCATION: WESTLAKE. Beside Schroeder's apartment in "Upon Reflection." Also in the alley as you exit the Hobo Camp in "The White Shoe Slaying."

CHEVROLET VAN

Showroom Number	3/19
Year	1937
Power	85 HP
Top Speed	70 MPH

LOCATION: WESTLAKE. You can also find one of these parked in the lot to the east of the bloodstained door in "Upon Reflection."

CHEVROLET CIVILIAN VAN

Showroom Number	4/19
Year	1949
Power	90 HP
Top Speed	80 MPH

LOCATION: DOWNTOWN, CENTRAL. Also parked at the gas Station across the street from the fire station in "Manifest Destiny." Find another in the parking lot beside Eagleson's Gun Store during "Buyer Beware."

CHEVROLET PICKUP 2

Showroom Number	5/19
Year	1940
Power	85 HP
Top Speed	70 MPH

LOCATION: DOWNTOWN, CENTRAL. Also parked at Clemen's Worksite in "The Gas Man." You can find one in the fenced parking lot across the street from Cavanagh's Bar in "The Driver's Seat."

GMC PICKUP

Showroom Number	6/19
Year	1947
Power	93 HP
Top Speed	76 MPH

LOCATION: DOWNTOWN, CENTRAL. You can usually find one parked in the lot across the street from the Central Police Station during "The Driver's Seat."

NASH DELUXE 600 ARMY

Showroom Number	7/19
Year	1942
Power	99 HP
Top Speed	90 MPH

LOCATION: SOUTH HOLLYWOOD. Hughes Airplane Company on 813 Van Ness Avenue.

AMERICAN LA FRANCE FIRE TRUCK

Showroom Number	8/19
Year	1946
Power	160 HP
Top Speed	80 MPH

LOCATION: WILSHIRE. You can easily find one of these as you leave the Vice Precinct at the beginning of "Manifest Destiny." The fire station is adjacent to the police department.

BUICK AMBULANCE

Showroom Number	9/19
Year	1947
Power	110 HP
Top Speed	86 MPH

LOCATION: CENTRAL. This ambulance is actually a rare find. It's not the same make as the ones the city has in service. This Buick model can be found in the west Central area on 8th between Beacon and Union.

CHEVROLET TOW TRUCK

Showroom Number	10/19
Year	1947
Power	140 HP
Top Speed	85 MPH

LOCATION: WILSHIRE. There are many of these driving around the Demolished Elysian Fields house in "House of Sticks." Look near 1st and Normandie. They also frequent McArthur Park.

DESOTO CUSTOM SUBURBAN TAXI

Showroom Number	11/19
Year	1946
Power	95 HP
Top Speed	90 MPH

LOCATION: DOWNTOWN, CENTRAL. Found driving all around the Central area.

DODGE FUEL TRUCK

Showroom Number	12/19
Year	1939
Power	150 HP
Top Speed	65 MPH

LOCATION: WILSHIRE. Often seen driving around where 3rd, 4th, and Alameda St meet in the south Central Division 1 area.

FORD AMBULANCE

Showroom Number	13/19
Year	1948
Power	110 HP
Top Speed	75 MPH

LOCATION: CENTRAL. Your first easy chance to get in one is at the Central Coroner's office during "A Marriage Made in Heaven." There's one parked beside the entrance.

INTERNATIONAL METRO KB1M

Showroom Number	14/19
Year	1949
Power	84 HP
Top Speed	70 MPH

LOCATION: WILSHIRE. Found around the streets near the garage where Hidden Vehicle 2 (the Chrysler Woody) hides. This is south Wilshire where Vermont Ave turns into 8th St.

INTERNATIONAL KB5

Showroom Number	15/19
Year	1946
Power	100 HP
Top Speed	82 MPH

LOCATION: HOLLYWOOD. In the alley behind the building you circle around to sneak up on the rooftop sniper in "Manifest Destiny."

INTERNATIONAL D SERIES

Showroom Number	16/19
Year	1939
Power	82 HP
Top Speed	75 MPH

LOCATION: CENTRAL. Parked in the lot to the east of the bloodstained door in "Upon Reflection."

HEIL COLECTO-PAK

Showroom Number	17/19
Year	1947
Power	95 HP
Top Speed	70 MPH

LOCATION: CENTRAL. This is a somewhat difficult find. Look for them cruising around The Mayfair Hotel landmark.

INTERNATIONAL KB8

Showroom Number	18/19
Year	1946
Power	100 HP
Top Speed	80 MPH

LOCATION: EAST DOWNTOWN. This vehicle can be found driving around east downtown.

INTERNATIONAL KB6

Showroom Number	19/19
Year	1946
Power	100 HP
Top Speed	82 MPH

LOCATION: EAST DOWNTOWN. You can also find one across the street from Schroeder's Apartment behind a tall, climbable fence in "Upon Reflection."

POLICE (9)

POLICE (9 9)

STUDEBAKER
COMMANDER

YEAR
1947
POWER
94 HP
TOP SPEED
90 MPH

CHEVROLET FLEETMASTER 2DR

Showroom Number	3/9
Year	1947
Power	90 HP
Top Speed	96 MPH

LOCATION: CENTRAL. This is the vehicle used by Jack Kelso during his Arson cases.

BUICK SUPER

Showroom Number	1/9
Year	1947
Power	110 HP
Top Speed	96 MPH

LOCATION: Used during Traffic cases.

CHEVROLET CORONER'S VAN

Showroom Number	4/9
Year	1949
Power	85 HP
Top Speed	90 MPH

LOCATION: Parked near many crime scenes.

CADILLAC SERIES 62 CONVERTIBLE

Showroom Number	2/9
Year	1947
Power	150 HP
Top Speed	95 MPH

LOCATION: Used during Vice cases. This is Roy Earle's vehicle.

FORD POLICE SPECIAL

Showroom Number	5/9
Year	1947
Power	100 HP
Top Speed	95 MPH

LOCATION: Used during Patrol cases. You begin the game behind the wheel of this vehicle.

HUDSON COMMODORE

Showroom Number	6/9
Year	1948
Power	128 HP
Top Speed	91 MPH

LOCATION: This vehicle is used during your Arson cases.

NASH SUPER 600

Showroom Number	8/9
Year	1947
Power	112 HP
Top Speed	98 MPG

LOCATION: Used during Homicide cases.

INTERNATIONAL POLICE WAGON

Showroom Number	7/9
Year	1940
Power	110 HP
Top Speed	75 MPH

LOCATION: Many of these are locked when you find them. Look for them at police roadblocks. During "Reefer Madness," you can find one unlocked in front of Parnell's Soup Co. Factory in Hollywood just before the raid.

STUDEBAKER COMMANDER

Showroom Number	9/9
Year	1947
Power	94 HP
Top Speed	90 MPH

LOCATION: Parked near many crime scenes, but first seen in "The Driver's Seat" parked beside your vehicle at the railroad crime scene in Central. You must enter the car before investigating or it will be gone when you leave the scene.

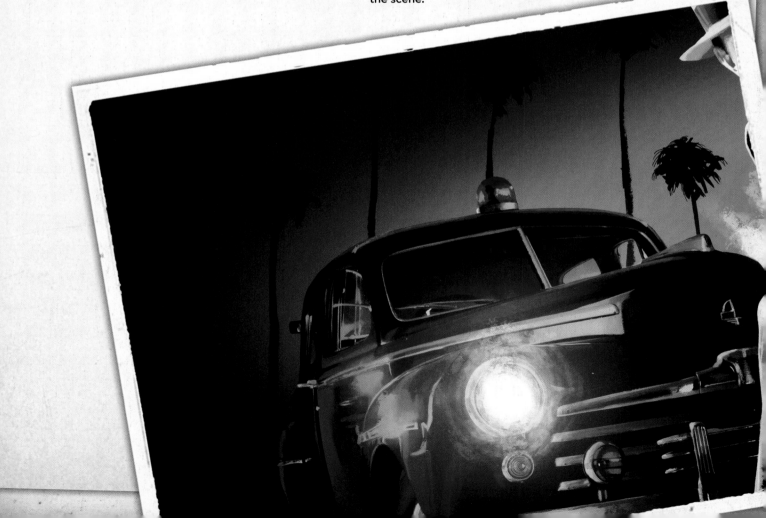

100% COMPLETION

COMPONENT	NUMBER TO COLLECT/COMPLETE	PERCENTAGE
STORY CASES	21	57%
STREET CRIMES	40	15%
VEHICLES	95	15%
FILM REELS	50	7%
LANDMARKS	30	3%
NEWSPAPERS	13	3%
TOTAL		100%

ACHIEVEMENTS & TROPHIES

PLAYSTATION 3 TROPHIES

NAME	TYPE	POINTS	CRITERIA
POLICE ACADEMY	BRONZE	15	COMPLETE ALL CASES ON THE PATROL DESK.
PAVED WITH GOOD INTENTIONS	BRONZE	15	COMPLETE ALL CASES ON THE TRAFFIC DESK.
THE SIMPLE ART OF MURDER	BRONZE	15	COMPLETE ALL CASES ON THE HOMICIDE DESK.
NO REST FOR THE WICKED	BRONZE	15	COMPLETE ALL CASES ON THE VICE DESK.
MOTH TO A FLAME	GOLD	90	COMPLETE ALL CASES ON THE ARSON DESK.
A COP ON EVERY CORNER	BRONZE	15	COMPLETE A SINGLE STREET CRIME CASES.
JOHNNY ON THE SPOT	SILVER	30	RESPOND TO 20 STREET CRIME CASES.
THE LONG ARM OF THE LAW	SILVER	30	COMPLETE ALL STREET CRIME CASES
THE CITY OF THE ANGELS	GOLD	90	REACH 100% GAME COMPLETION.
THE UP AND UP	SILVER	30	COMPLETE A STORY CASE WITH A FIVE-STAR RATING.
SHAMUS TO THE STARS	GOLD	90	COMPLETE ALL STORY CASES WITH A FIVE-STAR RATING.
THE BRASS	SILVER	30	ACHIEVE MAXIMUM RANK (20).
NOT SO HASTY	BRONZE	15	STOP A FLEEING SUSPECT WITH A WARNING SHOT AS AN LAPD DETECTIVE.
ASPHALT JUNGLES	BRONZE	15	CHASE DOWN AND TACKLE A FLEEING SUSPECT ON FOOT AS AN LAPD DETECTIVE.
TRAFFIC STOP	BRONZE	15	DISABLE A SUSPECT VEHICLE WITH HELP FROM YOUR PARTNER.
THE STRAIGHT DOPE	BRONZE	15	USE EVIDENCE TO PROVE A LIE AS AN LAPD DETECTIVE OR INVESTIGATOR.
ONE FOR THE FILE	BRONZE	15	FIND AND INSPECT A CLUE AS AN LAPD DETECTIVE OR INVESTIGATOR.
GOLDEN BOY	BRONZE	15	CLEAR A CASE, FINDING EVERY CLUE AS AN LAPD DETECTIVE OR INVESTIGATOR.
THE PLOT THICKENS	BRONZE	15	FIND AND SOLVE AN INSPECTION PUZZLE.
STAB-RITE	BRONZE	15	AT RAY'S CAF, FIND THE BLOODSTAINED KNIFE ON YOUR FIRST SWEEP OF THE CRIME SCENE.
ROUND HEELS	BRONZE	15	AT THE BAMBA CLUB, GET DICK MCCOLL TO GIVE UP THE LICENSE PLATE OF CELINE HENRY'S MALE COMPANION.
THE FIGHTING SIXTH	BRONZE	15	AT THE BUS SHOOTING, TALK FELIX ALVARRO INTO GIVING UP THE MARINES INVOLVED IN THE COOLRIDGE HEIST.
HUCKSTER	BRONZE	15	AT ELYSIAN FIELDS, OUTWIT LELAND MONROE WHEN DISCUSSING HIS DEVELOPMENTS OR ADVERTISING CAMPAIGN.
LEAD FOOT	BRONZE	15	KEEP THE NEEDLE ABOVE 80MPH FOR MORE THAN 10 SECONDS WHILE DRIVING.
MILES ON THE CLOCK	BRONZE	15	DRIVE MORE THAN 194.7 MILES.
WOODEN OVERCOATS	SILVER	30	BRING DOWN A TOTAL OF 30 BAD GUYS WITH HEADSHOTS.
DEAD MEN ARE HEAVIER	BRONZE	15	SHOOT AND KILL A TOTAL OF 100 BAD GUYS.
ROSCOE AND FRIENDS	BRONZE	15	KILL AT LEAST ONE BAD GUY WITH EVERY GUN.
MAGPIE	GOLD	90	FIND AND INSPECT 95% OF ALL CLUES.
THE SHADOW	BRONZE	15	TAIL A SUSPECT WITHOUT BEING SPOTTED IN A SINGLE CASE.
THE THIRD DEGREE	SILVER	30	CORRECTLY BRANCH EVERY QUESTION IN EVERY INTERVIEW IN A SINGLE STORY CASE.
THE HUNCH	SILVER	30	USE FIVE INTUITION POINTS IN CONVERSATION WITH A SINGLE SUSPECT, CORRECTLY BRANCHING EACH QUESTION.
STAR MAP	BRONZE	15	DISCOVER ALL LANDMARK BUILDINGS AROUND THE CITY.
PUBLIC MENACE	SILVER	30	RACK UP $47,000 IN PENALTIES DURING A SINGLE STORY CASE.
THE MOOSE	BRONZE	15	TAIL CANDY EDWARDS FROM THE PARKING LOT TO HER DESTINATION WITHOUT USING COVER OR GOING INCOGNITO.
KEEP A LID ON	BRONZE	15	COMPLETE THE HOBO CAMP, RANCHO ESCONDIDO, OR AMERICAN LEGION STADIUM BRAWL WITHOUT LOSING YOUR HAT.
AUTO ENTHUSIAST	BRONZE	15	DRIVE 5 DIFFERENT VEHICLES.
AUTO COLLECTOR	BRONZE	15	DRIVE 40 DIFFERENT VEHICLES.
AUTO FANATIC	SILVER	30	DRIVE EVERY VEHICLE IN THE CITY.
HOLLYWOODLAND	SILVER	30	FIND AND INSPECT ALL GOLDEN FILM REELS.
PLATINUM TROPHY	N/A	N/A	COLLECT ALL OTHER TROPHIES TO GAIN THIS TROPHY.

XBOX 360 ACHIEVEMENTS

NAME	POINTS	CRITERIA
POLICE ACADEMY	15	COMPLETE ALL CASES ON THE PATROL DESK.
PAVED WITH GOOD INTENTIONS	15	COMPLETE ALL CASES ON THE TRAFFIC DESK.
THE SIMPLE ART OF MURDER	15	COMPLETE ALL CASES ON THE HOMICIDE DESK.
NO REST FOR THE WICKED	15	COMPLETE ALL CASES ON THE VICE DESK.
MOTH TO A FLAME	70	COMPLETE ALL CASES ON THE ARSON DESK.
A COP ON EVERY CORNER	15	COMPLETE A SINGLE STREET CRIME CASES.
JOHNNY ON THE SPOT	30	RESPOND TO 20 STREET CRIME CASES.
THE LONG ARM OF THE LAW	30	COMPLETE ALL STREET CRIME CASES.
THE CITY OF THE ANGELS	80	REACH 100% GAME COMPLETION.
THE UP AND UP	30	COMPLETE A STORY CASE WITH A FIVE-STAR RATING.
SHAMUS TO THE STARS	80	COMPLETE ALL STORY CASES WITH A FIVE-STAR RATING.
THE BRASS	30	ACHIEVE MAXIMUM RANK (20).
NOT SO HASTY	15	STOP A FLEEING SUSPECT WITH A WARNING SHOT AS AN LAPD DETECTIVE.
ASPHALT JUNGLES	15	CHASE DOWN AND TACKLE A FLEEING SUSPECT ON FOOT AS AN LAPD DETECTIVE.
TRAFFIC STOP	15	DISABLE A SUSPECT VEHICLE WITH HELP FROM YOUR PARTNER.
THE STRAIGHT DOPE	15	USE EVIDENCE TO PROVE A LIE AS AN LAPD DETECTIVE OR INVESTIGATOR.
ONE FOR THE FILE	15	FIND AND INSPECT A CLUE AS AN LAPD DETECTIVE OR INVESTIGATOR.
GOLDEN BOY	15	CLEAR A CASE FINDING EVERY CLUE AS AN LAPD DETECTIVE OR INVESTIGATOR
THE PLOT THICKENS	15	FIND AND SOLVE AN INSPECTION PUZZLE.
STAB-RITE	15	AT RAY'S CAF, FIND THE BLOODSTAINED KNIFE ON YOUR FIRST SWEEP OF THE CRIME SCENE.
ROUND HEELS	15	AT THE BAMBA CLUB, GET DICK MCCOLL TO GIVE UP THE LICENSE PLATE OF CELINE HENRY'S MALE COMPANION.
THE FIGHTING SIXTH	15	AT THE BUS SHOOTING, TALK FELIX ALVARRO INTO GIVING UP THE MARINES INVOLVED IN THE COOLRIDGE HEIST.
HUCKSTER	15	AT ELYSIAN FIELDS, OUTWIT LELAND MONROE WHEN DISCUSSING HIS DEVELOPMENTS OR ADVERTISING CAMPAIGN.
LEAD FOOT	15	KEEP THE NEEDLE ABOVE 80MPH FOR MORE THAN 10 SECONDS WHILE DRIVING.
MILES ON THE CLOCK	15	DRIVE MORE THAN 194.7 MILES.
WOODEN OVERCOATS	30	BRING DOWN A TOTAL OF 30 BAD GUYS WITH HEADSHOTS.
DEAD MEN ARE HEAVIER	15	SHOOT AND KILL A TOTAL OF 100 BAD GUYS.
ROSCOE AND FRIENDS	15	KILL AT LEAST ONE BAD GUY WITH EVERY GUN.
MAGPIE	80	FIND AND INSPECT 95% OF ALL CLUES.
THE SHADOW	15	TAIL A SUSPECT WITHOUT BEING SPOTTED IN A SINGLE CASE.
THE THIRD DEGREE	30	CORRECTLY BRANCH EVERY QUESTION IN EVERY INTERVIEW IN A SINGLE STORY CASE.
THE HUNCH	30	USE FIVE INTUITION POINTS IN CONVERSATION WITH A SINGLE SUSPECT, CORRECTLY BRANCHING EACH QUESTION.
STAR MAP	15	DISCOVER ALL LANDMARK BUILDINGS AROUND THE CITY.
PUBLIC MENACE	30	RACK UP $47,000 IN PENALTIES DURING A SINGLE STORY CASE.
THE MOOSE	15	TAIL CANDY EDWARDS FROM THE PARKING LOT TO HER DESTINATION WITHOUT USING COVER OR GOING INCOGNITO.
KEEP A LID ON	15	COMPLETE THE HOBO CAMP, RANCHO ESCONDIDO, OR AMERICAN LEGION STADIUM BRAWL WITHOUT LOSING YOUR HAT.
AUTO ENTHUSIAST	15	DRIVE 5 DIFFERENT VEHICLES.
AUTO COLLECTOR	15	DRIVE 40 DIFFERENT VEHICLES.
AUTO FANATIC	30	DRIVE EVERY VEHICLE IN THE CITY.
HOLLYWOODLAND	30	FIND AND INSPECT ALL GOLDEN FILM REELS.

THE ASSIGNED CASES

THE "PERFECT" PATH

L.A. Noire's main story takes place over the course of 21 police cases, each one a separate "mission" but all linked by a multi-layered central plot. The first four cases are tutorial missions that introduce your main character, Cole Phelps, and the basics of gameplay. You must then complete 17 deep, complex, richly detailed cases as Phelps works his way through four divisions or "desks" of the Los Angeles Police Department: Traffic, Homicide, Administrative Vice, and Arson.

Our walkthrough details the ideal path through each case. We'll guide you through every crime scene investigation and all witness/suspect interviews with a perfect score: find all key clues and assess every interview response correctly. It's important to note, however, that each case offers multiple ways to a successful conclusion. You can "solve" a case without getting a perfect score in the Case Report at mission's end.

So we highly recommend forging ahead through your current case, even if in-game music cues indicate that you're missing a clue at a location or one of your interview assessments was incorrect. You can often complete a case even after missing a few clues or misjudging an interviewee's responses to your interrogation. Sometimes a "mistake" leads to an alternate way of solving the case.

THE STORY

Our story opens with a voiceover narrator giving an overview of Los Angeles in 1947. It sets a classic noire tone:

"A city on the verge of greatness. A new type of city, based not on the man but on the automobile. The car—the symbol of freedom and vitality."

"Where every man can own his own home, and have room to breathe, and not be overlooked by his neighbors. A city where a man's home is his castle. A quarter acre of the dream made possible by victory."

"The city of opportunists. The city of dreams where Hollywood will shape the thoughts and desires of the entire planet."

"A city of pioneers. A city of dreamers."

"A city of undercurrents, where not everything is as it seems. A twentieth century city that will become a model for the world. A city that has no boundaries. That will stretch as far as the eye can see."

THE PATROL CASES

The game designates this first set of four missions as tutorial cases. These teach you the basics of gameplay in L.A. Noire. As the game opens, your character is Officer Cole Phelps, a young patrol cop based in the Los Angeles Police Department's Wilshire Division. Your partner is Officer Ralph Dunn, and your unit's call sign is 14 Adam.

In 1947, the LAPD designates each two-man unit of uniformed officers with the letter A combined with the team's beat number—for Phelps and Dunn, the beat is 14. Using the LAPD phonetic alphabet, their patrol car is thus referred to as "14 Adam."

WHAT IS KGPL?

Throughout L.A. Noire, the LAPD communicates with its two-man units via radio. The police radio station is known by the call letters KGPL, operating at 1730 kHz, just above the commercial radio broadcasting frequencies.

UPON REFLECTION

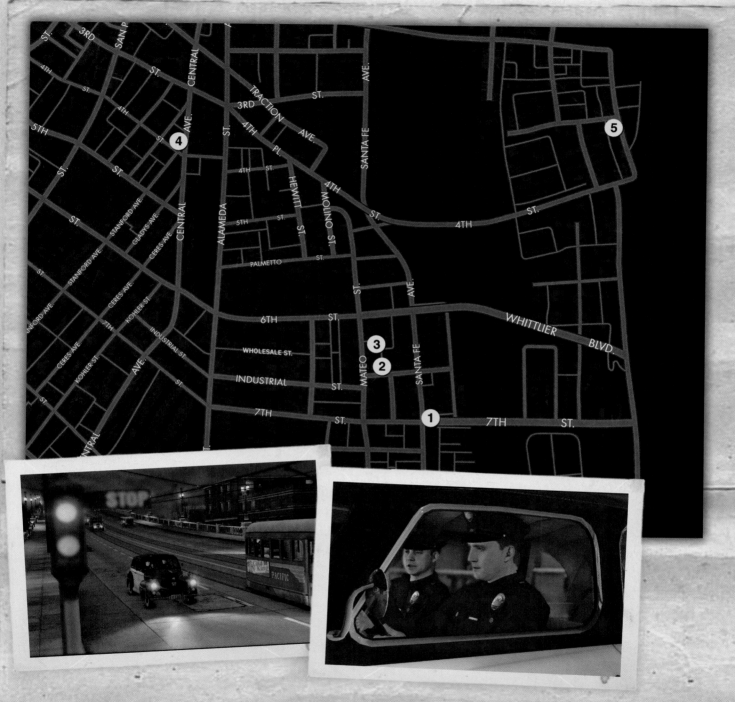

Officers Phelps and Dunn take a call from KGPL, directing them to provide uniformed assistance for an evidence search. A detective unit ("16 William") is investigating a shooting in an alley between Sixth and Industrial Streets, down in L.A.'s warehouse district by the river. Onscreen, your first objective appears: "Investigate Crime Scene."

LAPD CODES

The LAPD designates all detective units with the letter W, or "William." A Code 2 means "respond immediately to location, no lights or siren, obey all traffic laws."

Objectives

* Investigate Crime Scene.
* Investigate Gun Store.
* Investigate Schroeder's Apartment.
* Search Schroeder's Apartment.

CASE REPORT

TOTAL NUMBER OF KEY CLUES	4
TOTAL NUMBER OF INTERVIEW QUESTIONS	N/A

Fail Conditions

* Phelps dies.
* Any friendly NPC dies.
* Crime scene contaminated (e.g., drive a car through it).

LOCATION:
ALLEYWAY CRIME SCENE
DRIVE TO THE CRIME SCENE.

First, press the Pause button and select Map for a quick overview of the trip. Your current location ① is the white arrow icon. Move the cursor over the nearby yellow flag on the map just a couple of blocks to the northwest ② to see its popup designation: "Alleyway Crime Scene." This is your first destination.

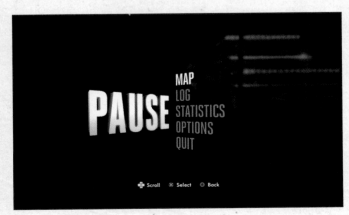

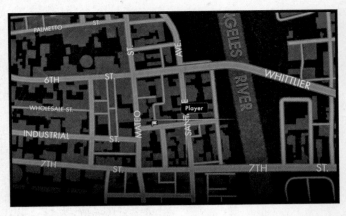

Use the car controls to drive the short distance to the alley, where other uniformed officers have cordoned off the crime scene. The L.A. County Coroner's wagon is parked at the head of the alley. Approaching it triggers the next cutscene.

As the coroner drives off, Phelps meets Floyd Rose, the lead Homicide detective at the scene. He reports that the victim (the "vic"), Scooter Peyton, has already been bagged up and sent to Central Morgue. A witness reports that the shooter, a tall white man, shot Peyton twice and then tossed his gun (the "gat"). Rose wants you to find the weapon.

PERSONS OF INTEREST

Whenever you get information about someone associated with the current case (a victim, suspect, witness, or even a fellow cop like Detective Floyd Rose), that "person of interest" (P.O.I. for short) is listed on the People page of your notebook. You can select their name to review what you know about them.

Later, if you conduct an interview of that P.O.I., the topics for questioning are listed on that person's Questions page in the notebook. (We'll cover the details when we get to that part of an investigation.)

INVESTIGATE THE CRIME SCENE.

You start out at the head of the alley with your partner, Dunn, who immediately moves ahead. The onscreen directive says, "Search locations thoroughly to discover clues." Take that to heart, and keep in mind that crime scenes are generally littered with objects you can pick up, but only a few that can be categorized as "clues."

Follow your partner down the alley and start looking for clues. If you have Clue Hints turned on in the Menu, each examinable object will trigger a chime when you get near it, plus you'll feel your controller vibrate (assuming you have Vibration turned on as well). Press the button indicated onscreen to pick up the examinable object. Officer Dunn stops at the first set: discarded beer bottles and a newspaper (see the next section) on the right side of the alley. Examine a bottle or two for practice.

Partner Advice

Consult your partner for investigative tips during an evidence search by pressing the Advice button when you're near him. Press the same button while driving to get directional tips from your partner.

Once you're holding an object, it's important to use the left controller stick to manipulate it. Turn the item from side to side and look for markings or other information. In many cases it's not enough to simply pick up the object; you'll need to also find key information written or etched somewhere on it.

TRIGGER A "STORY BEHIND THE HEADLINES."

The newspaper in the alley is a copy of the **Los Angeles Inquisitor**. Its headline reads, "Shrink Says: The Mind Is the Final Frontier." Pick up the paper and press the button indicated onscreen to trigger a cinematic sequence revealing "the story behind the headline."

Watch the scene set in a lecture hall at the University of Southern California's Keck School of Medicine: A second-year medical student named Courtney Sheldon approaches a famous psychiatrist, Dr. Harlan Fontaine, after his lecture. Sheldon asks questions about what was then called "battle fatigue" (known today as post-traumatic stress syndrome, or PTSD); he's a World War II vet and has a war buddy who suffers from the affliction. Dr. Fontaine offers to make a prognosis for Sheldon's friend in exchange for volunteer service in one of Fontaine's L.A. psychiatric clinics. Sheldon enthusiastically agrees to the deal.

NEWS CLUES

Thirteen special newspapers are scattered throughout the game. When examined, each one triggers a special "story behind the headlines" cinematic sequence. Watch these cinematic scenes to gain important perspective on the larger story in L.A. Noire.

The special newspapers are not technically key clues-i.e., they don't count as one of the "Clues Found" listed on the Case Report at the end of each detective story mission. But the investigation music for that location will keep playing until you examine all key clues at the scene and the newspaper, too.

EXAMINE THE MURDER SCENE.

Soon Officer Dunn calls out, "Cole, come take a look at this." He stands at a blood-splattered door, the spot where the victim was shot. Approach the door. When you hear the chime, examine the **bloodstain**. An onscreen message reports that you've found your first official clue: "NEW CLUE: Bloodstain."

Found clues are automatically added to the Evidence list in your notebook and can be viewed at any time during a case.

FIND THE MURDER WEAPON.

Now turn and continue down the alley to the left of the door, past the dumpster until you hear another

chime. Press the Examine button: Phelps looks up at the open window above and spots the image of a revolver reflected on the glass from the opposite roof. An onscreen message tells you to find a ladder or drainpipe to climb up ③.

Next move: yep, find a drainpipe. Follow the alley around the left turn and find one on the left wall. Walk toward the pipe—when you reach it, Phelps automatically starts climbing.

At the top, turn left and find the **Smith & Wesson revolver** lying on the roof. Pick up the weapon and use your left control stick to turn the gun in your hand until you see its engraved name (Smith & Wesson) and serial number (S71893). The camera automatically zooms in when you manipulate the gun to the correct

angle. Don't stop there, though— examine the gun even further! Phelps flips open the cylinder and notes that two rounds have been fired.

This officially marks the gun as a clue: "Smith & Wesson revolver" is now listed on the Evidence page

of your notebook, along with "Bloodstain." Note also that the investigation music has stopped playing, which indicates that you've found all of the key clues at this location.

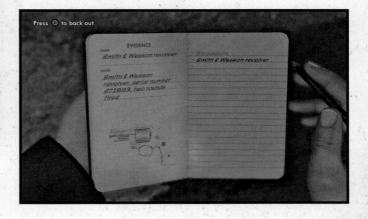

Return to the drainpipe and climb back down to the ground to trigger a short scene with your partner, Dunn. Phelps wants to show some initiative by tracking down the gun's owner; he wants to check with a local gun store. Dunn says there's one just a few blocks away.

SET YOUR NEXT DESTINATION.

This puts a new objective onscreen: "Investigate Gun Store." To set the gun store as your next destination, open your notebook, select Locations, and then select Gun Store. Move the pencil cursor down to "Set As Destination" and choose that option. This marks the Central Avenue gun store location ④ on your map with a yellow flag.

LOCATION: CENTRAL GUNS
INVESTIGATE THE GUN STORE.

Your patrol car is marked as the blue automobile icon on your map. Return to the car, then get in and drive to Central Guns by following the yellow map flag. Remember that you can ask your partner for directions at any time. Upon arrival, your approach to Central Guns triggers a quick cutscene of the store.

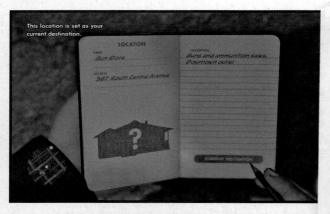

Walk to the Central Guns front door. Note that it has a gold handle. Any gold-handled door can be opened or interacted with when you approach it. Entering triggers another cutscene: The storeowner knows the Smith & Wesson revolver well—in fact, he sold it. He hands you his **gun store ledger** with the proof. This automatically adds a new clue to your Evidence list: "Gun store ledger."

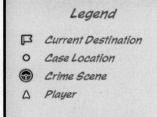

Open the ledger and move Phelps' finger across to the fifth entry on the second page: a Model 27 with a pearl grip. The purchaser is listed as Errol Schroeder, 203 South Gless Street. Select the entry to add Schroeder to your "P.O.I." list and trigger a new objective: "Investigate Schroeder's apartment."

FLAGS AND BLIPS

All locations important to your current case are marked as yellow icons on the map. Your current destination (which you select in your notebook or on your map) is marked as a yellow flag.

Legend

⚑ Current Destination
○ Case Location
◎ Crime Scene
△ Player

Before exiting the store, you can pick up and examine the bird decoys and an ammo box on the glass counter if you want, but they offer nothing pertinent to the case. Again, you'll find many examinable objects at locations you visit, but only a few of these items will be critical to the investigation.

Open your notebook, select Locations, and set Errol Schroeder's apartment as your current destination. This puts a new yellow flag ⑤ on your map, showing the place as almost due east of your current location.

LOCATION: ERROL SCHROEDER'S APARTMENT

INVESTIGATE SCHROEDER'S APARTMENT.
Follow the yellow map flag. The route takes you over the 4th Street bridge to a building that houses Moxley's Menswear on the ground floor. Schroeder's apartment is upstairs.

Enter the door (left of the storefront) and examine the mailboxes on the right to learn that Schroeder lives in

Apartment 2. Climb the stairs and approach this unit to knock on the door.

Schroeder answers and admits to owning the Smith & Wesson. When Phelps confronts him about the Scooter Peyton murder, Schroeder seems surprised and tries to present the gun... but the drawer is empty.

Phelps informs the suspect that he's under arrest, but Schroeder refuses to go quietly and coldcocks Dunn. This triggers your first brawling sequence.

DEFEAT SCHROEDER IN A FISTFIGHT.

Face up to Schroeder and hold down the controller button indicated to put Phelps in brawl mode. Press the controller buttons shown onscreen to punch or block/dodge. When the fight's over, Phelps cuffs Schroeder and you get your final objective for this case.

SEARCH SCHROEDER'S APARTMENT.

There are a number of examinable objects scattered around the place, but the only one of substance is in the nearby open drawer where Schroeder sought his gun. Find **Schroeder's notebook** in the drawer and turn a page to find Floyd Rose's name listed. (This puts the clue "Schroeder's notebook" in your Evidence list.) Recall that Rose was the lead detective on the scene of Scooter Peyton's murder.

Officer Dunn strongly recommends leaving the notebook where you found it to avoid stirring up a hornet's nest. Phelps calls in the arrest, and then a murky flashback sequence plays showing Phelps during the war.

Key Clue Checklist: Schroeder's Apartment

✓ Schroeder's notebook

We walked you step by step through the previous case because it introduced a lot of L.A. Noire basics. From this point on, our walkthrough will assume your knowledge of game basics and controls. The next case is quick and uncomplicated. Phelps and Dunn get a radio report of a "211" (LAPD radio code for an armed robbery) in progress with shots fired at Westlake Savings & Loan. 14 Adam isn't far from there, so Phelps takes the call.

Objectives

* Subdue Robbery Suspects.

CASE REPORT

TOTAL NUMBER OF KEY CLUES	N/A
TOTAL NUMBER OF INTERVIEW QUESTIONS	N/A

Fail Conditions

* Phelps or Dunn dies.
* Suspects escape.
* Kill a bystander.

Red Blips

Suspects are always marked on your radar mini-map as red blips. This is particularly helpful during a chase or a gun battle.

SUBDUE THE ROBBERY SUSPECTS.

Open fire! You start out leaning against the back panel of a truck for cover. Follow onscreen directions for using cover, then gun down the bad guys posted outside the bank. Once they fall, hustle across the street and take cover just outside the Westlake Savings & Loan's front entrance.

LOCATION: WESTLAKE SAVINGS & LOAN

DRIVE TO THE BANK.

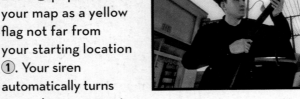

Westlake Savings & Loan ② pops onto your map as a yellow flag not far from your starting location ①. Your siren automatically turns on, and cars veer out of your way as you speed to the location. (Activate your siren whenever you're in a hurry and you want to clear traffic.) Your arrival triggers a brief cutscene: the robbers spot your patrol car and open fire. Phelps retrieves a police-issue shotgun from the trunk and sets up just across the street from the bad guys.

One thug pops out from a column on the left, another is holed up behind the desk at the end of the center aisle, and a third shooter sets up on the balcony directly above the desk. If incoming fire is too intense, you can "blind-fire" around the corner, firing your weapon without leaning out from cover. But in this case, you should be able to pop out and pick off targets without taking major damage.

Once you eliminate the final gunman, the mission ends with a quick exchange between Phelps and Dunn. Then another war flashback plays.

WARRANTS OUTSTANDING

Officers Phelps and Dunn ride patrol on a steamy
L.A. night. Dunn can't get his partner to talk about
the war—Cole Phelps is a decorated hero, cited for valor on Okinawa where he won a Silver Star. Suddenly, Dunn
spots Wendell Bowers, a bum who jumped parole. He tells Phelps to get after Bowers on foot while Dunn tries to
cut him off with the car.

Objectives

* Pursue Suspect.
* Subdue Suspect.

CASE REPORT

TOTAL NUMBER OF KEY CLUES	N/A
TOTAL NUMBER OF INTERVIEW QUESTIONS	N/A

Fail Conditions

* Phelps dies.
* Bowers escapes.

LOCATION: MAIN AND 6th STREETS

PURSUE THE SUSPECT.

You start out on Main Street near 6th ①. Bowers sprints up an alley, so give chase using the controls indicated onscreen to run. When you reach the

chain-link fence in the first alley, simply run right into it—Phelps automatically scales low obstacles. Bowers takes a hard right just past the fence. If you lose sight of him, remember that he's the red blip on your radar mini-map.

Officer Dunn drives into the alley up ahead and cuts off Bowers, but the suspect veers left and climbs a fire escape ladder. As with the fence earlier, just run right at the ladder until Phelps grabs on and starts climbing. Follow Bowers all the way up to the roof.

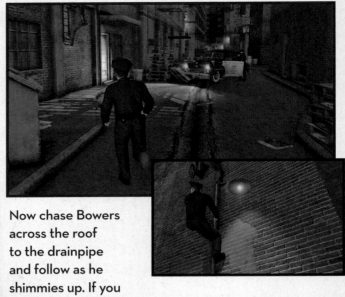

Now chase Bowers across the roof to the drainpipe and follow as he shimmies up. If you get too close, he kicks you in the head! At the top, your suspect leaps off the next ledge onto a narrow section of roof below. Just run toward the gap and Phelps automatically leaps. Climb up to the next roof, then follow Bowers across another gap as he works his way right back toward Main Street where the chase started.

If you haven't caught Bowers before you round the rooftop power shed, a cutscene plays: Bowers clotheslines Phelps! Then he squares up, ready to brawl.

SUBDUE BOWERS.

Employ the same fighting controls used to subdue Errol Schroeder back in "Upon Reflection." You owe

Bowers a few good shots for that nasty clothesline trick. Note that this thug is a much tougher customer than Schroeder. Keep punching, ducking, and grappling until you finish him off. When the fight's over, Dunn hustles Bowers into the paddy wagon and congratulates his partner for another job well done.

> ### ROOF TOSS
> Phelps can throw Bowers off the rooftop during the fight. This ends the fight and you see the thug loaded into an ambulance instead of a paddy wagon. The exchange between partners is different, as well.

BUYER BEWARE

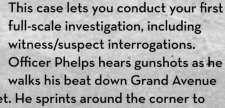

This case lets you conduct your first full-scale investigation, including witness/suspect interrogations. Officer Phelps hears gunshots as he walks his beat down Grand Avenue across 7th Street. He sprints around the corner to the scene of a shooting outside the Nunn Bush Shoes store. A patrol car pulls up and Phelps' partner, Ralph Dunn, hops out. He tells Phelps to take charge as first reporting officer, then goes off to set up a perimeter around the crime scene.

Objectives

* Search Crime Scene & Talk to Witness.
* Interview Incident Eyewitness.
* Investigate Gun Store.
* Investigate Hartfield's Jewelry.
* Apprehend Edgar Kalou.
* Obtain a Murder Conviction.

CASE REPORT

TOTAL NUMBER OF KEY CLUES	7
TOTAL NUMBER OF INTERVIEW QUESTIONS	5

Fail Conditions

* Phelps dies.
* Crime scene contaminated.

LOCATION: NUNN BUSH SHOES

SEARCH THE BODY.

You begin on the sidewalk in front of the shoe store ① with the first clue already listed on the Evidence page of your notebook: "Shooting." Phelps automatically stands over the victim, ready to examine the body.

Make sure Phelps' hand is pointing at the left breast pocket of the victim's suit jacket. (It's on your right as you face the dead man.) Then press the Examine button to open the suit and pull a layaway voucher from the inside pocket. Scroll down the voucher to examine it fully and add "Layaway voucher" to your notebook in two places: the Clues page and the Evidence list that you use when interviewing a subject.

The layaway voucher shows a series of payments made to Bank of Arcadia by someone named "C. Galletta" on a pair of pearl earrings.

FIND THE BULLET CASINGS.

After examining the victim, walk toward the curb—you should see a glint on the ground (circled in our screenshot). When you hear the chime, examine one of the five **.32 shell casings** scattered on the sidewalk.

An onscreen notification states that they've been added as a New Clue to your notebook.

FIND THE HANDGUN.

Now walk over to the trashcan next to where Officer Tate holds back the crowd. When you hear the chime, examine the trashcan to find a revolver. Be sure to examine the gun closely to see it's an **FN Browning handgun**, serial number 01138.

Phelps mentions he should run it by a gun store. Dunn remarks that Eagleson's is just a couple of blocks away. This adds "Eagleson's Gun Store" to your Locations list.

TALK TO THE WITNESS.

Now walk toward the onlookers at the opposite end of the sidewalk. Approach the fellow in the reddish shirt to trigger a quick cutscene: The witness reports that he heard gunshots and saw a girl run into the shoe store.

(Note that if you try to enter the store to interrogate the girl before finding all three of the key clues, Officer Dunn says, "We should make sure we've combed the whole crime scene before questioning the witness.")

INTERVIEW THE INCIDENT EYEWITNESS.

Walk into Nunn Bush Shoes and approach the young female clerk to trigger a cutscene that opens your interview with her. Her name is Clovis Galletta, 27, and the shooting victim was her boss, Everett Gage. This adds both to your P.O.I. page—it also automatically brings up the Questions page of your notebook.

In L.A. Noire, you conduct interviews using your notebook. All topics for questioning are listed on the right-hand page. Move your pencil

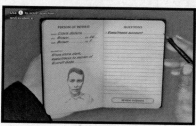

to the topic you want to discuss and then select it to trigger a question. In this case, you have only one topic listed so far: "Eyewitness account." Select it to trigger Phelps' first question.

Get All the Clues First!
Clues provide new leads and evidence for interviews. Be sure to carefully scour crime scenes and other locations for all possible clues. Keep searching until the investigation music stops, indicating that you've found all key clues.

If you lack key clues when questioning someone later, you may not be able to catch him/her in a lie.

Key Clue Checklist: Nunn Bush Shoes
✓ Shooting
✓ Layaway voucher (on victim)
✓ .32 shell casings
✓ FN Browning handgun

INTERVIEW: CLOVIS GALLETTA

TOPIC: *EYEWITNESS ACCOUNT*

Phelps asks Miss Galletta what happened. She describes how her boss accosted her in another store during her lunch break, accusing her of being late. Then as she walked ahead of him back to Nunn Bush Shoes, she heard shots behind her and saw Mr. Gage fall. And that's it.

Now watch her demeanor for a few seconds: Miss Galletta looks uncomfortable. She swallows, licks her lips, and glances evasively from side to side.

In this case, she's lying... and because the Patrol cases are tutorial missions, the game tells you onscreen to select "Lie" as your response. But keep in mind that you must have evidence to support any accusation of lying. If you don't, you let the subject off the hook—you "fail" that question and may lose out on key information, or cut off other lines of questioning.

For example, if you select "Doubt" here, you merely infuriate Miss Galletta and she clams up, refusing to speak further to Phelps. (Note: Despite this setback, you can still solve this particular case by tracing the gun clue.)

But if you've been following our walkthrough, you have the evidence you need. Select "Lie."

CORRECT ASSESSMENT: *LIE*
EVIDENCE: *LAYAWAY VOUCHER*

Officer Phelps presses Miss Galletta, who responds indignantly and challenges him to "prove different." This automatically brings up the Evidence page of your notebook. Right now you have four pieces of evidence. Select the "Layaway voucher." Amazingly, it seems the woman is holding back information because she's afraid she'll lose the pearl earrings she has on layaway!

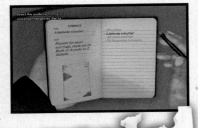

BACKTRACKING

If you select "Lie" and decide you don't have the evidence necessary to support the accusation, you can back out of the assessment and make another choice.

Now Phelps turns up the heat, so Miss Galletta admits that Edgar Kalou, the man who owns the jewelry store, got into a loud argument with Gage. This adds the Jewelry Store as a new Location and Edgar Kalou as a new P.O.I. in your notebook. (Again, if you fail this question you can still acquire Kalou's information later at the gun store.) Then she re-describes the shooting. When she finishes, two new topics are added to your Questions page.

Listen to the Music: Pt. 2

When you correctly select Truth or Doubt, or present the correct evidence after selecting Lie, you hear an ascending three-note musical cue that ends in a harmonized chord. This cue will, indeed, become music to your ears as the game progresses.

However, if you make the wrong assessment or present incorrect evidence, you'll hear a four-note musical cue that ends in a lowered tone.

THE NOTEBOOK MARKS

If Phelps puts a checkmark beside a topic on the Questions page, it means you made the correct assessment-Truth, Doubt, or Lie (including selection of the correct evidence to refute the Lie).

Phelps puts an X beside a notebook topic if you make an incorrect assessment or fail to produce the correct evidence to support your choice of Lie.

TOPIC: *POSSIBLE MURDER SUSPECT*

This topic is added upon successfully completing the first topic, "Eyewitness account." Miss Galletta provides the location of the jewelry store, Hartfield's. She also verifies that Kalou was, indeed, the shooter. But once again she appears nervous— lowering her gaze when she makes eye contact with Phelps, then glancing side to side.

If you accept her answer as the full story and select "Truth," you won't get a plausible motive for the murder. But again, as this is a tutorial case, the game offers the correct answer in an onscreen message.

CORRECT ASSESSMENT: *DOUBT*

Phelps keeps up the pressure, demanding a reason for the shooting. And Clovis obliges by providing a possible religious motive: Gage hated Jews, and Kalou is Jewish. This suggests that Gage's critique of Kalou's merchandise as shoddy was fueled by bigotry and perhaps triggered Kalou's violent reaction.

TOPIC: *DETAILS OF SHOOTING*

This topic is added if you successfully completed the first topic, "Eyewitness account." Phelps asks how

many gunshots Miss Galletta heard. She struggles to remember at first, but looks directly at Phelps several times and speaks with what seems like honest emotion.

CORRECT ASSESSMENT: *TRUTH*

Phelps gently urges her to concentrate. Eventually, she recalls five shots, which matches the number of .32-caliber shell casings you found out on the sidewalk. The interview ends with Officer Phelps thanking Miss Galletta for her bravery; she agrees to make a formal statement of testimony. When Phelps steps outside, he has a brief conversation with his partner Dunn and a new objective appears: "Investigate Hartfield's Jewelry."

Key Clue Checklist: Clovis Galletta Interview

✓ *Suspect positively identified*

✓ *Possible religious motive*

LOCATION: EAGLESON'S GUN STORE
INVESTIGATE THE GUN STORE.

Miss Galletta's interview gives you all the reason you need to seek Edgar Kalou at Hartfield's Jewelry. But if you want an ironclad case, set Eagleson's Gun Store as your current destination and follow the yellow map flag to the location ②. Enter and approach the counter to trigger a conversation with the owner, a fellow named Fickman.

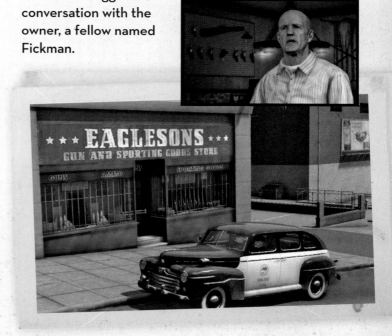

Fickman explains that the FN Browning handgun is a European favorite rarely seen in the States. He doesn't sell the model, but cleaned one a couple weeks ago. The owner, he recalls, is one Edgar Kalou. Fickman remembers that Kalou works at Hartfield's, the jewelry store up on Broadway.

If you don't already have this information from the Clovis Galletta interview, it is now added to your notebook. It's time to apprehend Mr. Edgar Kalou.

Key Clue Checklist: Eagleson's Gun Store
✓ Murder weapon serviced

LOCATION: HARTFIELD'S JEWELRY
GO TO HARTFIELD'S JEWELRY.

Set Hartfield's Jewelry as your current destination and follow the yellow map flag to the location ③. When you arrive, a new objective appears onscreen.

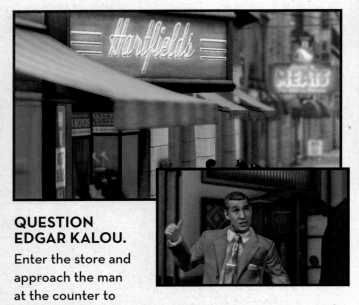

QUESTION EDGAR KALOU.

Enter the store and approach the man at the counter to trigger a cutscene: Phelps asks him if he's Edgar Kalou. The man says Mr. Kalou is resting out back. He offers to buzz him for you and walks toward the rear of the store. Then he starts running—he's actually Kalou! Sprint at the counter to leap over it and give chase.

APPREHEND EDGAR KALOU.

You automatically draw your weapon as you run. Kalou exits the building and turns right, following the alley out back. Stay as close as possible. Remember that you can track Kalou (the red blip) on your radar mini-map.

If you aim your weapon at Kalou during pursuit, a small circular gauge appears onscreen over the fleeing suspect. The gauge starts to fill up and continues to do so as long as your targeting cursor is on Kalou. If

you can keep the cursor on Kalou until the gauge fills up completely, Phelps fires a warning shot— and the suspect immediately skids to a halt and surrenders.

From the alley Kalou cuts through a restaurant, runs across Hill Street, and sprints through the park ④. If you can't get close enough to tackle him or target him with a warning shot in the park, Kalou continues down a lower-level drive-through that runs from Olive to Grand. Here you should be able to target him long enough to fill up the gauge and fire a warning shot, allowing you to apprehend him.

If all else fails, a multi-car pileup halts Kalou and lets you apprehend him there.

LOCATION: WILSHIRE POLICE STATION

Now the scene shifts to the Wilshire Division precinct station. A long cinematic plays: Captain Donelly gives Phelps the opportunity to interrogate the suspect. Donelly explains what you need for a conviction: "A motive, opportunity, hard evidence, and best of all, a confession." This gives you a new onscreen objective: "Obtain a Murder Conviction."

INTERVIEW: EDGAR KALOU

The opening topic on your notebook's Questions page depends on whether or not you got a complete statement from Clovis Galletta.

TOPIC: *ARGUMENT WITH GAGE*

This is your starter topic if you got "Suspect positively identified" from Clovis Galletta. Here Phelps lays out the simple facts as reported by the shoe store clerk. Kalou admits his disdain for Gage, but claims he had nothing to do with the shooting. (Note: If you failed to get a statement from Miss Galletta, this topic is replaced by "Nunn Bush shooting incident.")

CORRECT ASSESSMENT: *LIE*
EVIDENCE: *SUSPECT POSITIVELY IDENTIFIED (CLOVIS GALLETTA'S STATEMENT)*

When Phelps brings up Miss Galletta's statement, Kalou loses his temper and begins to show his true colors. He rages at Gage's anti-Semitism and is on the verge of losing control. Phelps knows to keep pushing Kalou's hot buttons and does so in the next topic, "Possible religious motives."

TOPIC: *SHOOTING INCIDENT*

This is your starter topic if you failed to get a statement from Clovis Galletta, but paid a visit to Eagleson's Gun Store to trace the murder weapon. After accusing Kalou of lying, present him with the evidence you collected from your discussion with Fickman at Eagleson's Gun Store. The murder was committed with Kalou's weapon. His response adds another topic to your Questions list.

CORRECT ASSESSMENT: *LIE*
EVIDENCE: *MURDER WEAPON SERVICED*

TOPIC: *POSSIBLE RELIGIOUS MOTIVE*

After Phelps sees Kalou's reaction, he presses hard on the bigotry angle, trying to force Kalou to crack. When Phelps reiterates that Gage hated Jews (learned from Miss Galletta's statement), Kalou suddenly tries to clam up, saying, "I don't know what you're talking about." Then he smirks, rolls his eyes, and tries to act nonchalant.

CORRECT ASSESSMENT: *DOUBT*

Phelps keeps up the pressure. Kalou cannot contain his anger now, and the truth spews out. Phelps pushes Kalou to admit that he despised Gage, whose bigotry carried over to business dealings. This gives you the last piece you need for a conviction: a powerful motive. And with that, Phelps makes his accusation... and Kalou is a broken man.

Afterwards, watch as a very pleased Captain Donelly congratulates Officer Phelps and hints at a promotion in the works. As he puts it, "The department needs heroes."

THE TRAFFIC CASES

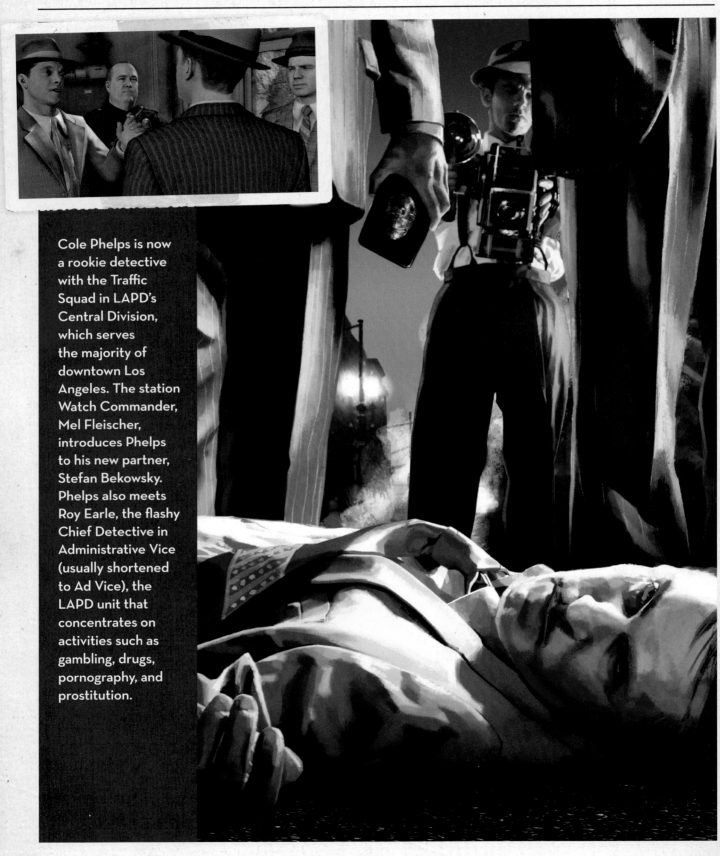

Cole Phelps is now a rookie detective with the Traffic Squad in LAPD's Central Division, which serves the majority of downtown Los Angeles. The station Watch Commander, Mel Fleischer, introduces Phelps to his new partner, Stefan Bekowsky. Phelps also meets Roy Earle, the flashy Chief Detective in Administrative Vice (usually shortened to Ad Vice), the LAPD unit that concentrates on activities such as gambling, drugs, pornography, and prostitution.

THE DRIVER'S SEAT

Bekowsky leads Phelps into the briefing room where they get the lowdown from Captain Gordon Leary on an **abandoned vehicle** with signs of foul play at the Pacific Electric Freight Depot.

Key Clue Checklist: Station Briefing

✓ Abandoned vehicle

Objectives

* Investigate P.E. Freight Depot.
* Interview Nate Wilkey.
* Investigate Black Residence.
* Interview Margaret Black.
* Investigate Cavanagh's Bar.
* Interview Frank Morgan.
* Investigate Morgan's Apartment.
* Apprehend Adrian Black.

CASE REPORT

TOTAL NUMBER OF KEY CLUES	14
TOTAL NUMBER OF INTERVIEW QUESTIONS	12

Fail Conditions

* Phelps dies.
* Crime scene contaminated.
* Lose/spook Morgan if you tail him.

LOCATION: P.E. FREIGHT DEPOT

TRAVEL TO THE PACIFIC ELECTRIC FREIGHT DEPOT.

Back at the Central Police Station ①, open your notebook to the Locations page and you'll see that the P.E. Freight Depot is already selected as your current destination down in L.A.'s warehouse district.

Exit the briefing room, then turn right and go downstairs. Head straight to the Exit sign on the ceiling and turn left to leave the station. Hop in the black unmarked car at the curb and wait for Bekowsky to join you. You can also let Bekowsky drive; see the Tip on this page.

Partner Driving

Stand beside the car then press and hold down the button designated for Partner Driving on your controller to let him take the wheel. When he "drives" to the current destination (set by you in your notebook, or set automatically by certain in-game situations), you actually skip to that location.

Note that any conversation, which would normally occur during that specific trip, still takes place before you skip.

If you choose to drive yourself, follow the yellow map flag to the P.E. Freight Depot ②. En route, listen as Phelps fills in Bekowsky on his background: He grew up in San Francisco and went to Stanford, then enlisted late in the war in the Marine Corps and signed up for Officer Candidates School (OCS) at Camp Elliott near San Diego. He shipped out to the Pacific in 1945 as a First Lieutenant... just in time to participate in the bloody battle of Okinawa. He was wounded there, but won the Silver Star for gallantry in action—the third highest military decoration awarded. After just a year as a beat cop, he landed in the Detective Bureau.

Trip Chat

Long cross-town trips usually feature some banter between Phelps and his partner; you often learn interesting bits about the case or other elements of back-story in these exchanges. If you ask your partner to drive, you can just relax and listen... and when the travel talk ends, you jump immediately to the set destination.

INVESTIGATE THE PACIFIC ELECTRIC FREIGHT DEPOT.

Your arrival at the depot triggers a brief cutscene: a patrol cop, Officer Clyde Hart, chats with the man who reported the vehicle, Nate Wilkey, as the coroner examines the bloody interior of the car. Other detectives comb the area, tagging evidence.

Walk across the lot and approach Officer Hart to get a rundown of the situation. This adds Nate Wilkey (the witness) and Adrian Black (the abandoned car's registered owner) to your P.O.I. list. You also get a new clue: **Blood splashes.**

EXAMINE THE CAR.

Accumulate more evidence before interviewing Nate Wilkey. Approach the coroner next to the car and press the Talk button to trigger a cutscene: Coroner Malcolm Carruthers points out the abundance of blood splattered all over the vehicle's interior. No sign of the victim anywhere, however, "unless he's in the trunk of the car"—a good place to search next. But first, examine the car's interior to find a significant amount of blood spilled.

EXAMINE THE TRUNK.

Walk around behind the car and open the trunk. You can examine the tire iron, but nothing about it appears unusual. However, to the left is a **receipt for a live hog** from Riverside Slaughterhouse, a new clue.

The purchaser is signed as "Mr. F. Morgan." This also adds F. Morgan to your P.O.I. list.

EXAMINE THE WALLET AND GLASSES.

Now walk a few feet in front of the car and check out the items next to the yellow crime scene evidence marker labeled "A": a pair of **glasses** and a **wallet**. Pick up the wallet and examine the driver's license on the left side to add the new clue, giving you Adrian Black's identity and home address and adding his wife as a P.O.I. (This also triggers a new objective: "Interview Mrs. Black.") You can examine the photo of the Blacks on the wallet's right side, as well. They look like a nice enough couple, don't they?

Put the wallet down, pick up the glasses, and turn them until you get a close-up of the name "Stenzel" on the temple piece. This adds the new clue "Glasses" to your evidence list. Note also that the glasses

bear the sign of what Phelps calls "home repair": tape wrapped around the frame's nosepiece.

EXAMINE THE BLOODY PIPE.

Turn left from marker A and cross the railroad tracks to evidence marker B. Pick up the **bloody pipe** and turn it until you can see the brand name, InstaHeat, etched on the side. Phelps suggests that this might give you something to go on.

INTERVIEW THE WITNESS.

If you've followed our directions, the investigation music stops here, indicating you've gathered all of the key clues at this location. Now it's time to interview Nate Wilkey. Walk right up to him and press the Talk button to trigger the interview

sequence. After Wilkey gives you some preliminary information, the Questions page of your notebook pops up.

Key Clue Checklist: P. E. Freight Depot
- ✓ Blood splashes
- ✓ Receipt for live hog
- ✓ Wallet
- ✓ Glasses
- ✓ Bloody pipe

INTERVIEW: NATE WILKEY

TOPIC: *PURPOSE AT SCENE*

When Phelps asks the witness what he was doing at the scene, Wilkey explains that he was on his way to work for the Railway. He looks directly at the detective and appears straightforward in his answer.

CORRECT ASSESSMENT: *TRUTH*

Wilkey seems like an honest man. He says he saw no one at the site until the police showed up.

TOPIC: *KNOWLEDGE OF ADRIAN BLACK*

Detective Phelps asks Wilkey if he knows Adrian Black, the owner of the vehicle. Wilkey says no, and once again his gaze appears honest and unflinching.

CORRECT ASSESSMENT: *TRUTH*

Wilkey reports that he noticed the same car a few nights ago in the parking lot. He says it stood out because he'd never seen it before.

TOPIC: *BLOODSTAINED PIPE FOUND*

Phelps asks Wilkey if he knows anything about the bloody pipe. Without hesitation Wilkey answers no. He returns to the direct gaze that you saw with the first two questions.

CORRECT ASSESSMENT: *TRUTH*

Wilkey ends his statement by noting that the blood was dark and looked dry already when he found the vehicle. This suggests that whatever deed created the bloody mess was enacted earlier elsewhere, and then the car was dropped off here.

TOPIC: *CONTENTS OF WALLET*

When Phelps asks if Wilkey found anything in the wallet near the car, the man gets riled up for the first time. His reaction is defensive, and afterwards he smirks and his eyes shift away. Clearly you've hit a nerve with this question, and he seems less than truthful. But you have no evidence to suggest he's lying, so your only recourse is to express doubt about his response.

CORRECT ASSESSMENT: *DOUBT*

Phelps threatens to have Wilkey searched. Now Wilkey answers honestly that he checked the wallet, but found no money inside.

After the Wilkey interview, Phelps decides that it's time to report the disturbing findings to Adrian Black's wife. The address, 620 Bunker Hill Avenue, is automatically marked as a new yellow blip on your map. Use your notebook to set it as your Current Destination.

LOCATION: BLACK RESIDENCE

TALK TO MRS. BLACK.

Travel to the Black residence ③. Approach the front door to knock, then follow Margaret Black into the living room after she answers. This triggers an automatic conversation: Detective Phelps reports of her husband's disappearance and she appears genuinely upset.

When Phelps asks about "InstaHeat," Mrs. Black knows the name: the Blacks just had a new InstaHeat water heater installed right outside the kitchen window. Phelps asks her to recall any details about the previous night while he searches the house.

INVESTIGATE THE BLACK RESIDENCE.

The home contains plenty of irrelevant objects you can pick up—cups, brushes, bibles, laundry detergent, and so forth—but we'll take you right to the seven key clues. Four are in one bedroom, two in the kitchen, and one outside the house.

SEARCH ADRIAN'S BEDROOM.

First, note that Adrian and Margaret seem to have separate bedrooms. Start by examining Adrian's, the disheveled room next to the kitchen. Look in the armoire to find a used **train ticket** to Seattle.

There's a **glasses case** on the nearby dresser. After picking it up, examine it further to discover that it's a Stenzel case, and it's empty.

Next to the glasses case is a photograph of Adrian Black in a frame. Examine this further, too; Phelps opens up the frame. This reveals a concealed message—a breathless love note—written on the back of the photo. But it's not from Margaret Black!

The author signs her name "Nicole." This adds the **concealed message** clue to your Evidence page.

Finally, find the **Cavanagh's matchbook** on the small nightstand next to the bed. It provides you with the name of Cavanagh's Bar in Los Angeles, which gives you a new objective: "Trace Address of Cavanagh's Bar." Phelps says R&I should have an address and you get an onscreen message to look for a phone.

```
CHECKING WITH R&I
The LAPD Records and
Identifications Division (R&I)
can provide you with critical
information such as ownership
records, addresses, crime/arrest
records, and other case-specific
data. Phelps can call in to R&I
from any standard telephone or use
a "gamewell," one of the police
call boxes found on many corners
throughout Los Angeles.
```

SEARCH THE KITCHEN.

Enter the kitchen and approach the small table where you see two items. Pick up the **InstaHeat receipt** on the right to verify that the Blacks did recently install a new water heater. Phelps notes that it might be time to check the installation outside.

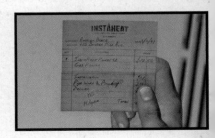

But before you go, pick up the **InstaHeat flyer** on the left. Once you get the close-up, examine it further to mark it as a new clue: Phelps turns it over to see a pipe-fitting diagram for the installation. Now you can exit the kitchen, although you can find

another Cavanagh's Bar matchbook on the counter in case you missed the one in Adrian's bedroom.

NEWSPAPER CINEMATIC

Don't overlook the newspaper on the dining room table with the headline "Alienist Fontaine." It provides another important piece of background information in its "story behind the headlines."

CALL IN FOR THE BAR ADDRESS.

Before going outside, use the phone in the front entry hall. Phelps calls into R&I and gets the address of Cavanagh's Bar. This puts that location on your map and adds another objective: "Investigate Cavanagh's Bar."

ASSEMBLE THE WATER HEATER PIPES.

Exit the front door, turn left, and walk around the house until you find the InstaHeat water heater on the wall. The installation is not complete—four pipe segments still lie on the ground. The camera focuses on these loose pipes.

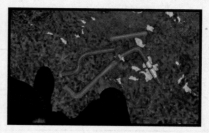

Pick up any one of the pipes; the camera shifts to view the installation. Remember the diagram on the flyer in the kitchen? Place the pipe in its proper place. (An incorrect placement causes Phelps to say, "That can't be right.")

When all four pipes are correctly placed, you can see that one pipe is still missing. Of course, it matches the shape of the bloody InstaHeat pipe you found near Black's abandoned vehicle. This gives you the **water heater** clue. It also updates the information in your notebook on the "Bloody pipe" clue.

INTERVIEW MARGARET BLACK.

The investigation music stops, indicating that you've found all key clues. Time to talk to Mrs. Black. Go back inside and approach her in the living room to trigger the interview sequence.

Key Clue Checklist: Black Residence

✓ Train ticket

✓ Glasses case

✓ Concealed message

✓ Cavanagh's matchbook

✓ InstaHeat flyer

✓ InstaHeat receipt

✓ Water heater

INTERVIEW: MARGARET BLACK

TOPIC: *SLAUGHTERHOUSE RECEIPT*

When Phelps asks about the receipt made out to F. Morgan for a live pig found in Adrian's trunk, Mrs. Black looks stumped. "A pig? Adrian runs a tool business," she says. But she identifies the recipient as Frank Morgan, someone she clearly doesn't care for. Then she makes steady eye contact with the detectives.

CORRECT ASSESSMENT: *TRUTH*

She explains that Frank Morgan is the foreman at her husband's plant and calls him a very shady character. Morgan is also Adrian's drinking buddy.

TOPIC: *STENZEL GLASSES CASE*

Phelps asks if Adrian Black was wearing his glasses when she last saw him. She says yes, and adds that he just bought a new pair—an interesting detail. Once again, she looks right at Phelps.

CORRECT ASSESSMENT: *TRUTH*

Margaret Black goes on to say that she urged her husband to throw away his old pair, which he'd repaired with tape. These old glasses, of course, are what you found near the abandoned car next to Adrian Black's wallet. If he left home wearing his new glasses, why were the old ones found at the scene?

TOPIC: *LOCATION OF ADRIAN BLACK*

Phelps asks Mrs. Black where her husband said he was going last night. Margaret answers that he simply said he was going to meet Frank for a drink. She seems sad, but no hint of duplicity.

CORRECT ASSESSMENT: *TRUTH*

Pressed for more detail, Mrs. Black notes that Adrian came home early from work—unusual because "he never comes home early." He also left early for the bar.

TOPIC: *PHOTOGRAPH SIGNED "NICOLE"*

Mrs. Black seems a bit flustered by Phelps' question about Adrian's photo in his bedroom. She glances sideways as she explains that it's from his most recent business trip to Seattle. Although she maintains some composure, Margaret clearly knows more than she's telling.

CORRECT ASSESSMENT: *LIE*
EVIDENCE: *CONCEALED MESSAGE*

Phelps accuses Mrs. Black of withholding information. When she insists she told what she knows about the picture, she sounds upset. Phelps confronts her about Nicole, the name on the back of the photo, and Mrs. Black admits she's seen the photo frame. She knows what's going on. There's another woman in Seattle.

TOPIC: *CAVANAGH'S BAR MATCHBOOK*

When Phelps asks about Cavanagh's Bar, Mrs. Black says her husband "practically lives there" after work. No reason to doubt this.

CORRECT ASSESSMENT: *TRUTH*

Lately, however, Adrian hasn't been frequenting the bar as often because he's been away in Seattle a lot... on business, says his wife.

TOPIC: *ALIBI FOR MRS. BLACK*

Phelps presses a little harder with this question, asking if she can account for her movements last night. She reacts with honest indignation and says she made dinner, then waited for her husband to come home.

CORRECT ASSESSMENT: *TRUTH*

Mrs. Black admits she was alone, so nobody can vouch for her story. Then she holds steady eye contact with the detective. She's clearly an honest woman suffering the pain of a failing marriage.

Once you've called in for the Cavanagh's Bar address, its location appears on your map as a yellow blip. Exit the Black residence and return to your car. Open your notebook, select Locations, and then select Cavanagh's Bar in your notebook to designate it as your current destination and mark its map location with a yellow flag.

LOCATION: CAVANAGH'S BAR
FIND AND INTERVIEW FRANK MORGAN.

Drive (or let your partner drive) to Cavanagh's Bar ④. Enter, approach the bartender, and press the Talk button to trigger a quick exchange: Phelps asks about Frank Morgan, and the bartender points him out.

Walk to the back of the bar and approach the man sitting alone in a Saval Tool Co. jumpsuit. Press the Talk button to trigger an interview sequence: Detective Phelps asks if he knows Adrian Black is missing, and Morgan replies, "No. Tough break." His answer doesn't seem very believable, does it?

INTERVIEW: FRANK MORGAN

TOPIC: *LINK TO ABANDONED VEHICLE*

Morgan denies knowing anything about the blood-covered, abandoned vehicle. Bekowsky isn't buying it, and you certainly have evidence to suggest it's a lie. Watch Morgan for a few seconds. Although he makes eye contact, his face is restless—he raises his brow nervously.

CORRECT ASSESSMENT: *LIE*
EVIDENCE: *RECEIPT FOR LIVE HOG*

When Phelps calls his bluff, Morgan gets nasty and demands proof he was at the railyard. When Phelps brings up the slaughterhouse receipt, Morgan cracks like an egg. Your correct assessment adds a new topic to your Questions list.

```
SECOND CHANCE
If you get this first assessment wrong, you have another chance to catch
Morgan being less than truthful with a new topic: "Knowledge of Adrian
Black." Again, Morgan lies and you must use the slaughterhouse receipt to
refute him.
```

TOPIC: *LOCATION OF ADRIAN BLACK*

When Phelps asks for Black's whereabouts, Morgan returns to his smarmy tone, claiming to have no idea. "I think he took off for Seattle," he says, then tries to smile. More like a smirk, don't you think?

CORRECT ASSESSMENT: *DOUBT*

When Phelps and Bekowsky get tough, Morgan quickly changes his tune. He admits that Adrian Black is holed up at Morgan's place. He spills the address, adding Morgan's Apartment to your Locations list. Select it as your current destination to mark it on your map as a yellow flag.

Spill it or we take you out in the alley and we knock it out of you.

ARREST FRANK MORGAN.

Now you can simply walk away and let Frank Morgan go—hey, he was just helping out a buddy, right?. Alternatively, press the button indicated to put Frank Morgan under arrest. We recommend arrest because we don't like the guy.

```
THIRD CHANCE
If you fail the
interview with
Frank Morgan and
he doesn't admit
that Adrian Black
is at his apart-
ment, you can tail
Morgan back to
his place to find
Black.
```

DRIVE TO FRANK MORGAN'S APARTMENT.

Get in your car and drive (or let your partner drive) to Morgan's apartment at Temple and Figueroa. As you proceed, KGPL calls in with a report from Technical Services on the blood found in Black's car. No surprise: the blood is not human, and most likely swine. (This adds a new clue.)

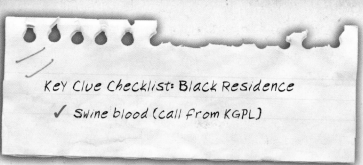

LOCATION: MORGAN'S APARTMENT

FIND APARTMENT 2.

Enter the building—the entrance to Morgan's apartment is just left of Geiger's Rare Books. You already know that Morgan lives in Apartment 2, but you can check the mailboxes just inside the entrance just to make sure.

Climb the stairs, turn left, and approach the first door on the left to trigger a quick scene. Phelps knocks on the door and none other than Adrian Black answers. When Phelps announces he's under arrest, Black apologizes and says he'll go quietly. But then he suddenly slams the door and bolts.

APPREHEND ADRIAN BLACK.

Run at the door to kick it open, then veer left into the bedroom and approach the open window—Phelps

automatically climbs through onto the fire escape. Black went up, so climb the fire escape ladders to the roof.

On the rooftop, turn left and leap down to the next lower roof. Follow Black down to another lower roof, then run to the drainpipe and slide down to the ground. Chase after Black until you find Bekowsky holding the suspect at gunpoint.

Afterwards, watch the cutscene as you end up back at the Central Police Station in the office of Captain Gordon Leary. If you performed well, the captain commends Phelps for his work.

A MARRIAGE MADE IN HEAVEN

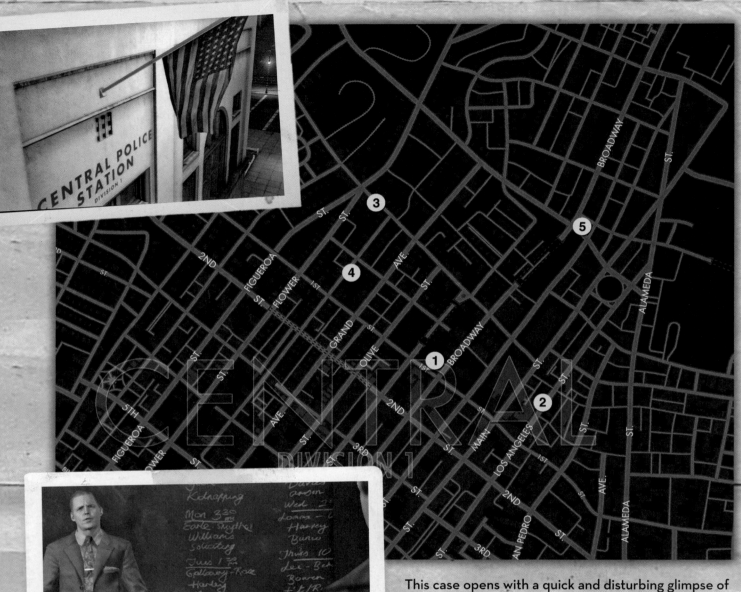

Key Clue Checklist: Station Briefing

✓ Hit-and-run vehicle

This case opens with a quick and disturbing glimpse of the crime: A man staggers from the sidewalk into the path of a speeding red automobile. After the impact, the vehicle veers around the shattered body and roars off into the night.

The scene shifts to the Central Police Station briefing room where Captain Leary reports the fatal hit-and-run incident. It happened just outside of Ray's Café on North Los Angeles Street, not far from the station. He sends his detectives to the scene to investigate and seek witnesses who can provide details on the car.

Objectives

* Investigate Ray's Cafe.
* Interview Shannon Perry.
* Interview Dudley Lynch.
* Investigate Shelton Residence.
* Apprehend William Shelton.
* Notify/Interview Mrs. Pattison.
* Report to Central Morgue.
* Apprehend Lorna Pattison.
* Apprehend Leroy Sabo.

CASE REPORT

TOTAL NUMBER OF KEY CLUES	9
TOTAL NUMBER OF INTERVIEW QUESTIONS	10

Fail Conditions

* Phelps dies.
* Crime scene contaminated.

LOCATION: RAY'S CAFÉ
INVESTIGATE RAY'S CAFE.

Follow the yellow map flag to the crime scene on the street outside Ray's Café. Approach the uniformed patrol officer to get the details: the victim is Lester Pattison, hit by a car as he stepped into the street after leaving Ray's. A young female witness, Shannon Perry, waits for you near the entrance. She lives above the bar. Investigate the crime scene before you approach her for a statement.

Start with the victim's body. Examine Lester's right breast pocket to find his **wallet**. This clue adds the Pattison address to your map. Then check Lester's left pocket for an **insurance letter** from California Fire & Life; it shows an increase in premium and payout, with a note of consternation scrawled in hand.

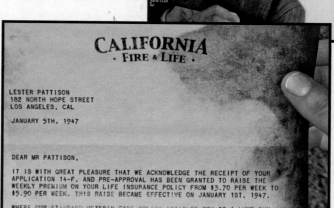

CALIFORNIA
· FIRE & LIFE ·

LESTER PATTISON
182 NORTH HOPE STREET
LOS ANGELES, CAL

JANUARY 5TH, 1947

DEAR MR PATTISON,

IT IS WITH GREAT PLEASURE THAT WE ACKNOWLEDGE THE RECEIPT OF YOUR APPLICATION 14-F, AND PRE-APPROVAL HAS BEEN GRANTED TO RAISE THE WEEKLY PREMIUM ON YOUR LIFE INSURANCE POLICY FROM $3.70 PER WEEK TO $5.90 PER WEEK. THIS RAISE BECAME EFFECTIVE ON JANUARY 1ST, 1947.

WHERE OUR STANDARD VETERAN CARE POLICY ENTITLED YOU TO A LUMP SUM

When you finish examining the body, Phelps automatically talks to Mal Carruthers for his **coroner's report**. Carruthers notes that the victim was intoxicated and likely died on impact. When Phelps points out the victim's chest wound, the coroner suggests it's not unusual in car accidents: "Look for a car with a prominent hood ornament."

Now explore the area. The blood smear at evidence marker C shows the body traveled a good 20 feet after impact. Marker B shows a blood splatter at what appears to be the point of impact, quite a distance from the body. The car's skid marks at marker A suggests that the driver managed to brake before the impact. (Note: None of these observations is listed as a new clue in your notebook.)

INTERVIEW THE EYEWITNESS.

Now that you've got the basic facts, approach the young woman standing alone outside the café to trigger an interview sequence. Her name is Shannon Perry.

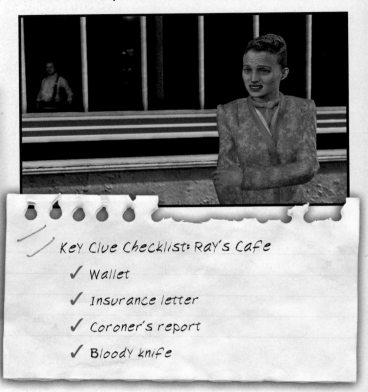

Key Clue Checklist: Ray's Cafe
- ✓ Wallet
- ✓ Insurance letter
- ✓ Coroner's report
- ✓ Bloody knife

Head down the alley to the left of Ray's Café and approach the upright garbage can beside the first dumpster. Examine it to find a **bloody knife**. Turn it in Phelps' hand until you can read "STA BRITE Stainless Steel" etched in the blade—this adds the knife to your Evidence page.

INTERVIEW: SHANNON PERRY

TOPIC: *EYEWITNESS REPORT*

Miss Perry says she looked out her second-floor window because of an **argument overheard** downstairs. She sounds like an uncomplicated girl, and there's no reason to doubt such a simple statement.

CORRECT ASSESSMENT: *TRUTH*

She goes on to report that she saw the car hit the victim and knock him down the street. This exchange adds the new clue plus a new Questions topic: "Argument overheard."

TOPIC: *SUSPECT VEHICLE DESCRIPTION*

Phelps asks her to describe the vehicle. Without hesitation she replies, "A dark **red Lincoln Continental**." She smiles slightly, as if proud of herself.

CORRECT ASSESSMENT: *TRUTH*

Phelps follows up by asking if she caught the license plate. She recalls the first three digits: 3C8. This adds a new objective: Call in the suspect vehicle.

TOPIC: *ARGUMENT OVERHEARD*

Phelps asks for more on the argument. Miss Perry reports hearing two voices, a man and a woman. That's all she'll say. The look on her face is fairly transparent—she chews on her lower lip and rolls her eyes. She's holding something back. But you don't have any evidence to the contrary yet.

CORRECT ASSESSMENT: *DOUBT*

When Phelps accuses her of holding out, Miss Perry apologizes and sheepishly admits she's a struggling actress and hoped to tell her story to the newspapers! She says the argument appeared to be between a married couple—the woman attacked the man with intimate, embarrassing comments.

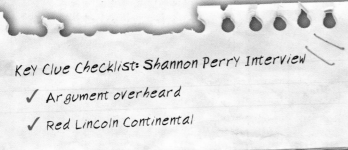

Key Clue Checklist: Shannon Perry Interview
✓ Argument overheard
✓ Red Lincoln Continental

INTERVIEW THE BARTENDER.

After talking to Miss Perry, the detectives decide to check with the patrons inside Ray's. Enter and approach the bartender and press Talk to trigger an interview sequence. The bartender gives his name as Dudley Lynch, and says he's covering for the owner who left to escort Pattison's wife, Lorna, to her home.

INTERVIEW: DUDLEY LYNCH

TOPIC: *HIT AND RUN INCIDENT*

Phelps asks what Lynch remembers about the accident. The bartender says he doesn't know much—the bar was busy, and all he heard was the impact. His gaze shifts away as he says this, then he squints and seems uncomfortable.

CORRECT ASSESSMENT: *DOUBT*

When Phelps brings up possible licensing violations, Lynch admits that Lester and Lorna Pattison were having an ugly fight. The owner made them take it outside.

TOPIC: *ASSOCIATION WITH VICTIM*

When asked if he knew the victim, Lynch tells Detective Phelps that he only knows Lester Pattison as a regular at the bar.

CORRECT ASSESSMENT: *TRUTH*

Lynch admits that Lester was not his favorite customer. Pattison's wife, Lorna, accompanied him to the bar that night, but "didn't seem too interested in the booze."

TOPIC: *ARGUMENT OVERHEARD IN BAR*

This topic appears after you learn details of the Pattisons' fight from Shannon Perry, the witness outside the bar. When Phelps asks Lynch, he corroborates that the argument was nasty and aired the couple's "dirty laundry." The statement seems straightforward, but then Lynch smirks and glances side to side a few times.

CORRECT ASSESSMENT: *DOUBT*

Phelps demands more information. Chastened a bit, Lynch explains that Lorna was very upset, so the bar's owner, Leroy Sabo, left to take her home. He divulges that Leroy and Lorna are close and recently discussed opening a new bar together. This adds **Lynch's statement** to your Evidence page and tacks on one more topic to your Questions list.

TOPIC: *JOINT BUSINESS VENTURE*

This topic only appears if you made the correct assessment on Lynch's previous answer. When Phelps asks for details on the plans for a new bar, Lynch tries to play dumb, saying, "I just serve the drinks." But again, his smirk is a dead giveaway.

CORRECT ASSESSMENT: *DOUBT*

When Phelps threatens to play rough, Lynch spits out the rest of the story: Lester Pattison was abusive to his wife, Lorna, when he was drinking, and was also a compulsive gambler. So Lorna pitched the bar idea to Leroy. But Lynch admits that Ray's Café is barely making it, kept afloat by the poker games in the back room. How would Lorna Pattison and Leroy Sabo fund a new venture?

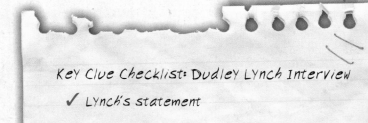

Key Clue Checklist: Dudley Lynch Interview

✓ Lynch's statement

NEWSPAPER CINEMATIC

Pick up the copy of the Los Angeles Inquisitor on the bar in front of Dudley Lynch. Press the button indicated onscreen to view the story behind the headline to get another snippet of interaction between Dr. Harlan J. Fontaine and Courtney Sheldon, the USC medical student.

CALL IN THE SUSPECT VEHICLE'S LICENSE NUMBER.

Use the payphone down the hallway and behind the bar in Ray's Café to phone in to LAPD dispatch and trace the partial plate number for the red Lincoln Continental. The only possible match is a car owned by someone named William Shelton. This puts Shelton's residence on West Temple Street onto your map and adds the objective to investigate the place.

LOCATION: SHELTON RESIDENCE

INVESTIGATE THE SHELTON RESIDENCE.

Travel to the Shelton residence ③. The red Lincoln Continental is parked out front with its front grille smashed. You also find Mr. William Shelton loading suitcases into the trunk, getting ready to skip town. Phelps and Bekowsky confront the young man, who readily admits to the accident. But then he speeds off in his Lincoln!

APPREHEND WILLIAM SHELTON.

Phelps automatically jumps into his car, giving you control of the vehicle. Chase Shelton's red Lincoln (easy to spot in traffic) as it makes a zigzag route across the city.

Try to run his car off the road, ram it until it stops running, or pull up beside it so Bekowsky can shoot out the tires. When the Lincoln finally comes to a halt, hop out and approach the vehicle to trigger the arrest scene.

> ## CAR TO FOOT
> If you don't halt Shelton's car before he reaches the train station, he hops out and starts running. At that point you must chase him down on foot.

Shelton admits hitting the victim, but claims it wasn't his fault—the guy suddenly jumped in front of his car, he says. Shelton makes another interesting claim: he says a woman and a man were standing right next to the victim just before the accident.

LOCATION: PATTISON RESIDENCE

NOTIFY MRS. PATTISON.

Travel to the Pattison residence ④ on North Hope Street and approach the front door. Lorna Pattison answers the knock and lets in Detectives Phelps and Bekowsky. You can look around the house and examine various objects, but you won't find anything of interest regarding the case, so just follow Mrs. Pattison into the living room to trigger a cutscene.

The detectives and the woman have a brief exchange in which Mrs. Pattison appears anything but grief-stricken about the recent loss of her husband. Then Leroy Sabo, the bar owner, appears from a back bedroom. The two explain what happened that evening, and Lorna adds that she was filing for divorce from Lester: mental cruelty.

INTERVIEW LORNA PATTISON.

When the cutscene ends, the interview with Mrs. Pattison automatically begins.

INTERVIEW: LORNA PATTISON

TOPIC: *HIT AND RUN INCIDENT*

Phelps asks Lorna how the accident occurred. She replies that Lester just walked into the path of the oncoming car. Her smirk is almost mocking. Clearly this is not the whole story, but you have no evidence to suggest otherwise.

CORRECT ASSESSMENT: *DOUBT*

Phelps jumps on her statement, but Lorna only adds that Lester's gambling was like a drug addiction, and he was yelling at her and others. She concludes by saying she almost felt sorry for the driver.

TOPIC: *NATURE OF ARGUMENT*

Phelps asks her about their argument and Lorna simply says that she and Lester were always arguing, adding, "So what?" As she says this, her gaze flits from side to side. Then she swallows heavily.

CORRECT ASSESSMENT: *DOUBT*

Phelps accuses Mrs. Pattison of baiting her husband. This prods her to provide more detail about the argument. Lester was losing at cards and made some impolite suggestions on how she could earn more money for him to get another stake in the game.

TOPIC: *PARTNERSHIP WITH LEROY SABO*

Phelps asks how Lorna planned to get money to invest in the new venture with Sabo. She claims she has a little money saved away. But the evasive look in her eye is classic prevarication. And in this case, you have a piece of evidence that can support a challenge to her lie.

CORRECT ASSESSMENT: *LIE* EVIDENCE: *INSURANCE LETTER*

When Phelps points out that she increased the premium on her husband's life insurance policy, she explains that it was Leroy Sabo's idea. The rationale was that Lester lived dangerously, so Lorna needed extra protection. Phelps suggests that the fact speaks to motive and premeditation, but Lorna reminds him that so far the physical facts point to a hit-and-run driver. And she's right... so far.

CALL IN ABOUT THE AUTOPSY RESULTS.

Exit the house and use the gamewell just down the street at the corner. Phelps gets a message from the coroner to report immediately to Central Morgue for results of the Pattison autopsy. This puts the location on your map.

LOCATION: CENTRAL MORGUE

REPORT TO CENTRAL MORGUE.

Travel to Central Morgue ⑤ and enter the door under the Mortuary Night Entrance sign. Veer right through

the open door and into the autopsy room to trigger a scene. Carruthers reports a surprise development: Lester Pattison was dead before the car struck him.

A puncture wound to the heart killed Pattison—a wound that most likely matches the

bloody knife you found in the alley at Ray's Café. As Bekowsky points out, your hit-and-run case just got upgraded to "murder one"—a first-degree murder charge, meaning premeditated murder.

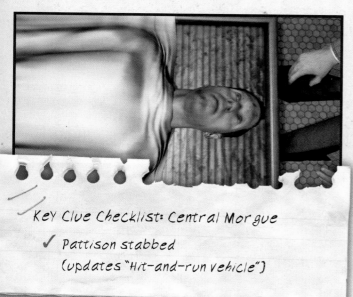

Key Clue Checklist: Central Morgue

✓ Pattison stabbed
(updates "Hit-and-run vehicle")

LOCATION: PATTISON RESIDENCE

APPREHEND LORNA PATTISON.

Return to the Pattison residence ④ and approach the front door to trigger a scene: Phelps reports the cause of death to Lorna Pattison, who immediately points the finger at Leroy Sabo. Leroy emerges from

the bedroom waving a gun and raving at Lorna, suggesting the murder was entirely her plan. The scene's tragic ending is inevitable...

APPREHEND LEROY SABO.

Chase down Leroy! He exits via the back door and sprints up the alley to the left. You can use a warning shot to trigger his surrender, or you can just gun him down. Either way, you wrap up the case and can earn Captain Leary's praise when you meet him back at Ray's Café.

THE FALLEN IDOL

This case opens on a rainy night. We see a Chevy Styleline idling on a wet hilltop, and a murky figure—a man in a suit and hat—jamming something onto its floorboard. Suddenly the car accelerates and flies off the escarpment just ahead.

Now cut to the next day in the Central Police Station briefing room. Captain Leary assigns Phelps and Bekowsky to the case: Two women were in that car, but incredibly, both survived. The vehicle got caught on a Cola King billboard on the embankment instead of diving off the cliff. Ironically, the hill overlooks the police station. Leary reports that one of the women claims she was drugged; she alleges that the "accident" was actually attempted murder.

Key Clue Checklist: Station Briefing

✓ Victims drugged

✓ Chevy Styleline

Objectives

* Investigate Crash Site.
* Interview June Ballard.
* Interview Jessica Hamilton at Central Receiving Hospital.
* Tail June Ballard.
* Investigate Bishop's Apartment.
* Interview Gloria Bishop.
* Trace Address of Prop Store.
* Investigate Silver Screen Props.
* Interview Marlon Hopgood.
* Evade or Subdue the Mobsters.
* Investigate Movie Set.
* Get Bishop Off the Lot Alive.

CASE REPORT

TOTAL NUMBER OF KEY CLUES	18
TOTAL NUMBER OF INTERVIEW QUESTIONS	16

Fail Conditions

* Phelps dies.
* Bishop dies.
* Crime scene contaminated.
* Spotted while tailing June Ballard.

LOCATION: CRASH SITE
INVESTIGATE THE CRASH SITE.

Exit the building and travel the short distance from the Central Police Station ① to the crash site ②. Drive toward the police barricade to trigger a scene: The woman sitting in the ambulance looks familiar to Phelps. Bekowsky points out that it's June Ballard, the B-movie actress; she's married to Guy McAfee, also well-known.

The detectives meet Officer Enrique Gonzales, who provides a quick overview. He refers to Ms. Ballard as the driver and says that the car's passenger, a young girl named Jessica Hamilton, was beaten up pretty badly. The girl's been taken to Central Receiving Hospital.

Walk past the police cars and down the trail to the crash site where the coroner, Mal Carruthers, waits for you. He tells you to check out what's laid out on the trunk of the car. You can also approach the driver's side door of the Styleline and examine the interior. You see a bit of blood and signs that the passenger hit the windshield, but no notebook-worthy clues.

Now examine the two items on the trunk: a pair of women's **underwear** and a purse. Pick up the underwear to find they're torn; Carruthers says he found them stuffed in the young lady's purse. Open the purse to find the **letter from mother**—it's written from Mrs. Camille Hamilton to her daughter Jessica ("Jessie"), begging her to give up her Hollywood fantasies and return home to Wisconsin. It also mentions the girl's "Aunt Junie"— June Ballard?

12129 North Astor St
Milwaukee
WI 53202

Dear Jessie,

Please, please, dear, come home.

If you're worried about your father, don't be. All is forgiven. He has a hot temper and he can be very proud, but you're still his little girl and he loves you. I know he didn't mean those things he said.

You're a good, decent girl, dear, and you're not made for Hollywood. I was fifteen once myself, I wanted to be just like Clara Bow and wear lovely dresses and kiss handsome men. But once I grew up and married your father, I realized I would never have been happy in that life. You'll realize it one day too. I'm sure Aunt Junie's looking after you, but I can't help

Approach the coroner and press Talk to trigger a short conversation. He hands you a **prop shrunken head**. After a brief Shakespearian moment, Phelps gets serious and asks if it's real; Carruthers says it looks like a movie prop. Be sure you turn the head until the camera zooms in on the casting marks to officially add the prop to your Evidence list. Then the coroner drops a bombshell: the head was used to wedge the Styleline's accelerator to the floor. Whoever did that wanted the car's occupants dead.

Key Clue Checklist: Crash Site

✓ Underwear

✓ Letter from mother

✓ Prop shrunken head

INTERVIEW JUNE BALLARD.

Follow the path back up to the ambulance and approach the woman sitting on the back. This triggers your meeting with June

Ballard and begins the interview sequence. The cagy, veteran movie actress has a hard time being straight with you.

INTERVIEW: JUNE BALLARD

TOPIC: *DOPING ALLEGATION*

Phelps asks who drugged June and her passenger, as she has alleged. She says she can't remember. Fortunately, she's such a hack that it isn't too difficult to see through her act.

CORRECT ASSESSMENT: *DOUBT*

When Phelps reprimands her, June tries a tired trick: she flirts with him. But then she hardens as she vows that her husband will settle the score with Mark Bishop. Which, of course, begs the question: Who's Mark Bishop? This adds a new topic to your Questions page, and we'll ask it in a minute.

TOPIC: *INJURED FEMALE PASSENGER*

When asked about the passenger in her car, June truly goes into full-scale, B-movie acting mode. She says it's

been a rough day for Jessica, calling her a poor, young girl desperate to break into the movies. But you have some evidence to suggest that it's been more than just a "rough day" for Jessica Hamilton.

CORRECT ASSESSMENT: *LIE*
EVIDENCE: *UNDERWEAR*

Phelps suggests something happened to Jessica before the crash. June Ballard demands proof. When Phelps notes that the girl's underwear was physically torn from her body, June suggests it happened during a casting session with Mark Bishop.

TOPIC: *SUSPECT "MARK BISHOP"*

Phelps asks if June thinks this Mark Bishop had anything to do with the incident. She explains that Bishop's a movie producer. But as for his involvement—once again, she reveals nothing and says, "You just leave it to me and my husband to worry about." Her smile is chilly. She's not exactly lying, but she's certainly not telling much truth.

CORRECT ASSESSMENT: *DOUBT*

Phelps responds with restraint considering her vigilante answer, but he demands to know her dealings with Bishop. She claims the producer offered her a part in a film then reneged. She pressed him on the matter and, as she sees it, this incident is Bishop's response.

TOPIC: *FAKE SHRUNKEN HEAD*

Phelps mentions the shrunken head used to tamper with the car. Ms. Ballard says the last thing she remembers is getting behind the wheel. But then her eyes dart sideways and she avoids eye contact for the first time in the interview. Once again, she's hiding something.

CORRECT ASSESSMENT: *DOUBT*

Phelps tries to pressure her for more, but June claims ignorance of such mundane movie issues because she's the "talent." Again, she points the detectives toward Mark Bishop, suggesting they find out which prop company he uses for his films.

After you finish with June Ballard, Detective Bekowsky suggests your next destination: visit Jessica Hamilton, the other passenger in the car. When you return to your vehicle, KGPL reports that the car crash victim has regained consciousness. Perfect!

LOCATION: CENTRAL RECEIVING HOSPITAL
FIND JESSICA HAMILTON.

Follow the new yellow map blip to Central Receiving Hospital ①, the unit attached to Central Police Station. After you arrive, enter the hospital and approach the Reception desk to ask about Jessica Hamilton. The nurse directs you across the hall to Recovery Room 1.

Approach the white-coated doctor writing on a chart just outside Recovery Room 1. This is Dr. Elias Webley, the physician attending to Miss Hamilton. He reports she was indeed drugged, most likely with chloral hydrate. Worse, the doctor has found

clear **evidence of abuse**. This is particularly disturbing because the girl is only 15 and still a minor.

INTERVIEW JESSICA HAMILTON.

Enter Recovery Room 1 to find Jessica conscious and sitting up in bed. Before interviewing her, examine the patient chart at the foot of the bed to update the evidence of abuse. Then talk to the girl.

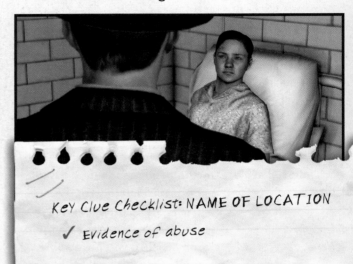

Key Clue Checklist: NAME OF LOCATION
✓ Evidence of abuse

> ### THE MICKEY FINN
>
> June Ballard referred earlier to being slipped a Mickey Finn. Chloral hydrate mixed in alcohol creates a solution called "knockout drops." These drops can be added to a bar drink to sedate the drinker—a concoction known as a Mickey Finn. The phrase commonly used is "slipping a Mickey."

INTERVIEW: JESSICA HAMILTON

TOPIC: *CRASH INCIDENT REPORT*

Phelps asks what Jessica remembers about the crash, and the answer is not much. But then she blurts out, "Nothing happened yesterday." The poor girl looks distraught, almost on the verge of tears. Her statement is clearly not true, and you have disturbing evidence to prove otherwise.

CORRECT ASSESSMENT: *LIE*
EVIDENCE: *UNDERWEAR*

Phelps brings up the torn underwear, prompting Jessica to admit that a liaison occurred. Her revelations about the rather cold advice she got from "Junie" angers Detective Bekowsky, but the girl defends Ms. Ballard, her aunt.

TOPIC: *CONTACT WITH PARENTS*

When Phelps says he needs to contact Jessica's parents, the girl says it's not necessary because they trust her Aunt June to take care of her. Poor Jessica isn't a very good liar, is she? Her discomfort is almost heartbreaking.

CORRECT ASSESSMENT: *LIE*
EVIDENCE: *LETTER FROM MOTHER*

Once Phelps points out that Jessica is a runaway teen, she makes an effort to remember what happened. She recalls going to a strange place with her Aunt June where she was given a drink that knocked her out: the Mickey Finn, no doubt.

TOPIC: *ASSOCIATION WITH BISHOP*

Phelps asks how Jessica met Mark Bishop. She answers that her aunt is a big movie star, but doesn't elaborate further.

CORRECT ASSESSMENT: *DOUBT*

Phelps tries to jolt her into revealing more by wondering why Bishop wants Jessica and June dead. The girl refuses to believe that's true. She admits she overheard some harsh phone conversations in which June Ballard screamed at Bishop. But she says the actor and producer seemed on better terms the previous day, just before the accident.

TOPIC: *EVIDENCE OF CRIMINAL ABUSE*

Now Phelps faces the unpleasant task of pressing for more details about the sexual abuse—in particular, where the incident took place. Jessica is understandably upset, and says it's hard to remember anything. She looks Phelps in the eye then starts to tear up.

CORRECT ASSESSMENT: *TRUTH*

Phelps gently coaxes Jessica to help. She says, "I remember the mermaid." This mermaid was on the front of a building where the abuse occurred.

When you leave the room after the interview's conclusion, you trigger a cutscene: As the two detectives step out of the recovery room, they spot June Ballard leaving the station with a male companion, who Phelps assumes is her lawyer. She seems in a hurry, and Bekowsky suggests that you tail her. The detectives hop into their car.

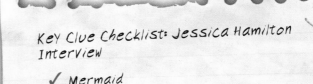

Key Clue Checklist: Jessica Hamilton Interview

✓ Mermaid

TAIL JUNE BALLARD.

Follow June's light green coupe. If you lose sight of the vehicle, note that its location is marked on your map as a red car icon. The icon flashes if you get too close to the coupe, fall too far back, or drive recklessly. Try to stay at least half a block behind and proceed carefully to avoid drawing attention. Avoid collisions.

Ballard's car takes a zigzag route. It starts down 1st, turns right on Spring, right on 3rd, then left on Broadway. Then it travels one long block before pulling to the curb just before 4th Street. June jumps out and walks quickly into Mallory's Café ③.

EAVESDROP ON JUNE IN THE CAFÉ.

Hop out of your car and take cover outside the café's front door (by pressing the Cover button indicated onscreen). You can see June waiting for a man to finish using the café's payphone. She looks around as she waits, so don't try to enter yet. After the man hangs up and leaves, June glances around some more, so don't be impatient or she'll spot you.

Stay in cover until June picks up the phone. Then step into the café and go to the empty booth on the left that has the newspaper on the table. Press the button indicated onscreen to "go incognito": Phelps

sits and opens the newspaper in front of his face.

Now you can eavesdrop on June's phone conversation. She appears to be talking to her husband—she calls him "Baby"—and demands action. She gives an address for Mark Bishop's apartment. The last thing she says is, "Sure, I got the film!" Then she exits the café and returns to her car.

You can let June go now—you've got a new objective. As Phelps says, "Sounds like Mark Bishop has a heap of trouble headed his way."

LOCATION: MARK BISHOP'S APARTMENT

TRAVEL TO BISHOP'S APARTMENT.

Set Bishop's apartment as your current destination and travel to the Wilson Apartment Hotel ④.

On the way, you hear a call from KGPL: there's a 415 in progress (LAPD radio code for "Disturbance") at Bishop's apartment 803! You are designated Code 3 (emergency call, lights and siren), so haul it fast to the Wilson. After the arrival cutscene, you run for the entrance.

Enter the building to trigger another quick cutscene: The bellman at the front desk says Mrs. Bishop is pretty upset, then directs you to the elevator and 803. Go left to the elevator and approach the call box to use it. On Floor 8, turn left down the hall to 803, the last door on the right. Gloria Bishop answers the door.

Mrs. Bishop is unhurt, but says you just missed thugs who ransacked the place. Phelps asks Gloria to gather her thoughts while he checks out the premises.

Thug Bout
If you get to Bishop's apartment fast enough you can catch the two thugs still there and engage them in a fight!

SEARCH THE APARTMENT FOR CLUES.

Start looking for clues. You can pick up a number of items, but only five are actual clues. Just inside the front door is a framed poster for the Bishop-produced movie "Gay Cowboys." It's not a key clue, but across the entry there's a prop saddle from that same film, presented to Mark Bishop by a company called Silver Screen Props. (Recall that June Ballard suggested you find out which prop house Bishop uses for his films.)

Enter the bedroom near the front entrance. Again, there are a number of examinable objects—ring, lipstick, hairbrush, and so forth—but the only item of interest is the **$20,000 check** from Mark Bishop to Lorna Hopgood on the floor near the armoire.

Now search the open office two doors down. You can examine more detritus scattered on the floor, but don't miss the **movie set photograph** and the **movie set replica**, both on the low cabinet. Each depicts the famous Great Wall of Babylon movie set for D.W. Griffith's 1916 film masterpiece, "Intolerance." As Phelps points out, the set still exists downtown.

Enter the living room where Mrs. Bishop sits and turn left to find a **prop store photograph** atop the credenza. The storefront sign for Silver Screen Props features a mermaid—no doubt the one that Jessica Hamilton recalled during her interview. When Phelps asks about the two men in the photo, Gloria Bishop says they're her husband Mark and Marlon Hopgood, owner of the prop store.

Finally, the investigation music stops, indicating that you've found all the key clues. But just for fun, step out onto the balcony before talking to Mrs. Bishop. Phelps points out the massive Babylon movie set looming in the distance: more foreshadowing. Then approach Gloria Bishop and press the Talk button to trigger the interview sequence.

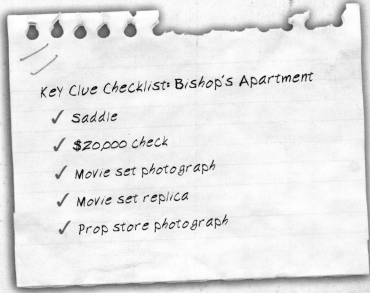

Key Clue Checklist: Bishop's Apartment

✓ Saddle
✓ $20,000 check
✓ Movie set photograph
✓ Movie set replica
✓ Prop store photograph

INTERVIEW: GLORIA BISHOP

TOPIC: *DOMESTIC DISTURBANCE*

You start with just one topic. Phelps tells Gloria that the thugs likely work for Guy McAfee, June Ballard's husband. She reacts with disdain, calling Ballard "that slut." She suggests that the recent incidents are related to Mark Bishop's new movie, but knows nothing about his business. Yet her smug look suggests otherwise.

CORRECT ASSESSMENT: *DOUBT*

When Phelps points out that June Ballard claimed a deal to be in the new picture, Gloria denies it, saying Mark repeatedly told June no. She explains Ballard made threats, and says she knows the woman from a previous film they were in together.

TOPIC: *WHEREABOUTS OF MARK BISHOP*

Phelps asks where to find Gloria's husband. She replies that Bishop said he'd be on set. That's all she knows.

CORRECT ASSESSMENT: *TRUTH*

When Phelps suggests that McAfee's men are looking for Mark Bishop with ill intent, Gloria says to check with Marlon Hopgood. This adds a new objective: "Trace Address of Prop Store."

TOPIC: *ABUSE OF JESSICA HAMILTON*

Phelps says Mark Bishop was at a casting with a young girl the previous day. Gloria Bishop claims no knowledge of this, saying her husband was scouting locations because the picture has already been cast.

CORRECT ASSESSMENT: *DOUBT*

When Phelps links Jessica's memory of a mermaid to the one on the prop store, Mrs. Bishop replies, "This is a sick town, detective." Then she admits her husband "likes them young." She herself was 16 when she met Bishop. She speaks of Hollywood's disillusionment, lechery, and shocking betrayals.

TOPIC: *CHECK FOR $20,000*

Phelps asks about the payment to Lorna Hopgood, who Gloria identifies as Marlon Hopgood's ex-wife. Then she asks, "Are you sure?" The question seems honest enough, but her face betrays more of the smugness you saw earlier.

CORRECT ASSESSMENT: *DOUBT*

Phelps presents his theory: somebody is trying to **blackmail** Mark Bishop. Whatever the blackmailers have on him must be bad if he's attempting murders to cover it up. When Phelps asks why the payment is going to Lorna Hopgood instead of McAfee, Mrs. Bishop explains that Lorna works at a check-cashing place in Hollywood.

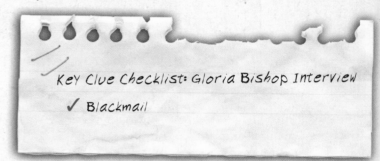

Key Clue Checklist: Gloria Bishop Interview

✓ Blackmail

GET AN ADDRESS FOR SILVER SCREEN PROPS.

Before leaving Bishop's apartment, use the telephone on the desk in the hallway. Phelps gets the address for Silver Screen Props from R&I. Then leave the apartment and take the elevator back down. Exit the building and go to your car.

LOCATION: SILVER SCREEN PROPS

INVESTIGATE SILVER SCREEN PROPS.

Travel to Silver Screen Props ⑤ at the corner of 3rd and Figueroa. Enter the store to trigger a scene: Detective Phelps meets Marlon Hopgood and asks if he holds castings here. Marlon admits having a soundstage out back. Follow Hopgood as he leads you to his seedy-looking stage.

Phelps decides to search the joint and asks Bekowsky to keep an eye on the prop storeowner. Walk up the two steps onto the stage, veer to the right toward the chaise lounge, and find the bottle of **chloral hydrate** on the nearby shelf.

Cross the room and approach the mirror on the wall to trigger a quick scene: Phelps discovers that it's a one-way mirror that looks into a small room that Bekowsky calls a "peep den."

You can see a camera in there, aimed through the mirror. Let's find that room.

Exit the soundstage and turn left in the lobby. Exit the door at the lobby's end to emerge into a storage alley. Turn left again and approach the workbench at the end of the alley. It holds paints, buckets... and several shrunken heads! Examine the **prop shrunken head molds** to add another clue to your Evidence list.

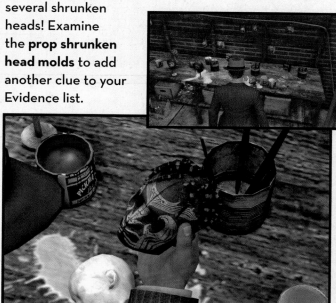

NEWSPAPER CINEMATIC

Don't miss the copy of the Los Angeles Inquisitor on the workbench in the storage alley. Its headline reads "Dope Floods Streets." Examining the story behind the headline triggers the scene of a meeting between Courtney Sheldon, the young medical student at USC, and the infamous mob boss Mickey Cohen.

FIND THE SECRET CAMERA ROOM.

Turn left from the workbench and approach what appears to be an empty dead-end alley. But when you examine it further you see it's actually a wall painted to look like an empty dead-end alley. Phelps kicks it to reveal an alley that has a locked door. Approach the door; Phelps kicks it open, too.

Inside you find the peep room with a camera aimed through the one-way mirror, plus walls covered with pornographic photos. There's a film canister with the names of Jessica Hamilton and Mark Bishop written on it. Be sure to investigate it further to discover it's an **empty film canister**.

News Clues

Just a reminder: the newspapers that trigger "the stories behind the headlines" are NOT key clues as numbered in your Case Report at the end of the case. But the investigation music for the scene will not end unless you examine the newspaper, as well as all other key clues.

Finally, you discover a "Jungle Drums" **film reel** that may reveal **Bishop's whereabouts**: apparently, he's using D.W. Griffith's old Wall of Babylon set downtown at the corner of 8th and Francisco. The investigation music stops, which means you can go back to Marlon Hopgood and get some answers.

Key Clue Checklist: Silver Screen Props

✓ Chloral hydrate

✓ Prop shrunken head molds

✓ Empty film canister

✓ Film reel

✓ Bishop's whereabouts

INTERVIEW: MARLON HOPGOOD

TOPIC: *ASSOCIATION WITH BISHOP*

Phelps asks if Hopgood has worked with Mark Bishop. The props proprietor says he mainly works for the big studios, and when Bishop does too, they cross paths. But he claims he hasn't seen Bishop around in a while. Hopgood is hard to read, but you have evidence that suggests he's not telling the truth.

CORRECT ASSESSMENT: *LIE*
EVIDENCE: *CHLORAL HYDRATE*

Once Phelps brings up the chloral hydrate, Hopgood spills it quickly, saying Bishop was indeed here with June Ballard and the girl just yesterday.

TOPIC: *WHEREABOUTS OF BISHOP*

Phelps explains that McAfee's thugs are looking for Bishop after his attempt to kill June Ballard. Hopgood says his advice to Bishop would be to skip town.

CORRECT ASSESSMENT: *TRUTH*

Phelps notes that Hopgood appears to be delivering props to the Jungle Drums movie set downtown. Hopgood says the place is old and dangerous, but might be a good place to hide. This adds a new objective: "Locate Mark Bishop."

TOPIC: *RELATIONSHIP WITH BALLARD*

When Phelps brings up the topic of June Ballard, Hopgood says he rarely gets to meet the "talent" unless they require some special prop.

CORRECT ASSESSMENT: *LIE*
EVIDENCE: *EMPTY FILM CANISTER*

Now Phelps springs his blackmail theory: Hopgood and Ballard are in cahoots, extorting money from Mark Bishop. When Hopgood proclaims his innocence, Phelps brings up the missing film reel of Bishop's "screen test" with Jessica Hamilton. Now Hopgood admits he filmed their liaison and included Bishop's face at June Ballard's request, for blackmail purposes. (You may recall June's last words on the phone in the café: "I got the film.")

TOPIC: *EVIDENCE OF BLACKMAIL*

Phelps wonders why money is involved if June Ballard got the blackmail film she wanted. Hopgood's disingenuous response: "What money?" Of course, you have proof he's lying again.

CORRECT ASSESSMENT: *LIE*
EVIDENCE: *$20,000 CHECK*

Phelps brings up the check made out to Hopgood's ex-wife. Marlon reveals June Ballard's plan to sell the Bishop/Hamilton smut film to Bishop after his new motion picture wraps. Lorna Hopgood works for a check-cashing company, so she can cash a check that large for Bishop.

MEET ROY EARLE AND THE MOBSTERS.

This scene happens automatically after you complete your interrogation of Marlon Hopgood. First, the Ad Vice detective Roy Earle arrives and announces that Hopgood is a Vice informant! He advises Phelps to release the storeowner and go rescue the movie producer.

Afterwards, Phelps and Bekowsky run into two of Guy McAfee's goons waiting in the lot outside the prop store. They're looking for Mark Bishop, of course, and Phelps warns them to back off. When Detective Bekowsky reiterates the message in less polite terms, the goons take offense... and start tailing your car with bad intentions.

EVADE OR SUBDUE THE MOBSTERS.

One option is to simply evade the mobsters; drive a zigzag route until you put a good distance between your vehicle and the mob cars. To subdue the mobsters, either nail them in a gunfight or disable their car—i.e., ram it or pull alongside so Bekowsky can shoot out its tires.

LOCATION: "JUNGLE DRUMS" SET
CHASE MARK BISHOP.

Travel to the Jungle Drums set ⑥ and get ready for a slam-bang action finale. When you arrive, the detectives immediately spot Bishop, who takes off

running. Run after him! Remember that the suspect is marked as the red blip on your mini-map. Stay on his tail as he dodges through the rickety old Babylon set that dwarfs the Jungle Drums set in the middle.

Bishop leads you up a towering staircase, then across gaps and collapsing platforms. Just keep running after him to get past hazards. Don't stop! Follow him up ladders and around the parapets of the great wall set. At one point, the planks of a ramp collapse behind him, so stick to the left side and leap across the gaps to stay on his tail.

Shortly after that, Phelps automatically pulls out his gun as he runs and finally corners Bishop, who surrenders. But then Bishop spots carloads of McAfee's goons arriving on the scene. He tells Phelps he knows another way out of the set, and leads the way.

GET BISHOP OFF THE LOT ALIVE.

Bishop is now the white blip on your map; a yellow blip shows the exit. Keep following Bishop until he stops and takes cover. Each time he does so, it means armed gangsters are deployed up ahead. Use cover and gun down the attackers. Look for explosive barrels that you can shoot to take out multiple targets in one shot.

Whenever the immediate area is clear, Bishop starts leading the way again. Stay with him! Follow as he

leaps across a big gap (created when you shoot explosive barrels), then nab the high-powered rifle leaning against the statue and use it to pick off McAfee's men on the far side of the set. Look for the lone sniper on a high platform above the wall. Keep looking for explosive barrels to detonate as you move with Bishop.

When you finally reach the long ladder, slide down to trigger a quick cutscene: Bekowsky steps up to cover you and leads Bishop down to the ground. More gunmen are posted below in the lot. You can pick off most of them from the platform above or slide to the ground and join your partner. Target the explosive barrels at the base of the huge column to bring it tumbling down onto enemy shooters.

Move across the lot with Bishop and Bekowsky, eliminating the last few goons before you reach the parking area. LAPD units are arriving, but a strong contingent of McAfee's thugs open fire from behind their cars in the lot. Pick them off to clear the way for your final escape.

WATCH THE TRAFFIC FINALE.

After the shootout, Captain Leary is pleased once again with the performance of young Detective Phelps. He informs his star that he's been promoted to a new assignment. But the moment is upstaged by the arrival of Roy Earle, who congratulates the Traffic detectives and takes them to The Blue Room Jazz Club for a celebratory drink.

Detective Earle bullies his way into the establishment and leads Phelps to the dressing room of singer Elsa Lichtmann, star of the club's current show. But Elsa is distraught and attended by none other than Doctor Harlan Fontaine, the same man we've seen earlier in some of the newspaper cinematic scenes. Roy Earle is not gentle with Miss Lichtmann... and Phelps is left bewildered.

THE HOMICIDE CASES

THE RED LIPSTICK MURDER

Six months later: As with the last case, this one opens with a shadowy, brutal depiction of the crime you must solve: A well-dressed man pulls a helpless girl from the back of an automobile, then bludgeons her with what looks like a crowbar.

Back in the Central Police Station briefing room, Captain Donelly announces the retirement of Floyd Rose, the Homicide detective you met in your first case, "Upon Reflection." The Chief of Police has replaced him with Cole Phelps, who inherits Rose's old partner, Rusty Galloway. Your first case is the murder you just witnessed. The crime scene is in a parkland area called The Moors, and the captain adds that the victim is "bearing all the signs of the werewolf"—a reference to the infamous Black Dahlia killer.

Objectives

* Investigate "The Moors" Crime Scene.

* Investigate the Bamba Club & Interview Dick McColl.

* Investigate Celine Henry's Residence & Canvass Neighbors.

* Investigate Jacob Henry's Apartment & Interview/Subdue Jacob Henry.

* Go to Central Station and Interview Jacob Henry Again.

* Investigate Mendez's Apartment & Apprehend Mendez.

CASE REPORT

TOTAL NUMBER OF KEY CLUES	19
TOTAL NUMBER OF INTERVIEW QUESTIONS	10

Fail Conditions

* Phelps dies.

* Crime scene contaminated.

* Mendez escapes.

LOCATION:
THE MOORS (CRIME SCENE)
INVESTIGATE THE CRIME SCENE.

Travel from the station ① to the crime scene at The Moors ②. Listen as Galloway mentions the Black Dahlia slaying and investigation.

Your arrival at the scene triggers a cinematic: After you push past the pack of reporters and get a preliminary briefing by Officer Houlihan, approach the coroner examining the body. Carruthers points out the victim's personal effects scattered about.

Start by examining the body; it was a gruesome attack. Examine the head and turn it to reveal the terrible **blunt force trauma** that likely killed the woman. A closer look at her left hand reveals a wound on her finger, most likely from the violent removal of a ring. This adds **missing jewelry** to your clue list.

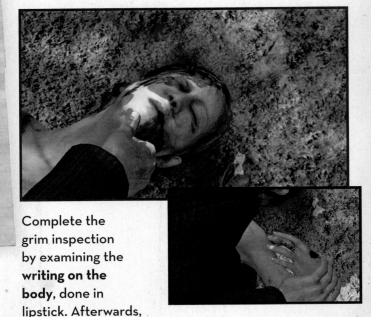

Complete the grim inspection by examining the **writing on the body,** done in lipstick. Afterwards, Carruthers suggests that the phrase scrawled on the torso may be a message about the Black Dahlia, but he admits it's pure speculation at this point. He has no idea what the "Tex" refers to.

Go to evidence marker C and examine the footprints. Carruthers reports that they're **size 8 shoe prints** from men's shoes. Ray Pinker of Technical Services took impressions of the prints to study back at the lab.

Key Clue Checklist: The Moors

✓ Writing on body
✓ Blunt force trauma (victim's head)
✓ Missing jewelry (victim's left hand)
✓ Size 8 shoe prints
✓ Lipstick
✓ Bamba Club lighter

At marker A, you find the victim's handbag and hairbrush. The brush is of little interest. Open the handbag to remove the **lipstick** inside. Examine it more closely to discover that it appears to be brand new and unused. So where did the killer get the lipstick for his writing?

At marker B you find a curious item: a globe puzzle. The trick is to rotate each section until the continents are aligned properly. The section near the base is fixed in place, so align the sections from the bottom up. This unlocks the globe, which opens up to reveal that it's a **Bamba Club lighter** engraved with the name and address of the club.

LOCATION: BAMBA CLUB
INVESTIGATE THE CLUB.

Travel to the Bamba Club ③ and enter the establishment to trigger an automatic conversation with the bartender. His name is Garrett Mason, an agency temp who fills in at bars around town. When Phelps describes the victim and asks if she came in last night, Mason gives the name Celine Henry and directs you to the bar's owner, Mr. McColl. (This gives you your first ID on the victim.)

The investigation music stops once you've found all five of the key clues in the vicinity. Galloway suggests going to the Bamba Club next. Good idea, Rusty. Open your notebook and set The Bamba Club as your current destination.

INTERVIEW DICK MCCOLL.

Walk toward the back of the club and approach the nattily dressed man wearing a hibiscus on his lapel and sitting alone in the booth. This triggers an interview sequence that begins a conversation with Dick McColl, the Bamba Club owner. He seems genuinely stunned that Celine Henry is dead. McColl says she's a regular customer; he and Celine and her husband Jacob "go way back."

INTERVIEW: DICK MCCOLL

TOPIC: *SUSPECT SEEN WITH VICTIM*

Phelps asks if Celine had any companions the previous night. McColl says she started out alone, but attracted the attention of several gentlemen as the night went on. One guy in particular was enamored with her stories. McColl seems honest enough about this topic.

CORRECT ASSESSMENT: *TRUTH*

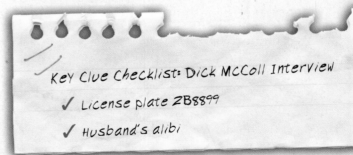

Celine left with the fellow about 11 PM. McColl doesn't know his name, but had enough foresight to copy the man's license number: **License plate 2B8899**. It's not surprising that McColl is this meticulous, given the way he dresses. This gives you the new objective to trace the plate.

TOPIC: *KNOWLEDGE OF HUSBAND*

McColl knows Jacob Henry. He was in the Marine Corps, met Celine on a furlough, and then married her after the war. He insinuates that Jacob put up with a lot of bad behavior from the woman. When Phelps asks if he thinks Jacob killed his wife, McColl says no... but his look is guarded and indirect, and he has trouble making eye contact.

CORRECT ASSESSMENT: *DOUBT*

Phelps tries guilt as a motivator, saying if Jacob Henry didn't do it, then McColl let Celine leave with a killer. But the bar owner won't bite, saying he tried to call Jacob to come get his wife—a regular occurrence, apparently—but Henry refused. When McColl called him back around 11:30, he didn't answer. This gives you the **husband's alibi**.

TOPIC: *RING STOLEN FROM VICTIM*

Phelps asks about the ring torn from Celine's finger in the attack. McColl says she always wore a large garnet ring. He adds that it dates back to her flying days. When Phelps asks if Jacob Henry gave the ring to Celine, McColl gets visibly nervous and says she got it "before Jacob." There's clearly something more to the story.

CORRECT ASSESSMENT: *DOUBT*

When pressed, McColl admits that he bought the ring for Celine years ago, before Jacob came along. He also admits that he's carried a torch for Celine all these years.

Before Phelps leaves, he gets Celine Henry's address from McColl, putting that new location on your map. Use your notebook to select it as your current destination.

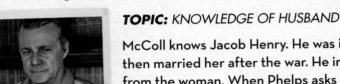

Key Clue Checklist: Dick McColl Interview
✓ License plate 2B8899
✓ Husband's alibi

CALL IN THE LICENSE PLATE NUMBER TO R&I.

Use one of the payphones at the front of the Bamba Club, next to the coat check desk. Phelps calls in the license plate he got from McColl. R&I will check with the DMV (Department of Motor Vehicles) for the registered owner and relay the answer via KGPL to your car radio.

LOCATION:
CELINE HENRY RESIDENCE

INVESTIGATE CELINE HENRY'S RESIDENCE.

Travel to the Henry residence ④. Interestingly, it's just a few blocks from The Moors. Approach the front door to trigger a scene: nobody answers the knock, so Galloway goes around back. He discovers a jimmied window, so he kicks in the back door and lets Phelps in the front.

NEWSPAPER CINEMATIC

Just inside the front door, find the newspaper with the headline "Family Burnt to Death" on the floor and watch the story it triggers. Once again Harlan Fontaine plays a prominent role as he discusses a house fire with a very disturbed man calling from a payphone.

Start searching the house. The place is a boozy mess; clearly, Celine had a drinking problem. Find the **female shoe**, a size 9, on the floor of the dining room; Phelps notes that a 9 is above average for a lady.

Enter the kitchen and examine the broken window for signs of **forced entry**;

the intruder used a pry bar to jack it open. Then find the note on the refrigerator door from Jacob. It says he can be found at an apartment on Huntley Drive, indicating that the Henrys have separated. It also puts the new location on your map and gives you a new objective: "Investigate Jacob Henry's Apartment."

After you examine the refrigerator note, Phelps tells Galloway to call in Burglary and get Technical Services to the house while he talks to the neighbors. But finish searching the house before you go outside.

Jacob's New Digs

Don't miss Jacob's note on the fridge! Without his address, your investigation is stalled.

In the bedroom, check the vanity dresser to examine an empty Tiffany box to update the **missing jewelry** clue in your cluelist. You also find a photograph of Celine in aviator garb piloting a plane called The Red Hawk. The photo shows her flashing a thumbs-up sign that reveals the distinctive and very large Tiffany ring.

CANVASS THE NEIGHBORS.

Exit the house via the back door, turn left, and climb over the brick divider into the backyard of the blue house next door. As you do this, a car pulls up the drive into the yard.

The woman who gets out is Jennifer Horgan, the next-door neighbor. Horgan says she's known Celine Henry for more than 10 years. She tells of a loud fight between the Henrys the previous night—Celine was drunk, then Jacob blackened her eye and stormed out, leaving his wife behind. Celine went out alone later, at 10:00 PM. Now you know about the Henrys' **marital problems**.

Key Clue Checklist: Celine Henry's Residence

✓ Female shoe

✓ Forced entry

✓ Missing jewelry (updated)

✓ Marital problems (from neighbor)

LOCATION: JACOB HENRY'S APARTMENT

INVESTIGATE JACOB HENRY'S APARTMENT.

Travel to Jacob Henry's place ⑤. When you arrive, just follow Galloway and watch the scene: Your partner kicks open the door and places Jacob under arrest. The man seems genuinely distraught to hear about his wife's death, and Phelps has him take a seat. Galloway sits with Henry in the living room, so you can search the place.

Go straight to the bedroom to find an open suitcase with a pair of shoes inside. Pick up and examine the **size eleven shoes**—a detail that works in Jacob's favor, since the killer wore size eights.

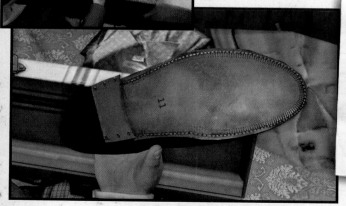

The only other key clue is on the counter between the kitchen and dining area. Find the notepad, then use the control shown onscreen to shade the pencil over the page. This reveals the impression of the previous note written on the pad, what appears to be a **death threat note**: "I need you to do something about my wife."

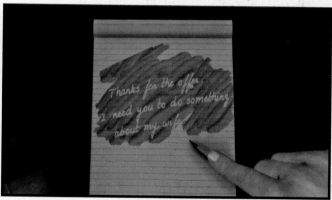

INTERVIEW JACOB HENRY.

Now return to the living room and approach Jacob Henry and press Talk to trigger an interview sequence.

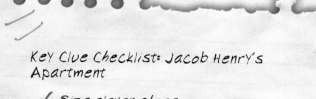

Key Clue Checklist: Jacob Henry's Apartment
- ✓ Size eleven shoes
- ✓ Death threat note

INTERVIEW: JACOB HENRY (FIRST TIME)

TOPIC: *MOVEMENTS OF VICTIM*

Phelps asks who could have killed Celine—where did she go last night? Jacob seems reluctant to talk, and mutters, "A bar, I suppose. I don't know." He won't make eye contact, and you have plenty of information that suggests he knew exactly where she was.

CORRECT ASSESSMENT: *LIE*
EVIDENCE: *BAMBA CLUB LIGHTER*

When Phelps brings up the Bamba Club, Jacob admits he got a call from the club, but refused to go pick up Celine. He says the phone rang again later and he ignored it. (This corroborates with what Dick McColl told you.) So Celine left the bar with someone else, and he has to live with that. Again, he seems devastated by the news.

TOPIC: *LAST CONTACT WITH VICTIM*

Phelps asks when Jacob last saw his wife. He says he saw Celine last night, things got out of hand, and he left. This is consistent with what the neighbor, Jennifer Horgan, told you, and he makes easy eye contact after this statement.

SUBDUE JACOB HENRY.

After the interview, Galloway pushes too hard on the suspect, insulting the memory of Celine Henry in the process. He calls her "a lush and a tramp," and this pushes Jacob over the edge. He suddenly punches Galloway, then squares up to fight Phelps. Take him down with a few good punches and finish him off.

CALL DISPATCH AND CHECK FOR MESSAGES.

Use the telephone on the counter in Jacob's kitchen (next to the notepad) to call for a patrol unit dispatch and get a message from the coroner. Carruthers gives you the autopsy report, saying Celine Henry was basically stomped to death. The head wounds are consistent with a socket wrench handle.

Phelps also gets through to R&I for a report on the license number. The plates belong to a brown 1936 Pontiac registered to Alonzo Mendez. Getting his address puts the location on your map. Finally, you get a message from Captain Donelly, who wants all suspects returned to Central Police Station for immediate questioning. You'd better obey the captain's orders.

CORRECT ASSESSMENT: *TRUTH*

A little more pressure from Phelps prods Jacob to remember that he last saw his wife around 9:00 PM. This also fits with the neighbor's timeline of events.

TOPIC: *MOTIVE FOR MURDER*

This topic appears on your list only after you reveal the death threat note on the notepad in the kitchen. Phelps tries a direct accusation of murder, and Jacob chooses to answer by saying, "I never gave up on my wife." But he looks uncomfortable after saying it.

CORRECT ASSESSMENT: *LIE*
EVIDENCE: *DEATH THREAT NOTE*

When Phelps brings up the impression of the note revealed on the pad, Jacob Henry says the meaning is that he wanted to have Celine committed to a hospital.

LOCATION: CENTRAL POLICE STATION
INTERROGATE JACOB HENRY.

Return to Central Police Station ①. Your arrival triggers a scene: Captain Donelly wants a conviction of Jacob Henry despite the lead on Mendez, the man with whom Celine left the Bamba Club. Phelps thinks Jacob may be the wrong man, but he enters Interview Room 2 anyway.

INTERVIEW: JACOB HENRY (SECOND TIME)

TOPIC: *LIPSTICK MARKINGS*

Phelps asks about the lipstick messages written on the victim, trying to rattle Jacob into giving some sign of recognition. But it appears that Jacob has no idea what Phelps is referencing, and he looks the detective right in the eye.

CORRECT ASSESSMENT: *TRUTH*

Jacob makes a pretty convincing "confession" that he's just a chump who loved his wife despite her scandalous behavior.

TOPIC: *DETERIORATION OF MARRIAGE*

When Phelps paints a picture of the evening—a marital fight that got out of hand—Jacob denies it.

CORRECT ASSESSMENT: *LIE*
EVIDENCE: *MARITAL PROBLEMS*

Phelps insists that Jacob got violent because the marriage was falling apart. When he presents the neighbor's report of a blackened eye, Jacob relents and admits he hit her. He's not proud of it, but he claims Celine was coming at him with a frying pan. He says he took her abuse for years, and finally just cracked.

TOPIC: *ACCESS TO MURDER WEAPON*

Phelps asks about Jacob's work. He's a mechanic, working on various engine parts... with access to plenty of tools. (The label on his jumpsuit suggests he works for Hughes Aircraft Company.) Phelps points out that Celine Henry was brutally beaten with a socket wrench handle. Jacob throws up his hands and simply says, "I was home in bed."

CORRECT ASSESSMENT: *LIE*
EVIDENCE: *HUSBAND'S ALIBI*

Now Phelps goes into high gear, accusing Jacob using details of the killing. When he denies it again, repeating that he was home, Phelps brings up McColl's assertion that he called Jacob and got no answer. Jacob responds by laying out the raw dynamic of his relationship to Celine.

TOPIC: *MISSING JEWELRY*

Phelps suggests that Jacob broke into Celine's house and stole her Tiffany ring. Jacob is almost dumbfounded by this. He says he has a key, and has no reason to break in.

CORRECT ASSESSMENT: *TRUTH*

When Phelps insinuates that Jacob stole the garnet ring because he knew it was a gift from Dick McColl, Jacob is even more dumbfounded. He clearly had no idea where the ring came from.

After the interview, a deeply disappointed Captain Donelly waits for Phelps out in the hall. Phelps assures the captain that Mendez is a good lead, but Donelly is not pleased with the police work.

LOCATION: MENDEZ'S RESIDENCE

INVESTIGATE MENDEZ'S RESIDENCE.

Travel to Mendez's apartment building ⑥. R&I told you he lives in Apartment 16, but you can double-check by looking at the
mailboxes on the
left side of the
entryway. Inside
you can also check a
directory that shows
Apartment 16 is on
the fourth floor.

Climb the stairs to the top floor and go straight down the hall to number 16. Phelps automatically kicks open the door.

Nobody's home, so search the apartment. There are plenty of mundane items, but only three key clues. Go down the hallway to the bedroom (second door on the left). First, pick up and examine one of the **size eight shoes** on the floor. (Be sure to turn the shoe until you zoom in on the sole.) Find the bloody box that contains **used lipstick** and a blood-covered **socket wrench**—pretty incriminating stuff right there.

APPREHEND MENDEZ.

Suddenly Mendez arrives home. When Phelps informs him that he's under arrest, the suspect bolts. Follow him through the window. Stay on his tail as he sprints across the rooftops then slides down a ladder and drainpipe to the ground. Just as Mendez reaches his car to escape,

Rusty pulls up in your vehicle. Hop in the driver's seat and follow Mendez.

Remember that in a chase, the suspect's vehicle is always marked as the red car icon on your map. Follow Mendez and ram him when possible. Pull up next to his left-rear fender to give Galloway a good shot at his tires to disable his car. When you finally accomplish this, hop out and approach the car to trigger an arrest cutscene. If you fail to disable his car, Mendez eventually crashes and you can apprehend him then.

Afterwards, a pleased Captain Donelly offers a toast with Galloway in honor of young Phelps. Then the scene shifts to the Blue Room Jazz Club, where Phelps takes in the main act.

THE GOLDEN BUTTERFLY

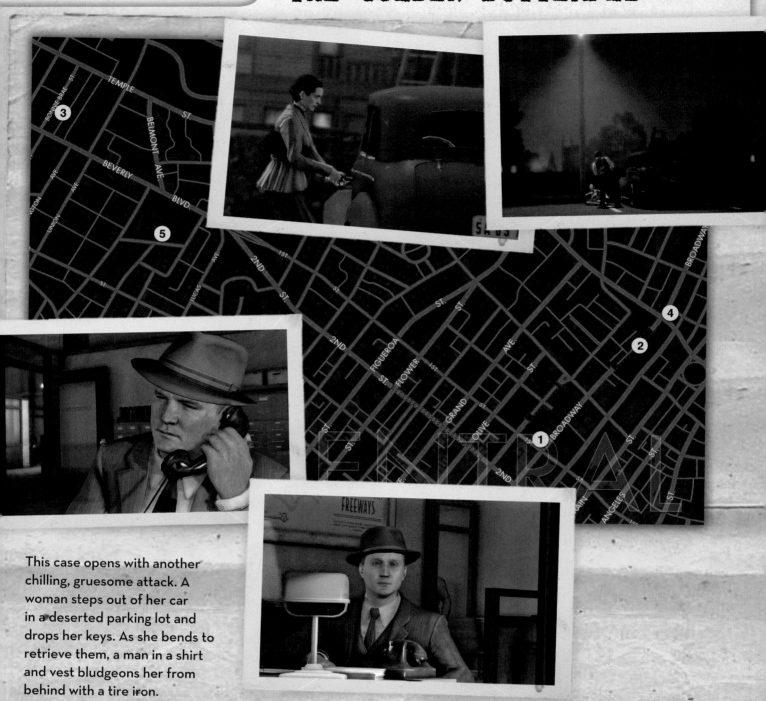

This case opens with another chilling, gruesome attack. A woman steps out of her car in a deserted parking lot and drops her keys. As she bends to retrieve them, a man in a shirt and vest bludgeons her from behind with a tire iron.

At Central Division the next day, Detective Galloway gets the call: the woman was murdered and dumped in the grass at the end of Hill Street. Phelps points out the similarity to the last case, but Galloway reminds him of the first rule of police work: Make no assumptions until you've seen the evidence.

objectives

* Investigate Crime Scene.

* Investigate the Moller Residence & Interview Michelle Moller and Hugo Moller.

* Speak to Moller's Neighbor & Apprehend Hugo Moller.

* Return to Central Morgue.

* Investigate High School & Apprehend the Molester.

* Return to Central Station & Interview Hugo Moller and Eli Rooney.

* Accuse a Suspect.

CASE REPORT

TOTAL NUMBER OF KEY CLUES	12
TOTAL NUMBER OF INTERVIEW QUESTIONS	15

Fail Conditions

* Phelps dies.

* Crime scene contaminated.

* Hugo Moller escapes.

* Eli Rooney escapes.

LOCATION: CRIME SCENE
INVESTIGATE THE CRIME SCENE.

Exit the police station ① and drive northeast to the yellow map flag that marks the crime scene ②. As you arrive, Captain Donelly tries to fend off the jackals of the press, who point out this slaying's similarities to the "Red Lipstick" murder of Celine Henry, as well as the "Black Dahlia" murder of Elizabeth Short.

Walk past the crime scene barricade and talk to the uniformed officer, Gonzales, who leads you to Coroner Carruthers and the victim at evidence marker A. The coroner notes the similar M.O. to the Celine Henry murder: severely battered, left on display, and stomped with a smallish men's shoe.

EXAMINE THE BODY.

Examine the victim's head to reveal the braided **rope pattern** on her neck. Carruthers notes that it's very distinctive; he'll work up some comparisons at the lab and get back to you.

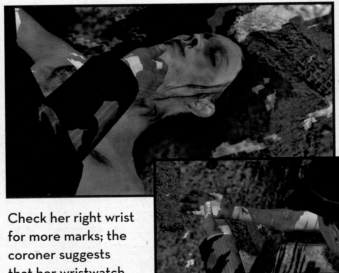

Check her right wrist for more marks; the coroner suggests that her wristwatch may have been torn off. Then examine her left hand to see that her ring has been violently removed, as well. This adds **missing jewelry** to your list of clues. You can also examine her chest to find the stomp marks of **small men's footprints**.

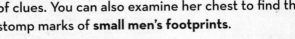

EXPLORE THE REST OF THE CRIME SCENE.

Step to evidence marker B beside the body and pick up the handbag on the ground. Examine the wad of cash in the purse; Phelps notes that the motive clearly wasn't robbery. Then pull out the PTA nametag to learn the victim's name, Deidre Moller. Phelps asks Officer Gonzales to run the name past R&I. Put down the purse.

LOCATION: MOLLER RESIDENCE
SEARCH THE MOLLER RESIDENCE.

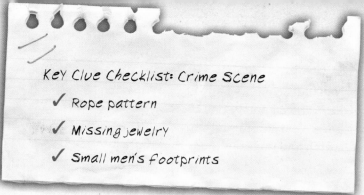

Now find evidence marker C on the other side of the nearby tree. Examine the **small men's footprints** (added to your Evidence list if you didn't find them earlier on the victim) leading to the body. Phelps asks if the stomping attack on Celine Henry was reported in the press; Carruthers confirms that it was and adds, "Every detail a copycat would want was there in the story."

Travel to the Moller residence ③ and approach the front door to trigger a scene. A young girl answers your knock—Michelle Moller, the 15-year-old daughter of Hugo and Deidre, invites the detectives inside. Phelps asks her to sit while he searches the premises.

Enter the hallway, turn right, and go into the master bedroom on the left. (You won't find anything of interest in Michelle's bedroom.) Examine one of the **size eight work boots** on the floor.

Once you've examined the evidence, Gonzalez returns: R&I says that Deidre Moller was reported missing by her husband Hugo Moller that morning. This adds the Mollers' address to the Locations page of your notebook and gives you a new objective.

Now examine the items on the dresser top. You find an empty Lady Elgin wristwatch case and an empty ring case. Be sure to get a close look at both to add the **missing watch and rings** update to your Clue list.

INTERVIEW MICHELLE MOLLER.

Return to the living room and approach Michelle Moller, then press Talk to trigger an interview sequence. Detective Phelps has to break the painful news about her mother to the poor girl, but she's a trooper about answering questions.

Key Clue Checklist: Moller Residence
✓ Size eight work boots
✓ Missing watch and rings (updates "Missing jewelry")

INTERVIEW: MICHELLE MOLLER

TOPIC: *LAST CONTACT WITH VICTIM*

Michelle says she last saw her mother the previous afternoon before the girl attended a dance at her school, Belmont High. When her mother didn't show to pick her up, her father came instead. But Michelle's demeanor—averted eyes and a small wince—indicates this isn't the whole story.

CORRECT ASSESSMENT: *DOUBT*

Phelps presses her on what happened, and she responds with distress. She admits that she called home repeatedly, but got no answer at first. Eventually, her father picked up the phone and then came straightaway to get her. This provides important details regarding the **husband's alibi**.

TOPIC: *MISSING WATCH AND RINGS*

Phelps asks about the missing jewelry. Michelle recalls that her mother had a ring and a watch, but claims she didn't really pay much attention to such things. Her gaze is steady and direct.

CORRECT ASSESSMENT: *TRUTH*

Michelle does manage to describe the rings and watch in some detail. She also reveals an interesting bit of info: her mother's Elgin watch was a makeup present from her father after a fight.

TOPIC: *STATE OF PARENTS' MARRIAGE*

When Phelps asks Michelle if her parents are happily married, she reacts somewhat defensively in affirming that they are.

CORRECT ASSESSMENT: *DOUBT*

Phelps expresses doubt and Michelle admits that her father hit her mother once. To make up, he bought his wife a golden **butterfly brooch**.

Key Clue Checklist: Michelle Moller Interview
✓ Husband's alibi
✓ Butterfly brooch

After Phelps lauds the girl for her bravery, Hugo Moller enters the house. He sends his daughter to her room, then reacts with apparent shock when informed of his wife's death. He sits and agrees to answer questions.

INTERVIEW: HUGO MOLLER

TOPIC: *FOOTPRINTS AT CRIME SCENE*

Phelps asks Hugo his shoe size. He replies that he wears size nines, but if you searched his bedroom beforehand you know better.

CORRECT ASSESSMENT: *LIE*
EVIDENCE: *SIZE EIGHT WORK BOOTS*

When Phelps brings up the work boots you found, Hugo admits that he's sensitive because he often gets teased about the smallish size of his feet.

TOPIC: *MISSING PERSONS REPORT*

Hugo confirms that he filed a missing persons report for his wife that morning. He says Deidre left home around 9:30 PM, but didn't arrive to pick up their

daughter at the high school dance. This seems true enough, but he's clearly nervous. He swallows repeatedly as he talks, and then glances away and closes his eyes several times after he finishes.

CORRECT ASSESSMENT: *DOUBT*

When Phelps asks if Deidre ever went to bars by herself, Hugo suddenly gets animated. He loses his cool and gets to his feet, asking if the detective is suggesting his wife is loose. He explains that their marital argument was about picking up Michelle from the dance.

TOPIC: *ALIBI FOR HUGO MILLER*

Phelps asks if Hugo stayed home all night, and he answers that he did. Of course, this contradicts what his daughter told you. (You can't correctly challenge this assertion as a lie unless you elicited the "Husband's alibi" clue when you interviewed Michelle Moller.)

CORRECT ASSESSMENT: *LIE*
EVIDENCE: *HUSBAND'S ALIBI*

When confronted with Michelle's statement, Hugo admits that he drove around for a while in order to relax. Now a new topic appears on your Questions list.

TOPIC: *HISTORY OF VIOLENCE*

Phelps describes the brutality of Deidre's murder and points out Hugo's history of domestic violence. Hugo denies it, of course, but you have evidence to suggest otherwise.

CORRECT ASSESSMENT: *LIE*
EVIDENCE: *BUTTERFLY BROOCH*

When Phelps brings up the golden butterfly brooch and calls it a "payoff" to buy Deidre's silence, Moller again vigorously denies that he's a violent man feared by his wife and daughter.

Interestingly, Phelps decides to allow Hugo to report on his own to Central Station for questioning. When Galloway protests and wants to cuff the suspect, Phelps points out that Moller's daughter is in the next room. He warns Hugo not to run.

Later, outside, Phelps explains more of his rationale to Galloway: despite Hugo's history of domestic violence, they still need to break his alibi because there's no

physical evidence tying Hugo to the crime scene. As they speak, a neighbor hails the detectives from across the street.

SPEAK TO THE NEIGHBOR.

Approach the woman to trigger a conversation. She reports that the Mollers had a loud argument the night before. She also saw Mr. Moller burning something in his incinerator that morning. Suddenly, she spots Hugo at the incinerator, giving you a new objective.

TAKE HUGO MOLLER INTO CUSTODY.

Approach Hugo Moller, who is now marked as the red blip on your radar mini-map. As you get close he takes off running. Chase him down! Follow Hugo as he sprints down the alley, and tries to cut through yards. When you get close, tap the Tackle button indicated onscreen to bring him down. (If you fail to tackle Moller during the chase sequence, you eventually catch him when he tries to open a locked door.) After the capture, you end up back at the incinerator in Moller's yard.

INSPECT THE INCINERATOR.

Examine the incinerator and pick up one of the **bloody shoes** (the undamaged one). When you turn it over, you find it's a size eight! Phelps places Moller under arrest for the murder of his wife, but Hugo insists he can explain the blood.

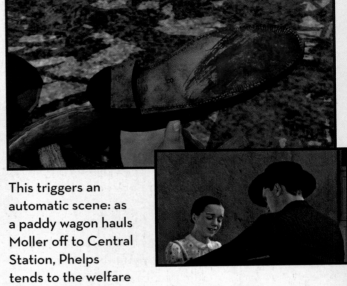

This triggers an automatic scene: as a paddy wagon hauls Moller off to Central Station, Phelps tends to the welfare of Michelle, instructing her to contact relatives and promising help from Juvenile Hall.

When the scene ends, use the nearby gamewell to get the Belmont High School address while Galloway calls in the request from your car. Soon you get a pair of KGPL calls. First, you learn that Coroner Carruthers has his report ready for you downtown. Swing by the morgue and pick it up.

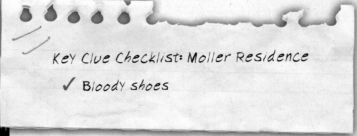

Key Clue Checklist: Moller Residence
✓ Bloody shoes

LOCATION: CENTRAL MORGUE
RETURN TO CENTRAL MORGUE.

Travel to Central Morgue ④, the new yellow flag on your map. Enter the mortuary night entrance; just inside, veer to the right into the examination room to trigger a scene.

Phelps asks if Coroner Carruthers can check the blood type on the shoes you found in the incinerator against the victim's type. Carruthers confirms strangulation as cause of death and directs you to view the samples on the bench. Examine the bench to see three rope samples next to a close-up photo of the ligature marks on Deidre Moller's neck.

The bottommost rope, the heavily braided one, is the obvious match. Select it to move it under the magnifying scope and over the photo for comparison. As Galloway points out, braided rope is commonly used on boats as mooring lines; the coroner adds that according to Ray Pinker of Technical Services, it's sometimes used as a bell rope in churches, too.

Carruthers notes that he found no sign of semen on the body, which suggests there was no sexual assault.

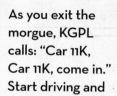

Now examine the plaster shoeprint molds taken from the murder scene, just to the right of the rope samples. They're **size eight footprints**; Carruthers notes that they're very similar to the prints in the Celine Henry case.

Before leaving, you can also take a look at the body and a sample of the autopsy organ removal on the scale. (You don't learn anything new from this viewing.)

As you exit the morgue, KGPL calls: "Car 11K, Car 11K, come in." Start driving and you get a report that Deidre Moller's green 1946 coupe has been found in a parking lot adjoining Belmont High School and its playing fields. Travel to that location now.

Key Clue Checklist: Central Morgue
✓ Size eight footprints
(update of "Small men's footprints")

LOCATION: BELMONT HIGH SCHOOL
MEET THE SCHOOL JANITOR.

Follow the yellow blip that marks the location of Belmont High School ⑤. Your arrival triggers a scene: Phelps questions the school janitor, James, who reports that he saw a man park the car in the lot around 1:00 AM. He mentions some recent problems with a child molester, but he doesn't know if it was the same man.

Before he can comment further, he suddenly spots the molester!

APPREHEND THE CHILD MOLESTER.

Sprint full speed through the first gap in the field bleachers on your right. (Remember: The suspect is marked as the red blip on your map.) Run at an angle

across the football field and aim for the gap between the blocking sled on the left and the track hurdles on the right.

Follow the fleeing suspect around the far bleachers and up the stairs to street level. Stay on his tail as he veers down the alley between

buildings on the right and hops over fences, trying to escape through yards. Then tackle him when you get close enough. (If you can't manage to tackle the suspect during the chase, Galloway eventually cuts him off at the end of an alley with the car; then you must defeat the suspect in a brawl.) This triggers a scene: after Phelps drags him back to the parking lot, he gives his name as Eli Rooney.

Eli claims no knowledge of the woman attacked the previous night, but when the detectives force him to turn out his pockets he produces Deidre Moller's golden **butterfly brooch**! He claims, however, that he found it in the parking lot.

SEARCH THE TRUNK OF DEIDRE'S CAR.

After Eli Rooney is hauled away in the paddy wagon, open the trunk of the 1946 coupe to find a trio of bloodstained items.

Examine the **rope**, the **bloody tire iron**, and the **overalls** stenciled with "H.M."—the same initials as Hugo Moller, who also happens to be a mechanic. Then walk away from the car to get a new objective.

CALL CENTRAL.

Follow the phone icon on your map to the gamewell on the nearby sidewalk. Use it to call in to Central Station and set up both Hugo Moller and Eli Rooney in interview rooms for interrogations.

Key Clue Checklist: Belmont High School
- ✓ Butterfly brooch (updated)
- ✓ Rope
- ✓ Bloody tire iron
- ✓ Overalls

LOCATION: CENTRAL STATION

INTERVIEW HUGO MOLLER.

Travel back to Central Station ① and enter the building. Your new objective is to charge one of the two suspects with murder. Approach the watch desk to trigger a quick scene with the Watch Commander, Mel Fleischer. He tells Phelps where the suspects are waiting.

Let's start with Moller. Find him in Interview Room 2. When you approach, Phelps lays out the case, but Hugo continues to protest his innocence. He even offers to take a lie detector test.

INTERVIEW: HUGO MOLLER

TOPIC: *DISPOSAL OF EVIDENCE*

When Phelps asks why Hugo was burning his bloody shoes, the suspect replies, "Because I knew you wouldn't believe me." The answer certainly seems straightforward and his look is direct.

CORRECT ASSESSMENT: *TRUTH*

Hugo claims that the blood came from a skinned rabbit. The coroner's report should confirm or deny that assertion easily enough.

TOPIC: *ACCESS TO BRAIDED ROPE*

Phelps asks if Hugo knows anything about ropes. The suspect says he was a Boy Scout and learned a bit more in the Army, but says he doesn't know much more than the average fellow.

CORRECT ASSESSMENT: *DOUBT*

Phelps pushes Hugo about strangulation. Moller answers aggressively, admitting that he learned various ways to strangle someone in the Army. He  openly admits that, if he had to choose, he'd use a triple-braid rope—the very kind used to strangle his wife. This would seem like an odd admission if he were indeed the killer.

TOPIC: *ACCESS TO TIRE IRON*

Phelps points out that Deidre was beaten savagely with a tire iron, then suggests that it's an appropriate choice of tool for a mechanic like Hugo. Hugo haltingly denies knowing anything about a tire iron. His eyes turn shifty.

CORRECT ASSESSMENT: *LIE*
EVIDENCE: *BLOODY TIRE IRON*

Deidre Moller drove a Chevrolet, but Hugo admits he drives a Chrysler Airflow—the same make as the tire iron that helped kill his wife.

TOPIC: *VICTIM'S VEHICLE RECOVERED*

Phelps tells Hugo about the discovery of Deide's car in the school parking lot, then asks where he keeps his work clothes. Hugo claims to keep them in his locker.

CORRECT ASSESSMENT: *LIE*
EVIDENCE: *OVERALLS*

When Phelps tells Hugo about the bloodstained overalls bearing his initials in the trunk of his wife's car, he denies that they could be his.

This ends your interview with Hugo Moller. You get the choice to either charge him with murder or exit the room without leveling charges. Let's talk to Eli Rooney before we jump to any conclusions.

INTERVIEW
ELI ROONEY.

Exit Interview Room 2 and head down the corridor in search of Rooney in Interview Room 1. You run into Captain Donelly just outside the door; he asserts that he'll be dealing personally with the accused. Enter the interview room to find a battered suspect. Pedophiles are a particularly despised class of criminal.

INTERVIEW: ELI ROONEY

TOPIC: *FOOTPRINTS AT CRIME SCENE*

When Phelps asks his boot size, Eli says he wears whatever he can get his hands on—currently size elevens, he claims.

CORRECT ASSESSMENT: *DOUBT*

Phelps doesn't believe it, based on Rooney's short stature. After a bit more prodding, he admits that he just might wear an eight. When Phelps asks why he "punishes" children with his iniquity, Eli seems to suggest it's a continuation of abuse he once suffered himself.

TOPIC: *PLACE OF EMPLOYMENT*

Phelps asks about Eli's job. He says he worked in San Pedro, but now he's looking for something new. Eli is not easy to read, but this answer leaves too much unanswered, and his folded arms and surly look suggest he's holding something back.

CORRECT ASSESSMENT: *DOUBT*

Eli says his ex-employer was Hennessy Marine— matching the initials stenciled on the bloody overalls found in Deidre Moller's trunk. Eli goes on to admit that the company gave him green coveralls to wear for work.

TOPIC: *ACCESS TO BRAIDED ROPE*

Phelps gets Eli to admit he uses rope to truss some of his victims. He claims to have no particular rope preference.

CORRECT ASSESSMENT: *TRUTH*

When pressed however, Eli admits that he prefers braid: "You tie a hitch in braid, it stays tied."

TOPIC: *MOTIVE FOR MOLLER MURDER*

Phelps suggests that Eli killed Deidre Moller in order to steal her jewelry. Eli flat out denies that, unlike his reactions to other accusations.

CORRECT ASSESSMENT: *DOUBT*

Now Eli tells what he claims to know: he saw the car enter the parking lot late the previous night. A man got out of the car and changed clothes, putting his coveralls in the trunk. Then the man dropped the butterfly brooch in the lamplight and walked away. Eli says he went to pick it up. And that's his story.

Before the interview ends, you're given the choice of selecting either Charge or Exit.

You have enough evidence to charge either Hugo Moller or Eli Rooney with the murder. Choose either one to close the case and complete The Golden Butterfly. Our preference is to lock up the admitted child sex offender, plus you earn the five-star award if you charge Rooney. Afterwards, Captain Donelly assesses your performance.

THE SILK STOCKING MURDER

This case opens in the Mirror Press Diner, a regular cop hangout just down Broadway from the Central Police Station. Detective Phelps arrives there for a breakfast meeting with his partner Rusty Galloway and Captain Donelly. The captain puts the pair on a new case: another young woman, this one Hispanic, murdered and left naked in an alleyway near City Hall.

Phelps can't help but comment on the similarity to the Henry and Moller cases. Galloway points out that his partner isn't convinced of Mendez's guilt in the Henry murder. But Donelly will have none of it, and expresses his happiness with the case built in the Moller murder, as well—the DA is on solid ground with the evidence, he believes.

Objectives

* Investigate Downtown Crime Scene.

* Investigate Antonia's Room & Interview Mrs. Lapenti.

* Investigate Maldonado Residence & Canvass Neighbors.

* Return to Central Station (Tech Services).

* Interview Angel Maldonado.

* Investigate El Dorado Bar & Interview Diego Aguilar.

* Investigate Just Picked Fruit Market & Interview Clem Feeney.

* Apprehend Feeney.

CASE REPORT

| TOTAL NUMBER OF KEY CLUES | 17 |
| TOTAL NUMBER OF INTERVIEW QUESTIONS | 13 |

Fail Conditions

* Phelps dies.

* Crime scene contaminated.

* Clem Feeney escapes.

LOCATION: DOWNTOWN CRIME SCENE

INVESTIGATE THE CRIME SCENE.

From the diner ①, travel to the crime scene ②. Approach the coroner, who says the cause of death is apparent. He waited for the detective team to arrive, so go ahead and examine the body.

EXAMINE THE BODY.

Start with the head. Phelps points out the great force indicated by the deep lacerations on the victim's neck. Examine her torso to find a lipstick message, another familiar touch. This one says: "Kiss the blood, B.D."

Examine the victim's left arm to see the marks of another wedding ring torn violently from the victim's

finger. Then examine her right hand to take the torn library card placed in her fingers—more grisly staging by the killer. It tells you her first name was Antonia and she was only 21 years old.

Afterwards, the four discuss the similarities to previous murders, including the Black Dahlia killing. Carruthers adds another similarity: bruising from a stomp attack by a small size of men's shoe. Pinker points out that the lipstick seems to be a similar color to the other cases.

SEARCH THE REST OF THE CRIME SCENE.

Examine the **bloodied stocking** on the ground next to the body, at evidence marker A. Note also the smeared **blood trail** leading away from the body. Follow it over to a blue cloche **ladies hat** on the ground near the blood-spattered door; it has the name Antonia written in the band.

The blood trail continues up the alley, past the squad car. Follow it to the trashcan near the blood smear on the wall and find the bloody ladies shoe inside, no doubt one of the victim's **personal effects**.

Keep following the blood trail to the water pipe and find the **key** dangling from a string. It's an apartment key etched with the number 5.

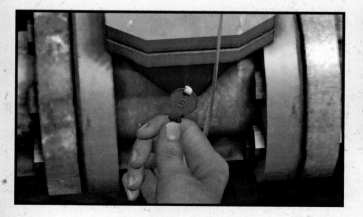

Again, follow the blood trail. Next, it leads you to a folded piece of paper on the ground. Examining this unfolds it to reveal an odd **dot pattern note** that shows dice pips for 2, 5, and 3. Phelps suggests that it must be some sort of code or cipher. It seems the killer left a deliberate trail for you to follow.

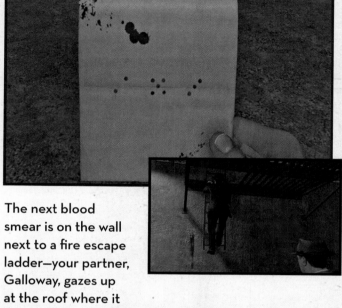

The next blood smear is on the wall next to a fire escape ladder—your partner, Galloway, gazes up at the roof where it leads, providing a hint for where to go next. Approach and examine the bloodsmear for a short cutscene: you look up the fire escape as Phelps says, "Where are you taking us?" Climb the fire escape to the roof.

The blood trail continues on the roof. Follow it into the pigeon coop to find an envelope with the name "Mrs. A. Maldonado" on the front. It's empty, and Phelps wonders where these odd clues are taking him.

Follow the blood smears again until you find an enameled and gold-plated makeup compact about halfway across the roof. Examine it to open it. Then continue along the grim, bloody trail to the pipe that runs up the wall. Climb it to the next rooftop.

Follow the blood to the box-like airshaft to find another item hanging from a string: Antonia Maldonado's wedding ring, torn from her finger. Phelps wonders: What's the significance?

MUSIC CUE

Remember that the "clue music" doesn't stop until you've found all pertinent clues in a location. The Maldonado crime scene has a lot of clues, so keep searching until the music stops.

Hop up to the next level of roof for the grisliest find so far: a bucket of what appears to be Antonia's blood and a blood-soaked paintbrush. Pick up the brush and examine it for a close-up. It appears that the killer used this brush to paint the **blood trail** (updates the existing clue) you've been following.

Follow the trail to the corner of the roof and pick up the victim's handbag. Open it and examine the second half of the torn **library card**. This verifies the victim's full name as Antonia Maldonado. It also gives you her address, which is added to your Locations page. This wraps up your crime scene investigation.

Key Clue Checklist: Downtown Crime Scene

- ✓ Bloodied stocking
- ✓ Blood trail (also updated on rooftop)
- ✓ Ladies hat
- ✓ Personal effects
- ✓ Key
- ✓ Dot pattern note
- ✓ Library card (found in two halves)

LOCATION: ANTONIA'S BOARDING HOUSE
SEARCH ANTONIA'S ROOM.

Travel to Antonia Maldonado's residence ③, a boarding house. Approach the front door to trigger a quick scene: Phelps knocks and Mrs. Barbara Lapenti, the owner, answers the door. After the meeting, follow Mrs. Lapenti into her parlor to trigger another scene: Detective Phelps reports the murder to the landlady and asks to search Antonia's room. Mrs. Lapenti directs the detectives upstairs.

Examine the suitcase on the bed to find an envelope addressed to "Mrs. Maldonado." Examine it further to open it; scroll down the **attorney's letter** to learn that Antonia had filed for divorce from her husband, Angel. The letter provides Angel's address and gives you a new objective.

Climb the steps and turn left, then approach Room 5 on the left side of the hall. Enter the room to find it's been broken into and ransacked. Turn right and examine the **broken window** to find an **iron picket** lying on the balcony outside the window. When you finish, Phelps automatically crawls through the window onto the balcony. Pick up the picket and examine it closely. Phelps wonders where it came from.

Crawl back into the room and search the dresser. Examine the framed **charm bracelet photograph** (it's turned face down)—you get a close-up of the bracelet on Antonia's wrist. Phelps notes that the bracelet wasn't among the crime scene evidence.

INTERVIEW MRS. LAPENTI.
Head back downstairs to the parlor and approach the landlady to trigger an interview sequence.

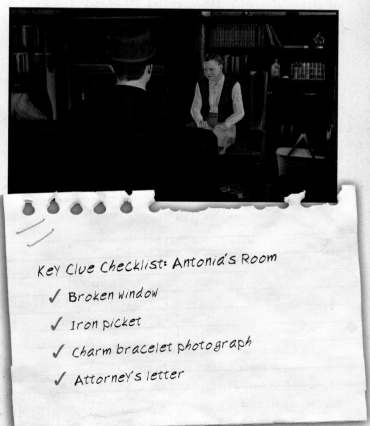

Key Clue Checklist: Antonia's Room
- ✓ Broken window
- ✓ Iron picket
- ✓ Charm bracelet photograph
- ✓ Attorney's letter

INTERVIEW: BARBARA LAPENTI

TOPIC: *POSSIBLE SUSPECTS*

When Phelps asks who might have wanted to hurt Antonia Maldonado, Mrs. Lapenti vehemently replies, "That rat of a husband, Angel." She mentions the divorce papers as a possible motive and gives the detectives a straight-in-the-eye, no-nonsense look.

CORRECT ASSESSMENT: *TRUTH*

Mrs. Lapenti claims that Angel was a cruel husband to Antonia, who was a good girl, if a little on the religious side.

TOPIC: *MOVEMENTS OF VICTIM*

Phelps asks when Antonia left and where she was going the previous day. Mrs. Lapenti gives her time of departure, but claims no knowledge of the young woman's destination. Her slight grimace suggests that she's not telling everything.

CORRECT ASSESSMENT: *DOUBT*

Phelps senses a cover-up and presses hard. The landlady admits that Antonia went to the El Dorado Bar, noting that she'd been drinking a lot lately. (This adds a new entry to your Locations page.) Galloway notes that it's near where the body was found.

TOPIC: *EVIDENCE OF BREAK-IN*

When Phelps asks about the break-in, Mrs. Lapenti tries to deny it. Of course, you have incontrovertible evidence.

CORRECT ASSESSMENT: *LIE*
EVIDENCE: *BROKEN WINDOW/IRON PICKET*

Mrs. Lapenti admits that she heard the noise in the early hours. She worries that her boarding house's reputation will suffer if word gets out.

TOPIC: *BREAKDOWN OF MARRIAGE*

Phelps asks about the state of the Maldonado marriage. The landlady says Antonia moved in two months earlier. When Phelps points out that Antonia

still wore her wedding ring, Mrs. Lapenti notes that she also wore a **religious necklace**, but no other jewelry. Her facial twitching and the wedding photo you saw suggest this isn't true.

CORRECT ASSESSMENT: *LIE*
EVIDENCE: *CHARM BRACELET PHOTOGRAPH*

Phelps asks about the bracelet, and Mrs. Lapenti at first claims to know nothing about it. But when Phelps mentions the wedding photo, the landlady says Antonia never wore it because Angel gave it to her. Instead, she kept it in her wooden jewelry box.

Key Clue Checklist:
Barbara Lapenti Interview
✓ Religious necklace

LOCATION: MALDONADO RESIDENCE
ARREST ANGEL MALDONADO.

Travel to the Maldonado residence ④ and examine the mailboxes on the right-hand side of the entry to find the apartment number, 304. Enter the building and climb the stairs to the third floor to trigger a scene: Galloway kicks in the door of 304 and places Angel Maldonado under arrest.

But as soon as the detectives tuck away their guns, Angel's brother, Hipolito, takes out Galloway with a flying tackle. When you regain control, you're faced off against Hipolito while your partner battles Angel. After you KO Angel's brother, go help Galloway if he needs it.

Once both brothers are cuffed and Galloway has called for a prowl car for backup, Phelps breaks the news about Antonia's murder to Angel. He seems honestly shocked. After the uniformed cops haul off the brothers, start searching the apartment.

SEARCH THE APARTMENT.

Enter the kitchen to examine the **bloodied shirt** hanging on a laundry line. Be sure to take a closer look at the bloodstains. Examine the fruit crate on the floor to get a new location, the Just Picked Fruit Market in Chinatown. Open the crate to find liquor inside.

You can also find a matchbook from the El Dorado bar on the counter. (This gives you the address if you don't already have it.) Now listen to Galloway's suggestion to check with the neighbors about Angel's movements the previous night.

The Mask

For fun, check in with the neighbor in 301, too.

CANVASS THE NEIGHBORS.

Exit the apartment and start knocking on doors. The man in 305 answers, but he works nights, so he's not very helpful. However, the woman in 302, Miss Aranda, heard the Maldonados fighting last night. She reports that Antonia lit out with Angel following her. Neither returned. This gives you information regarding the **husband's alibi**.

After this conversation, Galloway suggests investigating the El Dorado Bar next. But when you get in the car, you receive a KGPL call: Captain Donelly and Detective Sergeant Finis Brown urgently request your presence downtown—there's a new letter from the Black Dahlia killer. Better get back to the station right away.

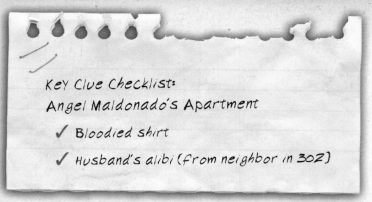

Key Clue Checklist:
Angel Maldonado's Apartment

✓ Bloodied shirt

✓ Husband's alibi (from neighbor in 302)

The Black Dahlia killer appears to have left two items to be found: a note made of letters cut from newspapers, and a poem by Percy Shelley—an excerpt from his four-act play, Prometheus Unbound. Phelps explains the play's premise and the team wonders about the excerpt's meaning.

HAVE CHANGED MY MIND, YOU WOULD NOT GIVE A SQUARE DEAL. FUCK YOU BD. TEX.

Heap upon thy soul, by virtue of this Curse,
Ill deeds, then be thou damned, beholding good;
Both infinite as is the universe,
And thou, and thy self-torturing solitude.
An awful image of calm power
Though now thou sittest, let the hour
Come, when thou must appear to be
That which thou art internally;
And after many a false and fruitless crime
Scorn track thy lagging fall through boundless space and time.

LOCATION:
CENTRAL POLICE STATION
MEET THE CAPTAIN IN TECH SERVICES.

Travel back to Central Station ①. When you enter, the Watch Commander calls out that the captain's

waiting for you downstairs. Turn right, then take the first left and follow the hallway to the stairs that lead down to Technical Services. (If you get lost, just follow Galloway.) Captain Donelly is waiting for you with Ray Pinker and Finis Brown.

INTERVIEW ANGEL MALDONADO.

Go upstairs to Interview Room 2, where Angel Maldonado is waiting. He admits his wife was at his apartment the night she died, but then she left and he never saw her again.

INTERVIEW: ANGEL MALDONADO

TOPIC: *LAST CONTACT WITH VICTIM*

When Phelps asks about his wife's visit last night, Angel says she stopped by around midnight and didn't stay long. But his extreme discomfort suggests some level of untruth, and you have evidence to share.

CORRECT ASSESSMENT: *LIE*
EVIDENCE: *HUSBAND'S ALIBI*

Phelps nails Angel with Mrs. Aranda's statement that he went after Antonia and didn't return. But Angel says his wife jumped into a **brown Ford coupe** at the corner; it was too dark to identify the driver.

TOPIC: *JEWELRY TAKEN FROM BODY*

Phelps asks if Antonia was wearing her religious medallion last night. Angel says yes, she always wore it. His steady look suggests he's not lying.

CORRECT ASSESSMENT: *TRUTH*

When Phelps asks about the charm bracelet, Angel confirms what Antonia's landlady, Mrs. Lapenti, told you earlier: she never wore it, keeping it locked in her jewelry box because "she didn't like the message."

TOPIC: *DIVORCE PROCEEDINGS*

When Phelps asks about the fighting and their impending breakup, a distressed Angel tries to deny that a divorce was in the works. You have plenty to refute this fantasy, however.

CORRECT ASSESSMENT: *LIE*
EVIDENCE: *ATTORNEY'S LETTER/DIVORCE PAPERS*

The attorney's letter works as evidence of the Maldonado divorce proceedings, but if you visited the El Dorado Bar before conducting this interview, the "attorney's letter" clue has been updated to "divorce papers." Angel gives more detail about what happened in the apartment. When he finishes, Phelps elicits his shoe size, too: size eight.

TOPIC: *BLOODSTAINED SHIRT FOUND*

When Phelps asks about the bloody shirt, Angel says he cut himself shaving—a lame explanation, and his face shows it.

CORRECT ASSESSMENT: *DOUBT*

Phelps threatens to have Angel charged if he doesn't get more cooperative. The suspect changes his story: the blood is from a fight with his brother, Hipolito. He goes on to recount that Antonia's visit to the El Dorado Bar reminded him of their visits to the nearby Just Picked Fruit Market, where a "creep" would ogle his wife.

*Key Clue Checklist:
Angel Maldonado Interview*
✓ *Brown Ford coupe*

LOCATION: EL DORADO BAR

INVESTIGATE THE BAR.

Travel to the El Dorado Bar ⑤ to trigger a scene: Phelps and Galloway enter and talk to Diego Aguilar, the bartender. He was working the previous night and says Antonia was so "hammered" she left a letter behind. When Diego sets it on the bar, pick it up and examine it to open the envelope and discover **divorce papers** (updates the "attorney's letter" clue) for Antonia and Angel.

INTERVIEW DIEGO AGUILAR.

Returning the papers to their envelope automatically triggers an interview sequence with the bartender.

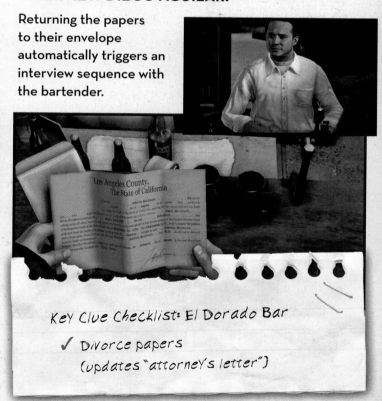

Key Clue Checklist: El Dorado Bar
✓ *Divorce papers
(updates "attorney's letter")*

INTERVIEW: DIEGO AGUILAR

TOPIC: *MOVEMENTS OF VICTIM*

Aguilar states that Antonia left the bar, saying she was going to serve the divorce papers on her husband. His look suggests he's telling all he knows.

CORRECT ASSESSMENT: *TRUTH*

When Phelps asks if Antonia attracted interest from any other bar patrons, Diego says yes, at first, but "she managed to scare them off."

TOPIC: *MISSING JEWELRY*

Aguilar says the victim was wearing a religious necklace and talked to the temp bartender much of the night. Again, he seems straightforward enough. But when Phelps asks what time Antonia left, Aguilar says he doesn't know, then looks uncomfortable, smiling oddly.

CORRECT ASSESSMENT: *DOUBT*

Phelps presses for more detail and Diego admits she asked for a cab, but his phone was out of order, so he sent her across the street to the fruit market.

SPEAK TO THE DELIVERY MAN OUT BACK.

Exit the El Dorado via its back door to trigger a meeting with a man pushing a handcart. (On the way, you find the phone with an "Out of Order" sign on it.) He says he's making deliveries to the bar from the Just Picked Fruit Market across the street. When Phelps mentions the Just Picked crate full of booze you just found, he denies knowledge of any such thing. Then he drives off in his delivery truck.

LOCATION: JUST PICKED FRUIT MARKET
INTERVIEW THE GREENGROCER.

Travel to Just Picked Fruit ⑥ and enter the market. Talk to the proprietor behind the counter—it's the same fellow you just saw making deliveries to the El Dorado Bar. His name is Clem Feeney, and he reports that Antonia did come by the store last night. This triggers an interview sequence.

INTERVIEW: CLEM FEENEY

TOPIC: *DISTINCTIVE NECKLACE*

Phelps asks if the woman was wearing a necklace; Feeney claims he didn't notice, and objects to the detective's tone. However, he finds it hard to maintain eye contact after he reacts.

CORRECT ASSESSMENT: *DOUBT*

When Phelps wonders how much fruit anyone could sell after midnight, Feeney admits he sells booze on the side.

TOPIC: *CONTACT WITH VICTIM*

Feeney says the young lady arrived around midnight, used his phone to call a cab, then left. But he looks awfully nervous about this statement.

CORRECT ASSESSMENT: *DOUBT*

The grocer admits he'd talked to Antonia before, but her husband grew quite jealous and he hadn't seen her again in a while before last night.

TOPIC: *MOVEMENTS OF VICTIM*

Feeney says Antonia Maldonado wasn't able to get a cab, so she got into a car that pulled up.

CORRECT ASSESSMENT: *TRUTH*

Feeney describes the car as a brown Ford coupe, the same make and model mentioned by Angel in his interview. Feeney adds that Antonia seemed to know the driver. When the interview ends, Phelps asks to look around. Feeney isn't too keen on the idea, but Galloway makes it clear that the grocer has no choice in the matter.

SEARCH THE FRUIT MARKET.

Approach the nearby green double-doors; they're locked, but Phelps kicks them open. This triggers

a quick scene: Phelps and Galloway discover a large cache of booze ready for shipment.

Approach the office desk on the left and examine the bloody **scalpel**. Then move to the open file drawer next to the other desk in the room. Take out the wooden box; Phelps notes that it requires a combination. The three locks resemble dice—remember the dot pattern diagram you found at the crime scene? Enter that sequence on the box locks: 2, 5, 3.

Inside, you find the pieces of Antonia Maldonado's charm bracelet... the one you saw on her wrist in the wedding photo in her boarding house room. (You can examine each charm individually, if you want, but it's not necessary.)

Once you've found both the scalpel and the charm bracelet, you get an urgent new objective and trigger a short cutscene: Clem takes off running, hops into his green delivery truck, and speeds away!

APPREHEND CLEM FEENEY.

Stay on the truck's tail as Clem veers down alleys and cuts across pedestrian-filled walkways. Be careful not to run down civilians as you give pursuit. Once Clem's truck gets out onto city streets, try to pull up beside him so Galloway can shoot out the tires. When you finally catch Clem, watch the case-closing scenes.

Key Clue Checklist: Just Picked Fruit Market
✓ Scalpel

THE WHITE SHOE SLAYING

An attractive and visibly inebriated woman steps off a city bus in the middle of a late night downpour. Oblivious to the precipitation, she staggers into the street and nearly gets hit by a car. Across the street, a male figure stoops to watch her with great interest through a railing....

The next day, the storm still rages. In the Central Police Station briefing room ①, Captain Donelly announces yet another case for Phelps and Galloway: a fourth woman dumped atop Signal Hill. As you leave the briefing room, other detectives ask Donelly about the latest letter in the Black Dahlia investigation.

Objectives

* Investigate Crime Scene & Interview Catherine Barton.
* Investigate Superior Laundry.
* Investigate Taraldsen Residence & Interview Lars Taraldsen.
* Investigate Baron's Bar & Interview Benny Cluff.
* Apprehend & Interview Richard Bates.
* Trace Yellow Cab.
* Interview James Jessop at Central Station.
* Investigate Interstate Bus Depot.
* Trace All American Bus 74.
* Investigate Hobo Camp & Arrest Stuart Ackerman.
* Interview Stuart Ackerman at Central Station.

CASE REPORT

TOTAL NUMBER OF KEY CLUES	/7
TOTAL NUMBER OF INTERVIEW QUESTIONS	/7

Fail Conditions

* Phelps dies.
* Crime scene contaminated.
* Bates escapes.
* Fail to charge Ackerman.

LOCATION: SIGNAL HILL CRIME SCENE
INVESTIGATE THE CRIME SCENE.

Travel to the crime scene ② on Signal Hill. Approach Carruthers and Pinker. You see an awfully familiar scene: a murdered woman, dumped at the end of a road, blunt force trauma to the head and likely strangled with triple-braid rope, according to the

coroner. He places **time of death** at around 2:00 AM. Pinker of Technical Services says much of the trace evidence has been washed away in the storm.

Phelps notes that she was left clothed with no writing on the body; her green silk dress is distinctive, and she's missing one of her white shoes. Carruthers also points out no handbag or other personal effects lying about, as well as tire tracks leading away from the body.

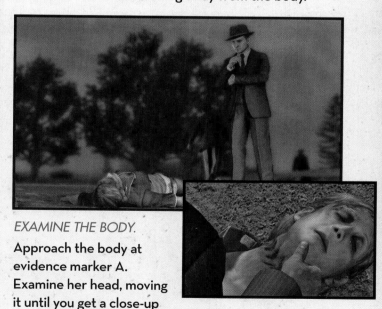

EXAMINE THE BODY.

Approach the body at evidence marker A. Examine her head, moving it until you get a close-up of a **laundry label** from Superior Laundry on the collar of her dress. Phelps notes the number: F1363. Examine both of the victim's arms to find that neither one of her hands shows signs of forcibly removed jewelry.

EXPLORE THE REST OF THE SCENE.

At evidence marker B, you find **boot prints** (but no drag marks) running from the body to a set of **tire tracks** at marker C. That does it for physical evidence at the scene. You need an address for Superior Laundry, so head for the gamewell hanging on the nearby telephone pole.

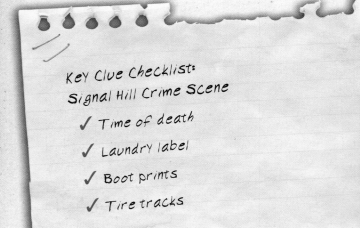

Key Clue Checklist:
Signal Hill Crime Scene
- ✓ Time of death
- ✓ Laundry label
- ✓ Boot prints
- ✓ Tire tracks

INTERVIEW CATHERINE BARTON.

Stepping outside of the crime scene triggers a cutscene: A squad car pulls into the lot, and the officer delivers a woman named Catherine Barton, who lives just across the way on Signal Hill. After she introduces herself, a short interview sequence begins.

INTERVIEW: CATHERINE BARTON

TOPIC: *SUSPICIOUS PERSONS*

Catherine Barton didn't see anybody around late last night, but earlier in the evening she spotted "that awful hobo" on the hill. (This adds "Hobo" to your P.O.I. list.) Catherine seems like an honest, respectable woman, so there's no reason to doubt her word.

CORRECT ASSESSMENT: *TRUTH*

She describes the hobo as a "very scary, angry man": tall, gaunt, and terribly disfigured. She mentions that he seems to be some sort of hobo leader—other hobos look up to him. She expects he can be found in one of the hobo camps around the area.

This updates the hobo's description in your P.O.I. section to "Disfigured Man" and gives you a new objective: Locate the disfigured suspect.

USE THE GAMEWELL FOR NEW LOCATIONS.

Now go to the gamewell on the nearby telephone pole to call in for the address of Superior Laundry Services. Phelps also asks for reports of hobo camps in the vicinity of Signal Hill. As it turns out, there's a large camp under the Grand Street bridge, not far from the hill. Both of these new locations now appear on your map. Time to head for your car.

LOCATION: SUPERIOR LAUNDRY SERVICES

INVESTIGATE THE LAUNDRY.

Travel to Superior Laundry Services ③ and listen to the partner chatter en route—Galloway notes the lack of messages on the body, which he says disconnects this case from the Maldonado murder and the others. When you arrive, enter and approach the service desk to trigger a scene: Phelps asks about laundry label F1363, and the owner gives you his **laundry ledger**.

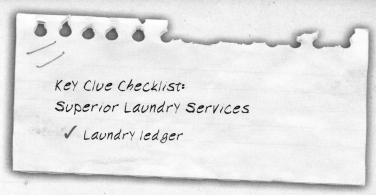

Open the ledger, then find and select the entry for F1363, a green silk dress, to get the name and address of "Mrs. T. Taraldsen." After Phelps closes the ledger, return to your car.

TICKET #	CLIENT NAME	CLIENT ADDRESS	ITEM(S) LAUNDER
F1355	MR. S. KARAYAN	2318 WEST SECOND ST.	1X SHIRT, 1X TROUSE
F1356	MRS. R. BROWNRIGG	141 NORTH MOUNTAIN VIEW AVE.	3X BUSINESS SHIRT
F1357	MRS. W. CAHALAN	128 NORTH BENTON WAY	1X SKIRT, 1X BLOUSE
F1358	MRS. A. MILLER	2716 HYANS STREET	1X BLACK TUXEDO
F1359	MR. R.G. TINGSON	339 VALLEY STREET	1X BLUE SUNDRESS
F1360	MRS. D. GOVING	447 CORONADO TERRACE	1X SPORTS COAT
F1361	MR. P. LABORDA	19 NORTH RAMPART BLVD.	X TROUSERS, 1X S
F1362	MR. J. SMITH	12 ND	HEETS
F1363	MRS. T. TARALDSEN		EN SILK DRE
F1364	MR. M. BROWN	98 HU	ACKET
F1365	MR. W. GORDON	229 LUCAS	
F1366	MR. B. WILLIAMS	109 CHILTON S	
F1367	MR. N. NEWTOWN	130 S FREMONT	

LOCATION: 43 EMERALD STREET (TARALDSEN RESIDENCE)

INVESTIGATE THE RESIDENCE.

Travel to 43 Emerald Street ④ and approach the front door to knock and trigger a scene: Lars Taraldsen answers and says that his wife hasn't returned since the previous night when they went to a party at the house of Bobby Ross. He describes her green silk dress and white shoes, which match those on the Signal Hill murder victim. Phelps reports the bad news, and Galloway tells Lars to look after his young girls while the detectives search the premises.

Step around the bookshelf to find the table with the chess set and pick up the Baron's Bar **matchbook**. This gives you the address and puts the location on your map.

Turn around and examine the dripping **wet jacket** hanging from the doorknob. Phelps notes that Lars must have been out in the rain last night. Then find and examine one of the **muddy boots** on the laundry room floor. Turn it over to discover that it's a size 8 boot. Phelps wonders if Pinker can match it to the impression at the crime scene.

SEARCH THE BEDROOM.
Go into the bedroom on the left and check out the dresser. You find another Baron's Bar matchbook and a framed photo, curiously turned face down; it's a picture of Lars and his wife.

SEARCH THE YARD.
Step through the door beside the hanging jacket to exit the house into the yard. Find the boat on the side of the house and walk around its bow to examine the **bow rope**. Phelps notes that its braid looks like a match to the ligature marks on Theresa Taraldsen's neck.

SEARCH THE LAUNDRY ROOM.
Now go through the kitchen into the laundry room and find the **victim's handbag** on the laundry sink. Open it and examine the lipstick—as Phelps points out, "at least she was spared that particular indignity." Then examine her driver's license: the victim was Theresa Taraldsen.

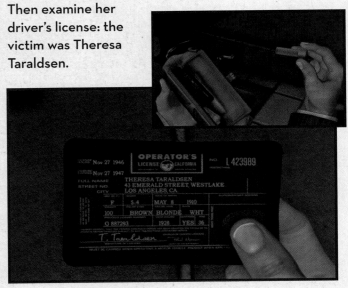

CALL KGPL.
Use the phone on the bookshelf to call in a request for the address of Bobby Ross and send a uniformed police unit to confirm Lars Taraldsen's alibi with Ross.

INTERVIEW LARS TARALDSEN.
Now go back to the living room and talk to Lars to trigger an interview sequence.

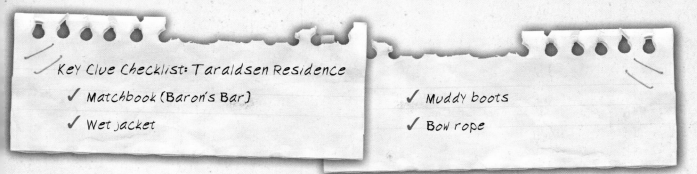

Key Clue Checklist: Taraldsen Residence

✓ Matchbook (Baron's Bar)

✓ Wet jacket

✓ Muddy boots

✓ Bow rope

INTERVIEW: LARS TARALDSEN

TOPIC: *POSSIBLE SUSPECTS*

Phelps asks if Lars knows anybody who might have wanted to harm his wife. He replies that everybody loved Theresa; it couldn't have been anyone who knew her. But after he says this he swallows uncomfortably and avoids eye contact, glancing up at the ceiling.

CORRECT ASSESSMENT: *LIE*
EVIDENCE: *BOW ROPE*

Phelps goes right for the jugular, accusing Lars of getting angry at Theresa for embarrassing him in front of friends, and then strangling her. When the detective notes the rope match to his boat's line, Lars just gets emotional about letting Theresa go.

TOPIC: *ALIBI FOR LARS TARALDSEN*

Phelps asks about the Bobby Ross party; Lars answers that people were having fun, but Theresa got bored and decided to leave. This may be true, but it's probably not the whole story.

CORRECT ASSESSMENT: *DOUBT*

More pressure reveals that Lars was enjoying the Ross party, but Theresa wanted to go dancing. Lars explains that she often goes to Baron's Bar, drinks too much, and then calls him to bring her home.

TOPIC: *VICTIM'S STATE OF MIND*

Phelps asks if Theresa was happy at home. Lars says yes, he thinks so. But he can't hide a tortured look in his eye.

CORRECT ASSESSMENT: *DOUBT*

When Phelps suggests that Lars is a prime suspect, he breaks down and spills some emotion. He let Theresa leave the party alone because he was tired of her impulsive nature—his anger is evident. Finally, he reveals that she left the party around 8:30 PM.

TOPIC: *LAST CONTACT WITH VICTIM*

Lars says that after Theresa left, he wrapped up his card game, came straight home, and went to bed. Then he looks you right in the eye. But you saw evidence in the laundry room that this isn't true.

CORRECT ASSESSMENT: *LIE*
EVIDENCE: *WET JACKET/MUDDY BOOTS*

When Phelps confronts Lars about the wet, muddy gear, the suspect claims that he met another woman at the party and walked her home before he came home himself. He seems genuinely distraught, although that doesn't exonerate him, of course.

Afterwards, Phelps lets Lars off the hook, asking him only to come downtown to identify his wife's body. He tells Galloway that Taraldsen's story "kind of rings true." It's time to check out Baron's Bar next.

LOCATION: BARON'S BAR

INTERVIEW BENNY CLUFF.

Travel to Baron's Bar ⑤ and enter the establishment to trigger a conversation with Benny Cluff, the bartender. He's heard about Theresa Taraldsen's murder on the radio and says he tried calling her husband that night, but the babysitter said he was out. This brings up your notebook for an interview sequence.

INTERVIEW: BENNY CLUFF

TOPIC: *LAST CONTACT WITH VICTIM*

Cluff says Theresa Taraldsen left the bar around 10:30 the previous night.

CORRECT ASSESSMENT: *TRUTH*

The bartender goes on to say the victim left in a cab, and he has the number. Cluff presents a bar tab with the information scribbled on it: **Yellow Cab 3591**. This adds a new topic to your Questions page.

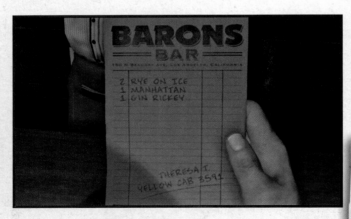

TOPIC: *VAGRANT MALE SUSPECT*

Phelps asks who Theresa was drinking with last night and describes the hobo. Cluff says he gets bums in his place, but nobody who fits that description. His facial expression suggests a hint of trouble; perhaps he's not telling all.

CORRECT ASSESSMENT: *DOUBT*

Phelps demands some detail. Cluff admits that two creeps were all over Theresa. One was a sailor in uniform with "USS Indiana" on his cap. The other guy was named Richard Bates... and Cluff says he's in the bar right now, the man in the red polo shirt.

TOPIC: *YELLOW CAB 3591*

This topic appears after you get the cab number from Benny Cluff. Phelps asks if Cluff knows where Theresa was going in the cab, but he has no idea.

CORRECT ASSESSMENT: *TRUTH*

Cluff does remember that she was trying to talk some of the guys at the bar into going to one of the dance halls. He adds that Theresa always wanted to go dancing after having a few drinks.

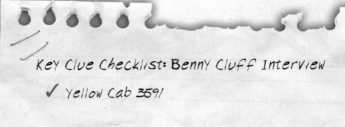

Key Clue Checklist: Benny Cluff Interview
✓ Yellow Cab 3591

After the interview, Cluff points out Richard Bates in the back of the bar. When the detectives present themselves, Bates takes off running out the back door.

APPREHEND AND INTERVIEW RICHARD BATES.

Chase down Bates! He sprints across the street, causing a Ford Custom to screech to a halt. When the driver hops out to yell, commandeer his car

because Bates jumps into his pickup truck and drives off.

Stay on his tail as he zigzags through dirt alleys and back roads, veers between the pumps of an Alaco gas station, and speeds down a hill. When you finally disable Bates' car, Phelps takes him into custody for questioning. (If you don't disable Bates' car, he eventually stops and tries to escape on foot. You can tackle him, halt him with a warning shot, or chase him until he's cornered and surrenders.) This triggers a short interview sequence.

INTERVIEW: RICHARD BATES

TOPIC: *CONTACT WITH VICTIM*

Bates was drinking with Theresa Taraldsen the previous night, but he claims he lost out to a sailor she preferred over him. But when his face screws up into a nervous squint, Phelps wants to know more—a lot more.

CORRECT ASSESSMENT: DOUBT

When Phelps threatens to turn Galloway loose on Bates, the suspect expands on the story. It sounds familiar: Mrs. Taraldsen was drunk, angry with her husband, and wanted to go dancing. Sounds like the truth.

TOPIC: *ACCOUNT OF MOVEMENTS*

Bates says that the sailor nailed him with a cheap shot after they left the bar. After that, he says he doesn't remember. But his look says otherwise.

CORRECT ASSESSMENT: DOUBT

Phelps forces Bates to admit that he did time for sexual assault and is currently on parole. But he sticks to his story that the sailor cold-cocked him, then took off in a taxi with Theresa.

CALL IN AN APB ON THE CAB AND THE SAILOR.

When the interview ends, Phelps has a uniformed officer haul Bates off to a Central Station cell as a material witness to a murder case. You can use a gamewell here to check for information about the sailor mentioned by Bates, but we'll hold off on that just a minute. Let's find that cab first.

Get in your squad car to have Galloway call in an all-points bulletin for Yellow Cab 3591, with all sightings relayed to Car 11K (yours). Start driving.

LOCATION: YELLOW CAB TRACE

FIND YELLOW CAB 3591.

Shortly after hitting the road, you get a radio call on the location of the Yellow Cab you're seeking. It's been spotted at a gas station on 7th Street near Garland ⑥, and it appears as a yellow blip on your map. Turn on your siren and drive as fast as you can to the Alaco gas station at that location.

Shortly after arriving, you get an update on the taxi's location—now it's at the corner of Wilshire and Witmer ⑦, just a few blocks away, again marked as a yellow map blip. Drive there quickly! As you get close, the yellow blip turns into a red car icon, so you can follow the cab easily if it takes off before you arrive.

If you aren't quick enough and miss the Yellow Cab, it will be reported at a new location. Keep racing to each new location until you finally spot the cab. Pulling

up to the halted cab triggers a scene: Phelps questions the cabbie, who gives you information about the **victim's movements**. He remembers the fare. He says the sailor was all over Theresa Taraldsen, but she rebuffed him, saying she just wanted to dance. The cabbie dropped them off at the Crystal Ballroom around 12:30 AM.

USE A GAMEWELL.

Now you can use the nearest gamewell (look for the blue phone icons on your map) to learn that a Navy sailor named James Jessop has information relevant to the case and is being detained at Central Station. Note that if you used a gamewell earlier to call in the APB on the Yellow Cab (instead of letting Galloway call it in on your car radio), you've already got this information on Jessop.

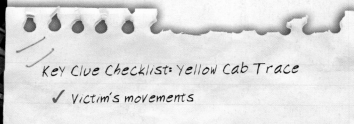

Key Clue Checklist: Yellow Cab Trace

✓ Victim's movements

LOCATION: CENTRAL POLICE STATION

INTERVIEW JAMES JESSOP.

Travel to Central Station ①. Enter and approach the watch desk to talk with Watch Commander Fleischer. He says the sailor is in Interview Room 2. Go there to meet US Navy Able Seaman James Jessop. He seems like a nice enough kid, but Homicide cops know better than to make snap judgments about people in trouble.

INTERVIEW: JAMES JESSOP

TOPIC: *CONTACT WITH VICTIM*

Jessop says he arrived at Baron's Bar around 7:00 PM, where he met Theresa Taraldsen. He says they had a couple of drinks, but then averts his eyes nervously.

CORRECT ASSESSMENT: *DOUBT*

Jessop admits he was trying to make it with the drunken woman, and they caught a cab to the Crystal Ballroom. This matches the cabbie's statement.

TOPIC: *INCIDENT WITH BATES*

When asked about his fistfight with Richard Bates, Jessop calls Bates a creep and suggests you look into him for the murder. Then he glances off to the side.

CORRECT ASSESSMENT: *DOUBT*

When Phelps says Bates is pointing the finger at Jessop, the sailor admits he punched Bates, but says he'd do it again. "She was better off with me," he says.

TOPIC: *CAB RIDE WITH VICTIM*

You get this topic only if you tracked down the Yellow Cab earlier. When Phelps reports the cab driver's assertion that Seaman Jessop was getting too friendly with Theresa, the sailor gives a crooked smile as he says, "That's not how I'd put it."

CORRECT ASSESSMENT: *DOUBT*

Jessop makes no apologies for his advances on Mrs. Taraldsen, but claims he got nowhere. At the Crystal Ballroom, she just got drunker and focused her attention on a bartender, according to Jessop.

TOPIC: *MOVEMENTS PRIOR TO MURDER*

You get this topic only if you tracked down the Yellow Cab earlier. Phelps asks where they went after the Crystal Ballroom. Jessop says Theresa caught a cab and he took a bus back to the base, but he looks nervous and evasive.

CORRECT ASSESSMENT: *DOUBT*

Phelps keeps pressing. Jessop finally admits that Theresa got on a bus with him—**All American 249**—and fell asleep on his shoulder. When it reached her neighborhood, she got off and he rode on.

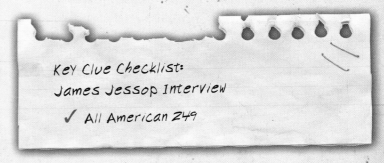

> Key Clue Checklist:
> James Jessop Interview
> ✓ All American 249

Phelps orders Jessop held until the detectives can clear his story with the bus driver. Then a patrolman reports the sighting of the disfigured hobo on Grand near the hobo camp. He also reports that the man is wanted in connection with two female assaults. Sounds like a hot suspect. But first, Phelps wants to check out Jessop's bus story.

LOCATION: INTERSTATE BUS DEPOT
INVESTIGATE THE BUS DEPOT.

Travel to the bus depot ⑧. Walk between the building and enter the depot to trigger a scene: Phelps and Galloway approach the counter and ask about the driver of All American 249. The clerk gives them the name Frank Zeferelli, currently out driving route 74. She gives you a **bus route map** so you can find him.

Open the bus route map to see the stops along the loop that route 74 follows. As Phelps says, you "need to run the loop." Close the map and return to your car. Take a look at your own map (including your radar mini-map) to see route 74 marked in red. Your goal now is to start following this red route until you find the All American 74 bus. Exit the terminal and return to your car.

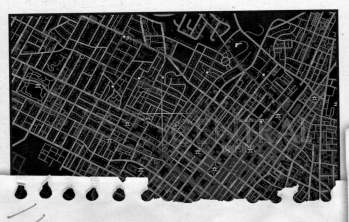

Key Clue Checklist: Interstate Bus Depot

✓ *Bus route map*

The driver remembers the pair, and says the sailor rode all the way downtown. But Zeferelli let off the woman near a hobo camp, which made him uneasy—she didn't seem to know exactly where she was. This gives you the clue: **victim last seen**.

Key Clue Checklist: Interstate Bus Depot

✓ *Victim last seen*

LOCATION: HOBO CAMP

ARREST THE DISFIGURED SUSPECT.

Travel to the hobo camp ⑨ to trigger a scene: Phelps and Galloway, who carries a shotgun loaded with six rounds, enter the unfriendly camp. The disfigured hobo leader emerges and calls out the detectives as "fascists" and a target for the campers. Galloway guns down as many attackers as he can, and others run away.

LOCATION: BUS ROUTE 74

FIND THE ALL AMERICAN 74 BUS.

Travel along the red route on your map. Just keep following the red line until you see the red vehicle blip on your mini-map and Galloway says, "There's the bus, Cole! Turn on your siren and pull her over!"

Exit your car and approach the bus driver, Frank Zeferelli, to trigger a scene: Phelps asks him about Jessop and Taraldsen the previous night.

Phelps ends up facing off with the hobo leader in a fistfight. Knock him out! After the fight, Phelps learns the bum's name: Stuart Ackerman. A uniformed officer arrives and hauls Ackerman downtown for questioning. Now you can search the camp for clues.

SEARCH THE CAMP.

Enter the corrugated tin shack directly ahead. The interior is lit with candles.

NEWSPAPER CINEMATIC

Inside Stuart Ackerman's shack, be sure to pick up the copy of the Los Angeles Inquisitor with the headline "Missing Morphine" to trigger another look behind the headline. Courtney Sheldon, the medical student we've seen earlier, pleads for help from Jack Kelso, his platoon sergeant during the war and now an insurance investigator.

Find the **bloodstained rope piece** on the nightstand next to the bed; be sure to examine it until you get a close-up view—looks like triple-braid. On the table across the room, you find a war photograph and a **purse** with the initials "T.T." on

Key Clue Checklist: Hobo Camp (Ackerman's Shack)

✓ Bloodstained rope piece

✓ Purse

it: Theresa Taraldsen, no doubt. Examine the purse further to find a Crystal Ballroom ticket stub tucked inside. Looks like awfully damning evidence.

LOCATION: CENTRAL POLICE STATION
INTERROGATE STUART ACKERMAN.

Travel back to Central Station ① and find Ackerman in Interview Room 1. Phelps guesses Ackerman's role in the Marine Corps when he recognizes the type of burns that disfigure the man.

INTERVIEW: STUART ACKERMAN

TOPIC: *MOTIVE FOR MURDER*

Phelps asks straight out why Ackerman killed Theresa Taraldsen. But instead of denying it, Ackerman gives a vague answer with a series of almost comically evasive looks. Of course, you have solid evidence to confront him.

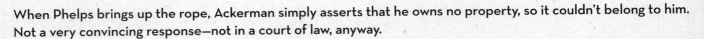

CORRECT ASSESSMENT: *LIE*
EVIDENCE: *BLOODSTAINED ROPE PIECE*

When Phelps brings up the rope, Ackerman simply asserts that he owns no property, so it couldn't belong to him. Not a very convincing response—not in a court of law, anyway.

TOPIC: *CONTACT WITH VICTIM*

The odd interview continues. When Phelps asks why Ackerman took his victim up to the hill after she got off the bus, he replies, "Which hill? I have many places."

CORRECT ASSESSMENT: *DOUBT*

Phelps suddenly takes another tack, suggesting that Ackerman is insane and thus won't face the death penalty. In response, he makes the strange admission that he's killed many women.

TOPIC: *ALIBI FOR STUART ACKERMAN*

Phelps wraps up with a simple question, asking for Ackerman's whereabouts at 2:00 AM the previous night. The suspect replies that he was at the camp.

CORRECT ASSESSMENT: *LIE*
EVIDENCE: *PURSE*

When Phelps presents the purse and ballroom ticket as proof of Ackerman's crime, the strange fellow gives another odd answer that seems incriminating, so Phelps formally charges him with the murder of Theresa Taraldsen.

An obviously drunk and unkempt-looking woman staggers through a trainyard late at night—a scenario that can't end up well. Then he appears: A man carrying a tire iron is stalking her. After the train passes, he makes his move...

Cut to the captain's office in Central Station, where Captain Donelly reports some unsettling news to Detectives Phelps and Galloway: somebody has pawned the distinctive rings taken by Deidre Moller's murderer (from "The Golden Butterfly"). The captain wants the pawnbroker quietly pressed for information—the Moller case goes before the grand jury soon, and the District Attorney is nervous.

Donelly also orders his detectives to a new crime scene at the rail freight depot on Sante Fe Avenue: another woman found murdered.

Key Clue Checklist: Captain's Briefing

✓ Pawned rings

Objectives

* Investigate Globe Loan & Jewelry.
* Investigate Railyard Crime Scene & Interview Jamison.
* Investigate Mensch's Bar & Interview McCaffrey.
* Investigate Levine's Liquor Store & Interview Robbins.
* Return to Mensch's Bar & Interview McCaffrey Again.
* Meet Captain at Central Police Station.
* Go to Rawlings Bowling Alley & Apprehend Tiernan.
* Investigate McCaffrey's Apartment & Apprehend McCaffrey.
* Interrogate Tiernan & McCaffrey at Central Police Station.
* Charge Tiernan or McCaffrey.

CASE REPORT

TOTAL NUMBER OF KEY CLUES	17
TOTAL NUMBER OF INTERVIEW QUESTIONS	16

Fail Conditions

* Phelps dies.
* Tiernan escapes.
* McCaffrey escapes.
* Fail the final interviews.

LOCATION:
GLOBE LOAN & JEWELRY
INVESTIGATE THE PAWNBROKER.

Exit the station ① and travel to Globe Loan & Jewelry ②. Enter the pawnshop and approach

the proprietor to trigger a conversation: his name is David Bremner, and he has the rose gold wedding and engagement rings in question. After a little hardnosed bargaining by Galloway, the broker gives up the rings for 10 bucks.

Examine each ring closely, making sure you get the close-up view of both. The band has a "22K" engraved on the inside; Bremner calls this engraving the "hallmark," indicating the quality. The other ring has an engraving, as well. Bremner calls it the "maker's mark," which shows who made the ring. In this case, the mark is for Hartfield's Jewelry down on Broadway.

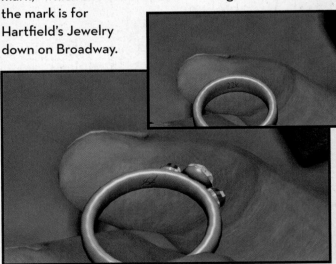

The pawnbroker reports that the man who pawned the rings gave his name as Percy B. Shelley, and left an address. Asked to describe the seller, Bremner isn't much help: dark hair, medium height and build, "one of those forgettable faces."

TRAVEL TO THE RAILYARD.

Exit the pawnshop and begin travel to the railyard location ③. This is a good place to let your partner drive so you can listen carefully to the travel chatter. Once again, Phelps' college education comes in handy: he knows the seller's name and address are a fake. He also makes a deduction about the connection between the Black Dahlia and Deidre Moller murders. The key is the Percy Bysshe Shelley clue.

LOCATION: RAILYARD CRIME SCENE

INVESTIGATE THE CRIME SCENE.

When you arrive at the railyard entrance ③, a uniformed cop tells you to follow him and hops in his squad car. Follow the car across the tracks to the crime scene. Galloway wants to keep the Moller ring development under wraps for now and follow the chain of command—i.e., Captain Donelly will decide when to release such information.

When you reach the crime scene, get out of the car and approach it to trigger a meeting with Officer Hart. He has two interviews for you: a fellow named Jamison and a rail worker, Nelson Gaines. Hart goes to keep an eye on Jamison until you're ready to interview him.

Approach the coroner at the body and talk to him. Carruthers points out lipstick smudges on her face but no writing, blunt force trauma to her head, and ligature marks that indicate strangulation as cause of death. He estimates **time of death** as sometime after midnight.

EXAMINE THE VICTIM'S BODY.

Approach the body. When you examine her head, Phelps notes a bad smell; Carruthers says it suggests a recent period of **vagrancy** (i.e., homelessness). Then examine her right hand to discover another **missing ring**, violently removed. Sound familiar?

EXPLORE THE REST OF THE CRIME SCENE.

Approach the items laid out on a mat near the body. Examine the **handbag** to open it. Take out the pink slip of paper, a studio pass. It gives you the victim's name, Evelyn Summers, and suggests she once had a **movie lot job** in the legal department. Unfortunately, as Galloway points out, the Keystone Film Company closed six years ago, in 1941.

Now take out the **upper half of the torn letter** to unfold and examine it. Looks like Evelyn had a bad

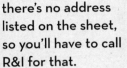

liquor problem. As Phelps says, "Somebody was trying to get her to come home." Now you can put down the handbag.

Next, pick up the sheet of paper. It's a list of personal items on stationery from Levine's Liquor Store. This adds the store to your notebook's Locations page, but there's no address listed on the sheet, so you'll have to call R&I for that.

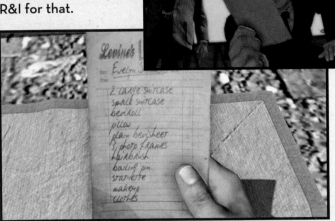

Finally, pick up the matchbook and examine it closely to see an address for Mensch's Bar. This gives you

another new location to investigate. Before conducting your interviews, you can also have a quick exchange with Ray Pinker, head of Technical Services—the guy on one knee over by the police barricade. Just approach him and press the Talk button indicated.

TALK TO THE SWITCHMAN.

Talk to the African American man in overalls near the power box to trigger a conversation: Nelson Gaines found Jamison on top of the victim at 7:30 that morning... hours after she was dead, according to the coroner's estimate.

INTERVIEW JAMISON.

Approach the man sitting on the stack of railroad ties next to Officer Hart. He introduces himself as John Ferdinand Jamison, another Pacific Electric employee. When Phelps asks what he was doing with the body, he admits he was kissing her. This elicits an involuntary reaction from Detective Galloway.

Phelps asks Ferdinand to turn out his pockets and he produces some red **lipstick**. You can extend the lipstick to see it's been used. He claims he found it on

the ground near the purse. This triggers the interview sequence.

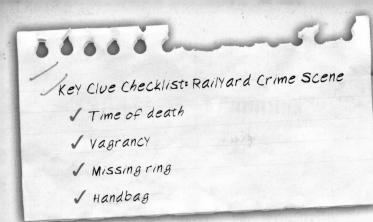

Key Clue Checklist: Railyard Crime Scene
- ✓ Time of death
- ✓ Vagrancy
- ✓ Missing ring
- ✓ Handbag
- ✓ Upper half of torn letter
- ✓ Movie lot job
- ✓ Lipstick

INTERVIEW: JOHN FERDINAND JAMISON

TOPIC: *DISCOVERY OF VICTIM'S BODY*

Jamison says he found the body as he was getting off his shift and headed home. You have no evidence to suggest otherwise, but his lowered eyes suggest more to the story.

CORRECT ASSESSMENT: *DOUBT*

When Phelps wonders how his story will seem to a jury, Jamison starts to panic. He says he came through this part of the yard around midnight and she wasn't here then. When he found her in the morning, Jamison says he knew she was dead.

TOPIC: *INTERFERENCE WITH EVIDENCE*

When Phelps asks if Jamison went through the victim's purse, he readily admits it, saying, "It wasn't as if she needed it." He looks directly at Phelps; no reason to think he's lying here.

CORRECT ASSESSMENT: *TRUTH*

Jamison goes on to say there was no money in the purse, and he found the lipstick and matchbook on the mat.

Phelps puts Jamison under arrest. The suspect complains once again that he did nothing illegal, which is just one complaint too many for Rusty Galloway.

USE THE GAMEWELL.

After Officer Hart hauls off Jamison, Galloway suggests you check out Mensch's place—a good idea, but make a call to R&I first. Use the gamewell on the telephone pole not far behind your car. Phelps gets the address of Levine's Liquor, adding that location to your map.

LOCATION: MENSCH'S BAR

INVESTIGATE THE BAR.

Travel to Mensch's Bar ④. You automatically enter the establishment and trigger a scene: Phelps chats with the owner, Walter Mensch, about Evelyn Summers.

Mensch paints a sordid picture: an unpleasant, penniless woman bumming drinks, living rough. He suggests you ask around about her.

Try the fellow by the front window—just approach and press the Talk button. He's reluctant to talk, but then says Evelyn was always mooching drinks. Not much else from the guy.

INTERVIEW GROSVENOR MCCAFFREY.

Approach the young man reading in the booth. His name is Grosvenor McCaffrey, and he calls himself a starving writer. He agrees to talk about Evelyn Summers, saying that he didn't know her well, but was "aware of her." This begins the interview.

INTERVIEW: GROSVENOR MCCAFFREY

TOPIC: *LAST CONTACT WITH VICTIM*

Phelps asks if McCaffrey saw Evelyn the previous night, and he replies no, he was home writing. His response isn't very convincing, is it?

CORRECT ASSESSMENT: *DOUBT*

When Phelps threatens to "get interested" in him, McCaffrey points the finger at someone named James Tiernan. He says Tiernan and Evelyn Summers spent time together at the library. Tiernan works at Rawling's Bowling Alley, a place Galloway and other cops frequent. This adds both Tiernan and the bowling alley to your notebook.

TOPIC: *CRIMINAL HISTORY*

Phelps asks if McCaffrey has a criminal record. He claims to have had a few minor "skirmishes," nothing serious. Again, he seems a bit skittish as he answers.

CORRECT ASSESSMENT: *DOUBT*

When Phelps gets angry, McCaffrey admits he's involved in strikes and workers' rights issues. For Galloway, this is code for a Communist—he's a pinko, a subversive "fifth columnist."

LOCATION: LEVINE'S LIQUOR STORE

INVESTIGATE THE LIQUOR STORE.

Travel to Levine's Liquor Store ⑤ to enter and talk to the owner, a man named Robbins. He knew Evelyn Summers; he was a good friend of her ex-husband, and kept some of her things in the store. When control returns, follow Robbins through the back storage rooms to a curtained-off area with a bed where Evelyn stayed.

Enter the area and turn left, starting in the corner. Pick up the statuette labeled "Keystone Films 1938." This triggers an exchange: Robbins tells you Evelyn worked in the studio's legal copyrights for music. You can also pick up a Keystone nameplate and a bowling pin from Rawling's Bowling.

Now check the opposite corner of the area. Pick up the framed photograph to see Evelyn wasn't always a loner. Then examine the **book**—Aristotle's Metaphysics, pretty heavy reading for a supposed broken-down alcoholic. Robbins comments that the only thing stupid about Evelyn was her need to drink. Be sure to examine the book further to open it and see the name inscribed on the inside cover: Grosvenor McCaffrey! This discovery adds a topic to your Questions lists for both Robbins and, later, McCaffrey. Before leaving, you can find one more framed photo of Evelyn as a young girl with her mother.

INTERVIEW ROBBINS.

When you finish investigating Evelyn's area, go back through the storage rooms to find Robbins. Approach him to trigger an interview sequence.

Key Clue Checklist: Levine's Liquor Store

✓ Book

INTERVIEW: MR. ROBBINS

TOPIC: *CONTACT WITH VICTIM*

Phelps wants to account for Evelyn Summers' movements the day before. Robbins reports that she stopped in early and bought a bottle of rye. Overall, he seems like an honest, direct man.

CORRECT ASSESSMENT: *TRUTH*

Robbins adds that although Evelyn didn't acknowledge where the money came from, she did say the **liquor purchase** was a make-up present for a boy with whom she'd been fighting.

TOPIC:
RELATIONSHIP WITH VICTIM

Robbins admits that he's probably one of the few people sad that Evelyn Summers is gone. His emotion is clearly real.

CORRECT ASSESSMENT: *TRUTH*

The liquor storeowner also admits that Evelyn was slipping deeper into her illness with no apparent motivation to get out; her mother made attempts to help with no avail. Robbins fears he may have been enabling her alcoholism by giving her a place to flop.

TOPIC: *KNOWLEDGE OF MCCAFFREY*

Robbins isn't quite as forthcoming when asked if he knows Grosvenor McCaffrey. He blinks several times when giving a slightly evasive answer: "Not personally."

CORRECT ASSESSMENT: *DOUBT*

Phelps presses, acknowledging his struggle to find good leads. Robbins says Evelyn idolized McCaffrey and his revolutionary stance on fixing society's ills. He seems to suggest that McCaffrey didn't care too much about Evelyn Summers in return.

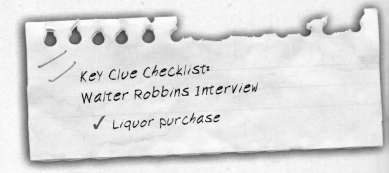

Key Clue Checklist:
Walter Robbins Interview
✓ Liquor purchase

When the interview ends, Robbins shows genuine concern for the murdered woman, and exhorts Phelps to capture the killer. Return to your car. You get a call from KGPL to return to Central Station, but your discovery of McCaffrey's book amongst the victim's belongings gives you something new to ask the writer back at Mensch's Bar.

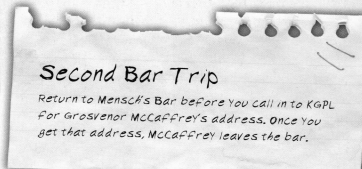

Second Bar Trip

Return to Mensch's Bar before you call in to KGPL for Grosvenor McCaffrey's address. Once you get that address, McCaffrey leaves the bar.

LOCATION: MENSCH'S BAR
INTERVIEW MCCAFFREY.

Travel back to Mensch's Bar ④. Enter and talk to Grosvenor McCaffrey, who still sits in the same booth reading his Sherlock Holmes.

INTERVIEW: GROSVENOR McCAFFREY (SECOND TIME AT MENSCH'S BAR)

TOPIC: *RELATIONSHIP WITH VICTIM*
Phelps notes that McCaffrey said he barely knew Evelyn Summers. McCaffrey affirms this, but looks nervous. You have a piece of evidence now that suggests he might be lying.

CORRECT ASSESSMENT: *LIE*
EVIDENCE: *BOOK*

McCaffrey's feeling the heat now, so he reports the **victim last seen** with James Tiernan entering Tiernan's hotel late with a bottle of booze. Now you can return to Central Station.

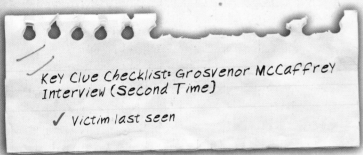

Key Clue Checklist: Grosvenor McCaffrey Interview (Second Time)

✓ Victim last seen

LOCATION: CENTRAL POLICE STATION
MEET WITH THE CAPTAIN.

Travel back to Central Station ①. Enter and approach Watch Commander Fleischer at the front desk; he tells you the captain is waiting for you with both Ray Pinker of Tech Services and Malcolm Carruthers, the coroner. Go downstairs to Technical Services.

Your arrival triggers a scene: Captain Donelly announces that Pinker and Carruthers have concerns about similarities in the Henry, Moller, and now even the Taraldsen and Summers cases. Donelly and Galloway see it as the work of copycats. But Carruthers points out the use of the same Classic Carmine lipstick, the messages to "B.D." and other details suggesting connections that seem more than coincidence or even copycat. The captain asks the detectives to keep the concerns quiet for now and focus on breaking the Summers case.

TRACE McCAFFREY'S ADDRESS.

As you leave the basement, Galloway suggests you find out where Grosvenor McCaffrey lives before heading off to your next stop, the bowling alley. Use the phone at the station watch desk to call R&I and get a home address for McCaffrey. Then exit the building and hop in your car.

LOCATION: RAWLING'S BOWLING ALLEY

INVESTIGATE THE BOWLING ALLEY.

Travel to the bowling alley ⑥. When you arrive, the detectives automatically enter the premises and talk to Florence at the desk. When asked about James

Tiernan, she says he works at the alley as a pinsetter and sends you to the back where he works.

Walk down the left side of the lanes (along Lane 1) to spot Tiernan leaping across lanes and then running through the "Staff Only" door on the left wall. Follow him through the door! This triggers a chase cutscene: Tiernan takes off running with Phelps and Galloway in hot pursuit. The suspect reaches his car and drives off... but the detectives commandeer a sweet, speedy Cisitalia Coupe, and the car chase is on.

APPREHEND JAMES TIERNAN.

Stay on Tiernan's tail until you can get close enough to ram him or let Galloway squeeze off shots at his tires. He takes a high-speed, crisscrossing route that leads you through Pershing Square (between 5th and 6th), then he veers left and tries to lose you in the Red Line tunnel.

When you finally bring Tiernan to a halt, a paddy wagon hauls him off to Central Police Station. He'll be waiting there for questioning later. But you have one more place to investigate before then.

LOCATION: MCCAFFREY'S APARTMENT

SEARCH MCCAFFREY'S PLACE.

Travel to Grosnvenor McCaffrey's apartment ⑦. Examine the mailboxes on the left side of the building

entrance to see that McCaffrey lives in unit number 6. Enter the building and climb the stairs on the right to the second floor to find apartment 6. Approach the door to knock, then kick it open.

Turn left into the living room area and find the bottom half of the **torn letter** you found at the Summers murder scene; it's on the desk. You see it is from Evelyn's mother, Augusta.

Not far away, on the floor to the right, there's a blood-spattered **tire iron** and a bloody shirt. Examine the tire iron for a close-up to see that it has "Rawling's Bowling" engraved on it.

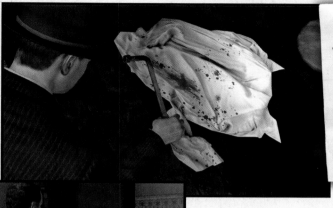

After uncovering these clues, a woman suddenly enters the room, calling for Grosvenor. She's a neighbor, and she says he has a pigeon coop on the roof. Exit the apartment, climb up one flight of stairs to Level 3, and go right to find the Roof Access sign. Climb that set of stairs to the roof.

APPREHEND MCCAFFREY.

Your arrival at roof level triggers a quick cutscene: McCaffrey spots the detectives and takes off running. Chase him as he crosses a walkway and heads down a fire escape. Remember that you can slide down ladders to speed your descent. McCaffrey sprints up a wooden staircase that runs up the hillside, then cuts through yards and down alleys.

When you finally get close, tap the Tackle button to bring him down. After the paddy wagon hauls him back to Central Station, it's time for you to head back there, too.

LOCATION: CENTRAL POLICE STATION
RETURN TO CENTRAL STATION FOR INTERROGATIONS.

Captain Donelly is waiting when you arrive. Phelps tells the captain he thinks Jamison is an "aberration." Thus Donelly wants a solid confession from either Grosvenor

McCaffrey or James Tiernan. Clearly, you're going to have to play these two suspects off each other.

This is one of the trickiest interrogation sequences in the entire game. Let's follow the room number order and start with Tiernan in Interview Room 1.

INTERVIEW JAMES TIERNAN.

Phelps asks Tiernan why he ran when spotted. His answer is almost disarmingly frank: Tiernan admits he was the last one to see Evelyn alive the night of the murder, and his guess is that the detectives assume he's the murderer.

INTERVIEW: JAMES TIERNAN (FIRST TIME AT STATION)

TOPIC: *RELATIONSHIP WITH VICTIM*

When asked, Tiernan claims that he barely knew Evelyn Summers. This seems like a stretch—he looks uncomfortable, and you have evidence to refute the claim.

CORRECT ASSESSMENT: *LIE*
EVIDENCE: *VICTIM LAST SEEN*

When Phelps brings up McCaffrey's testimony, Tiernan tells his story of the night in question. He asserts that Evelyn did go to his hotel to drink with him, but he passed out and she was gone when he woke.

TOPIC: *VICTIM'S BOOK FOUND*

Phelps asks about the copy of Aristotle's Metaphysics inscribed with McCaffrey's name. Tiernan says Evelyn was curious about it and McCaffrey mocked her for it. He suggests that she stole it,  wanting a part of McCaffrey. Tiernan's forlorn stare suggests that there's more to the story.

CORRECT ASSESSMENT: *DOUBT*

Phelps' threatening tone rattles Tiernan, and he suggests that McCaffrey's criminal record involves somewhat more than just the labor disputes.

TOPIC: *ALIBI FOR JAMES TIERNAN*

Phelps points out that the two were drinking the night of the murder and Evelyn had nowhere else to stay. His tactic is to tie the two together around the time of the murder. Tiernan continues to claim that he has no idea what happened that night. But his shifty-eyed look suggests otherwise.

CORRECT ASSESSMENT: *LIE*
EVIDENCE: *LIQUOR PURCHASE*

Phelps insists James and Evelyn were fighting, and offers Walter Robbins' statement about her whiskey purchase as evidence. This breaks down Tiernan a bit. He admits the relationship was more than friendship, but Evelyn's worship of McCaffrey clearly upsets him. He denies killing her however, saying he merely kicked her out of his room.

TOPIC: *ACCESS TO MURDER WEAPON*

Tiernan doesn't own a car, but he frankly admits he uses lug wrenches often at his bowling alley job. (Remember that the tire iron you found in McCaffrey's apartment was from Rawling's Bowling?) Again, his unease gives you reason to doubt that he's telling the whole truth.

CORRECT ASSESSMENT: *DOUBT*

When Phelps suggests he killed Evelyn Summers with such a wrench and then planted it in McCaffrey's apartment, Tiernan suddenly spills a fountain of information. He reports a visit to McCaffrey with Evelyn where she stole the Aristotle book while the writer was on the roof with his pigeons. According to **Tiernan's accusation**, McCaffrey was livid with anger and threatened Evelyn's life when he found out.

Although you can charge Tiernan with the murder here, you should question McCaffrey first before making a decision, so choose "Leave Interrogation." Before leaving, Phelps asks about Evelyn's missing ring. Tiernan describes it in detail and says he never saw her without it on.

Key Clue Checklist:
James Tiernan Interview
✓ Tiernan's accusation

INTERVIEW GROSVENOR MCCAFFREY.

Now you're loaded with ammunition for the Grosvenor McCaffrey interview. Go to Interview Room 2. The writer seems remarkably cocky, considering the distinct impression of guilt he created by running from the detectives. As he arrogantly remarks, "Let's see where this takes us."

INTERVIEW: GROSVENOR MCCAFFREY (FIRST TIME AT STATION)

TOPIC: *ALIBI FOR MCCAFFREY*

Phelps asks McCaffrey to remind him where he was when Evelyn Summers was murdered. The suspect reiterates that he was at home writing. Once again, he seems far less than convincing. And you have some evidence that connects him to the crime scene.

CORRECT ASSESSMENT: *LIE*
EVIDENCE: *TORN LETTER*

A little pressure from Phelps regarding the two pieces of the letter from Augusta Summers gets McCaffrey to change his story. McCaffrey claims to have no knowledge of the letter, and suggests somebody else planted it there.

TOPIC: *ACCESS TO TIRE IRON*

Phelps confronts McCaffrey with the physical evidence found in his apartment. The writer scoffs, saying if he'd killed someone he wouldn't be stupid enough to leave the proof in his own place. He insinuates that Evelyn Summers' was too insignificant to be worth the bother. But you have a statement that contradicts this attitude.

CORRECT ASSESSMENT: *LIE*
EVIDENCE: *TIERNAN'S ACCUSATION*

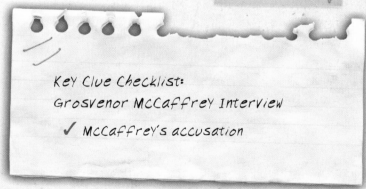

Key Clue Checklist:
Grosvenor McCaffrey Interview
✓ McCaffrey's accusation

When Phelps presents Tiernan's testimony about McCaffrey's threats to kill Evelyn, the writer turns the accusation right back at Tiernan. Now he claims the young pin setter killed Summers, then came to him for help. Phelps expresses doubt about **McCaffrey's accusation**, but the writer sticks to his story, saying he took Tiernan's bloodstained items with plans to dispose of them.

INTERVIEW TIERNAN AGAIN.

Time to discuss McCaffrey's new accusation with James Tiernan. Re-enter Interview Room 1. Tiernan seems happy to see the detectives again, incorrectly assuming that things are cleared up and he's free to go.

INTERVIEW: JAMES TIERNAN (SECOND TIME AT STATION)

TOPIC: *EVENTS PRIOR TO MURDER*

Phelps asks for clarification on events in his room while drinking with Evelyn. Tiernan continues to claim he simply woke up the next morning, hung over and with no idea where Evelyn went.

CORRECT ASSESSMENT: *LIE*
EVIDENCE: *MCCAFFREY'S ACCUSATION*

When Phelps tells Tiernan about McCaffrey's statement, he breaks down and tells the truth. He admits he was angry at Evelyn—angry enough to kill her, perhaps—but still has no memory of an attack. Then he plaintively asks: "Was it me?"

Here you have the option to formally charge James Tiernan with the murder of Evelyn Summers, and you can successfully conclude the case if you do so. However, you have another choice—one that may be preferable if you find Grosvenor McCaffrey insufferable and you pity poor James Tiernan.

CALL R&I ABOUT MCCAFFREY'S RECORD, THEN INTERVIEW HIM AGAIN.

Before you see Grosvenor McCaffrey again, pick up one more piece of evidence. Use the phone at the watch desk; Phelps calls R&I and learns about **McCaffrey's criminal record**. He was convicted of petty theft, but more importantly, he was dishonorably discharged from the Army during the Italian campaign for an assault on a Sicilian woman, who he almost beat to death. Now go talk to McCaffrey again.

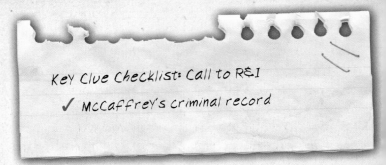

INTERVIEW: GROSVENOR MCCAFFREY (SECOND TIME AT STATION)

TOPIC: *MILITARY SERVICE*

McCaffrey says the war changed him; the terrible things he saw made him want to become a writer and lobby for change. When Phelps brings up his petty theft record, McCaffrey claims that the "salient point" is that he's never been convicted for anything violent. But you now have evidence that he's lying.

CORRECT ASSESSMENT: *LIE*
EVIDENCE: *MCCAFFREY'S CRIMINAL RECORD*

When Phelps confronts McCaffrey with the dishonorable discharge for beating a woman in Sicily, the writer's cool, arrogant demeanor shatters and he viciously blasts the woman as "a peasant whore" who tried to steal from his wallet. Of course, this is similar to the actions of Evelyn Summers, who stole his book. When Phelps points out this fact, McCaffrey's angry response is damning.

Phelps has what he needs to level an official charge of murder at Grosvenor McCaffrey. But over in the other interview room, James Tiernan has already all but confessed to the crime. Who will you accuse?

CHARGE MCCAFFREY OR TIERNAN WITH THE MURDER.

Either choice is correct for the purposes of completing your case, but only charging McCaffrey earns you the full five-star rating. Captain Donelly reacts to your accusation—he prefers charging the Communist rather than the "cry baby," but again, either charge works. Then Donelly orders the detectives to forget about the notion of a repeat offender.

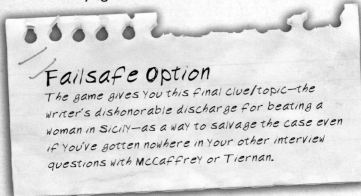

THE QUARTER MOON MURDERS

This Homicide desk grand finale features a deadly "treasure hunt" that leads you to a series of major city landmarks in search of clues, apparently placed by the Black Dahlia killer. The case opens with a short scene as Phelps and Galloway report to Technical Services to examine yet another taunting special delivery from the killer. Captain Donelly, Coroner Carruthers, and Ray Pinker all watch as Phelps takes a look at the latest letter.

Objectives

* Examine Items from Black Dahlia Killer.
* Search Pershing Square Fountain to Find Evidence and New Poem.
* Decipher Location Indicated in New Poem.
* Investigate New Location to Find Evidence and New Poem.
* Repeat Process at Five More Locations.
* Apprehend the Killer.

CASE REPORT

TOTAL NUMBER OF KEY CLUES	14
TOTAL NUMBER OF INTERVIEW QUESTIONS	NONE

Fail Conditions

* Phelps dies.

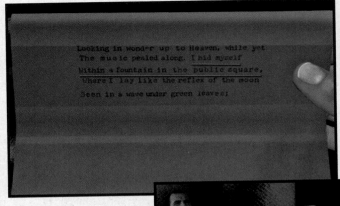

The Shelley excerpt contains a line that indicates a specific Los Angeles landmark. In this case, Phelps deciphers the key line during the cutscene: "I hid myself/Within a fountain in the public square." This gives you a new objective: Investigate the fountain in Pershing Square. As Phelps leaves, Pinker issues a warning. You're moving onto the maniac's turf now.

LOCATION: CENTRAL STATION (TECHNICAL SERVICES)
EXAMINE THE ITEMS ON THE TABLE.

Pick up the **Black Dahlia letter** constructed of cutout letters from newspapers. The message includes the same words that the coroner said were carved under the dress of Theresa Taraldsen. Only her killer would know it. Then it challenges you to "find me where I hid myself."

Pick up the red book of poems by Percy Bysshe Shelley and open it to find a passage from Prometheus Unbound bookmarked and underlined in red. Then pick up the sheet of paper and unfold it to read the **Shelley excerpt**. Setting it back down triggers a scene: the team tries to make sense of the new clues.

SHELLEY EXCERPTS

You don't have to manually copy any of the Shelley excerpts you find in this case. Each one is automatically transcribed in the Clue section of your case notebook. If you want to review a poem excerpt, just open the notebook and select that clue.

Key Clue Checklist: Central Station (Technical Services)

✓ Black Dahlia letter
✓ Shelley excerpt

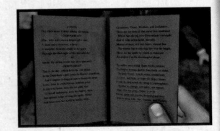

LOCATION: PERSHING SQUARE FOUNTAIN

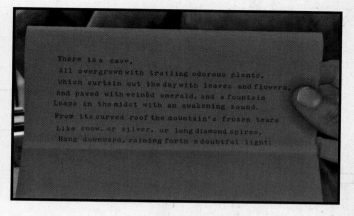

INVESTIGATE THE FOUNTAIN.

Travel from Central Station ① to Pershing Square ②. Upon arrival, approach the fountain and walk around it in the lower pool until you hear the evidence chime. Climb the fountain and find the two items at the base of the statue.

Pick up and examine the **social security card**. It belonged to Elizabeth Short, the Black Dahlia herself. Then examine the folded sheet of paper to reveal a **second excerpt** from Shelley. (This updates the clue in your notebook from "Shelley excerpt" to "First excerpt.")

DECIPHER THE SECOND EXCERPT.

The key words in this excerpt refer to an overgrown mountain cave with a frozen fountain hanging down from its curved roof. Open up your main map and move the cursor over the Hall of Records, just a few blocks northeast of your current location. Read the popup text about the hall's domed skylight and chandelier: sounds pretty familiar, doesn't it? Press the button indicated onscreen to set the Hall of Records as the current destination.

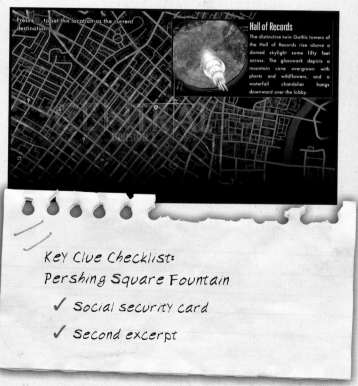

Press ▢ to set this location as the current destination

Hall of Records

The distinctive twin Gothic towers of the Hall of Records rise above a domed skylight some fifty feet across. The glasswork depicts a mountain cave overgrown with plants and wildflowers, and a waterfall chandelier hangs downward over the lobby.

Key Clue Checklist:
Pershing Square Fountain
✓ Social security card
✓ Second excerpt

LOCATION: HALL OF RECORDS

INVESTIGATE THE HALL OF RECORDS.

Travel to the Hall of Records ③, just a few blocks from Central Station. Enter to trigger a scene: Phelps asks the desk guard how to get to the top of the great chandelier hanging from the skylight. He sends you to a maintenance room on the top floor.

GET ATOP THE CHANDELIER.

Climb both flights of stairs and turn right at the top. Veer into the second corridor on the left and enter the door marked "Maintenance." Approach the ladder on the far side of the room, just to the right of the locker row. (The ladder starts a few feet from the floor.) Climb to the top and open the door to a small platform overlooking the atrium.

A length of cable runs from the platform out to the hanging chandelier. Proceed carefully across to the top of the chandelier; use the control stick as indicated onscreen for movement and balance. If you fall off the cable, Phelps manages to grab the line and can pull himself back up, but this only works twice; the third time, he falls to the floor and you must start over.

When you reach the chandelier, find and examine **Deidre Moller's watch** and a **third excerpt** from Shelley's poetry.

After examining the second item, the three stabilizing cables suddenly snap! Use the control shown onscreen to have Phelps create momentum and swing the chandelier. When you swing it far enough to the left, Phelps automatically jumps to safety.

DECIPHER THE THIRD EXCERPT.

Now open your Main map and find the Landmark that best matches the excerpt: the "high temple" of the LA Public Library with its torch-bearing sculpture at the top.

Turn right and go to the next section of scaffolding. Pull yourself up onto the first section and use the ladder to climb up to the next platform. Turn right and cross the narrow plank, balancing and moving carefully. You can fall twice and Phelps will catch the board so you can pull yourself back up. (A third slip causes a fall that forces you to go back to the scaffold again.)

Key Clue Checklist: Hall of Records
✓ Deidre Moller's watch
✓ Third excerpt

LOCATION: LA PUBLIC LIBRARY

CLIMB THE LIBRARY TOWER.

Travel to the LA Public Library ④. The building is undergoing renovation and has scaffolding all over the place. When you arrive, Phelps ends up at the foot of a staircase. The climbing route to the top of the tower is fairly linear, but we'll guide you through it anyway. First, climb the drainpipe at the top of the stairs on the right. Then use the low section of scaffold to climb to the next roof.

Climb the next drainpipe and ladder, then make a running leap across the subsequent pair of gaps, hopping across from one scaffold to the next. Climb another ladder up two levels of scaffolding to another narrow plank and cross it carefully. (You should see the names "Shakspere Goethe" etched on the wall next to the plank as you cross.) At the far side, you reach a ladder going back down!

But don't fret—as Phelps says, "Sometimes a step backwards is a step in the right direction." Slide back down through two levels of scaffolding, then go around the corner and hop down two more levels to reach a ladder with several broken rungs. Climb up to reach a series of steeply angled stairs and another ladder; these take you up to the base of the tiled roof pyramid.

Follow the walkway around to the far corner of the roof structure to find items on the ground. Examine **Antonia's medallion**—Our Lady of Guadalupe, torn from the slain woman's religious necklace—and a **fourth excerpt** from Shelley's poetry.

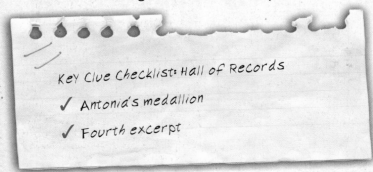

Round which death laughed, sepulchred emblems
Of dead destruction, ruin within ruin!
The wrecks beside of many a city vast,
Whose population which the earth grew over
Was mortal, but not human; see, they lie,
Their monstrous works, and uncouth skeletons,
Their statues, homes and fanes; prodigious shapes
Huddled in gray annihilation, split,
Jammed in the hard, black deep...

DECIPHER THE FOURTH EXCERPT.

Return to your automobile. Read the excerpt: monstrous "uncouth skeletons" and "prodigious shapes" that are "jammed in the hard, black deep." Then check your main map and move the cursor almost due west from your location to the Westlake Tar Pits on the edge of the revealed map.

Key Clue Checklist: Hall of Records
✓ Antonia's medallion
✓ Fourth excerpt

Press ✕ to clear the current destination

Westlake Tar Pits
Father Juan Crespi wrote of Los Volcanoes de Brea in 1769. By 1901 archaeological specimens were emerging, including the skeleton of a human female in 1914. Trauma to her skull suggests that she may have been LA's first recorded Homicide.

LOCATION: WESTLAKE TAR PITS

REACH THE ISLAND.

Travel to the Westlake Tar Pits ⑤ and approach the pits; Phelps automatically changes into waders for the trip across to the central island. Start at the broken gate and dock. The idea is to follow the old walkways made of wooden planks that are just below the surface. You can see these as the camera view moves overhead. The problem is that the planks are so old they collapse if you stand on them for more than a few seconds, so you must move quickly and without much hesitation or else you sink into the black muck and have to start over.

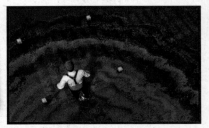

Here's the route:

Tar Pits Route

When you finally reach the island, walk straight ahead to find **Theresa Taraldsen's shoe** and a **fifth excerpt** from Shelley's poetry. This one speaks of a sphere set amongst wood rushes.

And from the other opening in the wood
Rushes, with loud and whirlwind harmony,
A sphere, which is as many thousand spheres,
Solid as crystal, yet through all its mass
Flow, as through empty space, music and light:

DECIPHER THE FIFTH EXCERPT.

After your partner Galloway rows you back to shore (where was that rowboat earlier, right?), open up your main map and find the Landmark that fits the clue. Move the cursor over the nearby LA County Art Museum to learn of its rose garden that holds a sphere-within-a-sphere celestial model called an "armillary sphere." Set the museum as your next destination.

LA County Art Museum

This site hosted racing and gambling until 1909, when concerned citizens had it recreated as a 'cultural center'. The museum kept fine art, while the rose garden hid wonders such as a sphere-within-a-sphere celestial model, or 'armillary sphere'.

Key Clue Checklist: Westlake Tar Pits
✓ Theresa Taraldsen's shoe
✓ Fifth excerpt

LOCATION: LA COUNTY ART MUSEUM

L.A. COUNTY ART MUSEUM

REACH THE CENTER OF THE MAZE.

Travel to the LA County Art Museum ⑥. Your arrival provides a peek at the armillary sphere. Follow the signs that say "This Way to Maze" and then start working your way through the hedges. Use our overhead map for quick passage to the sphere in the center.

Museum Maze Route

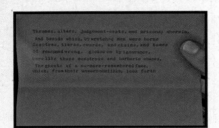

LOCATION: "INTOLERANCE" SET

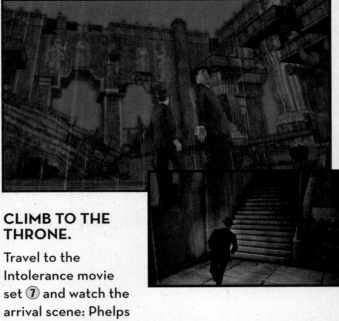

When you reach the sphere in the center, approach it to find the items on it. Examine **Celine Henry's garnet ring** and the **sixth excerpt** of Shelley's poetry. This one refers to thrones, altars, and obelisks. Sound familiar?

CLIMB TO THE THRONE.

Travel to the Intolerance movie set ⑦ and watch the arrival scene: Phelps points out the high throne you must reach, and you catch a glimpse of the staircase leading up toward it. After regaining control, jog straight ahead under the fallen column and through the big iron gates to the staircase. Then start climbing stairs.

It's a long way to the top. When you get there, run through the short corridor and hop onto the square wooden platform. Upon landing, much of the platform collapses around you, leaving only a small section where you stand. Use the control stick to have Phelps lean in counterbalance to whichever direction the platform starts tilting—e.g., if the platform tilts left, walk to the right.

DECIPHER THE SIXTH EXCERPT.

Open your Main map and move the cursor over the Landmark location of D.W. Griffith's "Intolerance" set. Return to your car.

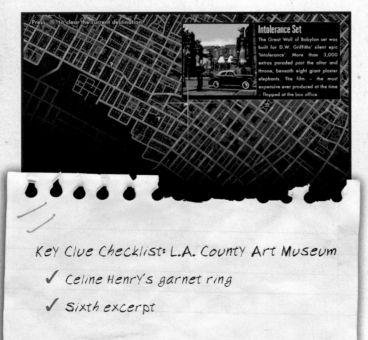

Key Clue Checklist: L.A. County Art Museum

✓ Celine Henry's garnet ring

✓ Sixth excerpt

Keep this up until Galloway can push down a wall section directly in front of you. Once he does this, walk forward (away from you) so the platform starts falling toward the collapsed wall section. Phelps automatically jumps across to that new platform as the one under his feet falls apart.

After reaching relative safety, proceed along the walkway to the first ladder on the left and slide down to the throne platform. Then approach the throne.

Pick up and examine **Evelyn Summers' ring**, the one made from a typewriter's E key. Then examine the **seventh excerpt** from Shelley's poetry. This one indicates that your search may be over. As Phelps says, "The place he calls home. End of the line."

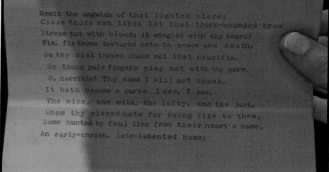

DECIPHER THE SEVENTH EXCERPT.

This excerpt speaks of a "thorn-wounded brow," tears, and a crucifix. The description certainly matches up with that of Christ Crown of Thorns, a Gothic Revival church now in disrepair. Set that landmark as your next destination and return to your car.

Key Clue Checklist: "Intolerance" Movie Set
✓ Evelyn Summers' ring
✓ Seventh excerpt

ESCAPE THE MOVIE SET!

When you finish examining both items, the platform starts to collapse. Run! Hurry through the arch ahead, then turn right and sprint down the walkway, hopping down from level to level until you reach the ground.

LOCATION: CHRIST CROWN OF THORNS

Picket Match

As you enter the front gate, notice that its spiked iron pickets match the one you found on the balcony outside the broken window of Antonia Maldonado's room—and one is missing.

INVESTIGATE THE ABANDONED CHURCH.

Travel to Christ Crown of Thorns church ⑧. Enter to trigger a dramatic cutscene: as the detectives move across the nave, they find candles lit on the altar and Phelps notices a light coming from the presbytery (the priest's residence). And then they confront, at last, their nemesis: a surprising and familiar face.

After the scene ends, rush toward the altar to trigger a quick follow-up sequence: the detectives discover that their suspect has disappeared into the tunnels

below the church. When control returns, exit the church via the side door to the right; it should lead you straight to the presbytery.

FIND A WAY INTO THE CATACOMBS.

Approach the door of the house; Phelps kicks it open. Work your way through the candlelit interior into the kitchen, then kick open the door in the back corner to reveal the killer's grisly "work room." Here you find a treasure trove of gruesome physical evidence, including dissecting tools, a tire iron, and a statue of Prometheus.

When you're finished exploring the bloody evidence, approach the open shaft leading into the catacombs and climb down the ladder.

KILL THE MURDERER.

Move cautiously along the catacombs, using cover and peeking carefully around each new bend. The killer is waiting for you! After taunting you and firing a few shots, he retreats from each corner, so move ahead when he withdraws. Keep chasing him deeper into the tunnels until you force him to step out. Then aggressively gun him down.

Watch the bittersweet conclusion as Captain Donelly appears with unexpected news about the shakeout. Although things don't play out as Phelps or Galloway expected, "young Phelps" receives a reward of sorts: a promotion out of Homicide to the LAPD's glamour desk, Administrative Vice, based in Hollywood.

THE VICE CASES

THE BLACK CAESAR

Lieutenant Archibald Colmyer welcomes Cole Phelps to the Ad Vice desk, working out of the Hollywood Police Station in LAPD's Hollywood Division. "Vice" in L.A., like everything else, seems to have more sizzle. With a new partner, the flashy cynic Roy Earle, Phelps now focuses on such leisure activities as gambling, drugs, pornography, and prostitution.

The team's first case is a pair of junkies found dead, both overdosed on pure, powerful **Army surplus morphine**. As they walk through the station, Phelps learns that Earle has personally requested his reassignment as partner... and that Phelps has become "the department pin-up boy."

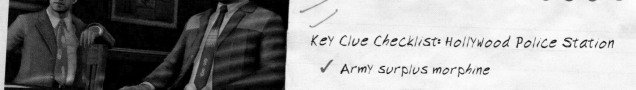

Key Clue Checklist: Hollywood Police Station

✓ Army surplus morphine

Objectives

* Investigate Crime Scene.
* Investigate Black Caesar Food Hut.
* Apprehend & Interview Fleetwood Morgan.
* Investigate Jermaine Jones' Booking Agency.
* Subdue Thugs & Interview Jones.
* Investigate Merlon Ottie's Numbers Operation.
* Apprehend & Interview Ottie.
* Investigate Ramez Removals.
* Disable Fleeing Truck.
* Use Crane to Gain Access to Ramez Cold Room.
* Chase & Subdue José Ramez.
* Investigate Polar Bear Ice Company.
* Eliminate Thugs to Reach Finkelstein.
* Examine Supply Crate.

CASE REPORT

TOTAL NUMBER OF KEY CLUES	13
TOTAL NUMBER OF INTERVIEW QUESTIONS	7

Fail Conditions

* Phelps dies.
* Merlon Ottie escapes.

LOCATION: YUCCA STREET CRIME SCENE

INVESTIGATE THE CRIME SCENE.

Travel from the Hollywood Station ① to the crime scene ②, an apartment building at Yucca Street and Ivar Avenue. Climb the stairs and follow the walkway to the open door, the last one on the left. Enter to trigger a scene: Coroner

Malcolm Carruthers greets the detectives and gives a preliminary report. Two overdose victims, Tyrone Lamont and Cornell Tyree, dead for two days, victims of too-pure Army-issue morphine lifted in a big robbery at the San Pedro wharves—a hit that has upended the L.A. dope scene. After Phelps and Earle have an interesting exchange of law enforcement philosophies, you can start investigating the scene.

SEARCH THE BODIES.
Start with the victim in the chair, Tyrone Lamont, to see that he used two of the morphine syrettes. Lamont's wallet is on the floor in front of the chair. Examine both sides to find his driver's license for positive ID and a **numbers slip**.

Move to the body on the floor, Cornell Tyree. Phelps notes that on Okinawa one syrette was enough for combat trauma, but "two of them will stop your heart." Tyree's arm is riddled with needle marks. Check his pockets for a wallet—examine both sides to see his driver's license and a **radio station note** that reads, "JJ always listens to 275 FM." As Phelps says, "Who is JJ? And why do these two care about his taste in music?"

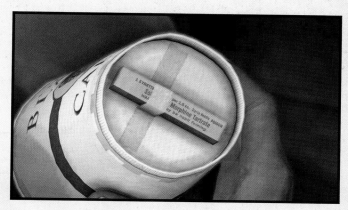

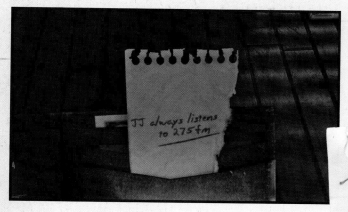

When the investigation music ends, exit the apartment with Roy Earle and head just down the street to the popcorn place, The Black Caesar.

SEARCH THE APARTMENT.

Start at the small table in the living room. You find some sheet music and a folded piece of paper with a **strange doodle**.

Pick up the Black Caesar cup on the table, one of many scattered about the place. Phelps turns it upside down to see that something was taped to the bottom, but is now removed. (This adds the **popcorn cups** clue to your Evidence list.)

Key Clue Checklist: Yucca Street Crime Scene
- ✓ Numbers slip
- ✓ Radio station note
- ✓ Strange doodle
- ✓ Popcorn cups (with morphine)
- ✓ Morphine syrettes

Enter the kitchen and pick up another popcorn cup on the counter. Phelps notes that it feels heavy for an empty cup. Examine it closer, turning it over to reveal an unopened box taped to the bottom that holds one of the **morphine syrettes**. (This also updates your previous clue to **popcorn cups with morphine**.) You can also find more syrettes on the floor near a popcorn spill, just outside the kitchen.

LOCATION: BLACK CAESAR FOOD HUT
APPREHEND THE FRY COOK.

Travel to Black Caesar Food Hut ③. (You can just walk if you want; it's just half a block up Ivar Avenue.) Your approach triggers a quick scene: Earle demands that the fry cook at the counter turn over the popcorn, but the cook takes off running out the hut's back door.

Chase him down! He leads you over the back wall, down an alley, then up a drainpipe to the rooftops. Try to tackle him, but if you can't, he eventually stops behind a roof stairwell exit and clotheslines Phelps, then calls over a friend named Eddie just as Roy Earle arrives. (Tip: You can avoid the clothesline move if you walk instead of run around the corner of the roof stairwell exit.) Keep fighting until you can arrest the fry cook. Afterwards, Phelps and Earle automatically haul the cook back to the food hut. He gives his name: Fleetwood Morgan.

Now inspect the cardboard box to open it. Inside, you find a shipment of **morphine for distribution**. Now you're ready to interview Fleetwood Morgan.

SEARCH THE FOOD HUT.

While Earle keeps an eye on the suspect, enter the hut and look for clues. Open the music case in the corner and examine the trumpet's mute to open it

and find **numbers racket** slips inside; you also get a Bronson Avenue address for the numbers operation, called "Ottie's." Examine the complimentary **Blue Room pass** in the case and turn it over to find its issuer: a booking agent named Jermaine Jones.

INTERVIEW FLEETWOOD MORGAN

Approach the suspect to trigger the interview sequence. Morgan seems agreeable, and promises to do his best. We'll see if he does.

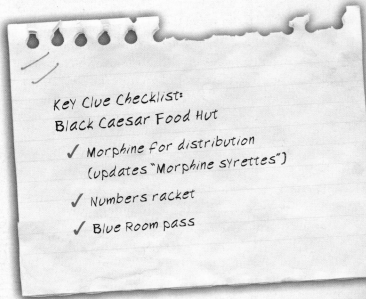

Key Clue Checklist:
Black Caesar Food Hut

✓ Morphine for distribution
  (updates "Morphine syrettes")

✓ Numbers racket

✓ Blue Room pass

INTERVIEW: FLEETWOOD MORGAN

TOPIC: *MORPHINE OVERDOSE VICTIMS*

First, Fleetwood denies that he sold the drugs to Tyree and Lamont, claiming he's just a burger flipper. Understandable that he won't make eye contact after telling a whopper like that one.

CORRECT ASSESSMENT: *LIE*
EVIDENCE: *POPCORN CUPS WITH MORPHINE*

Confronted by the evidence, Morgan gives up the name of the delivery contact and the boss, Jermaine Jones. With the **distributor identified**, you have good reason to visit Jones.

TOPIC: *NUMBERS SLIPS RECOVERED*

When Phelps asks him about the numbers operation, Fleetwood gives an angry, flippant response, calling it "the white man's tax on poor folk."

CORRECT ASSESSMENT: *DOUBT*

When Phelps threatens to give up Fleetwood as a snitch, he gets humble fast. The head of the numbers racket is named Merlon; Morgan calls him "a real slick dude... wears a hat and swings a cane."

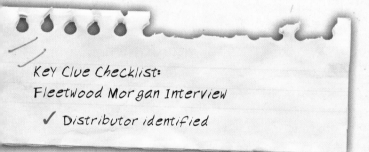

Key Clue Checklist:
Fleetwood Morgan Interview

✓ *Distributor identified*

CALL IN FOR JONES' ADDRESS.

You've got confirmation on the name of the drug supplier, Jermaine Jones. Use the public telephone booth next to the Black Caesar stand to call R&I and trace an address on Jones' booking agency.

LOCATION: JERMAINE JONES MUSICAL BOOKING AGENCY

INVESTIGATE THE AGENCY.

Travel to Jones' Booking Agency ④ on Santa Monica Boulevard. Climb the staircase and check out the building directory by the door to find the office number, 238. Then go inside and follow the hall, entering the first office on the left. Approach Jones and press Talk to trigger a scene: after some friendly coaxing from Earle, Jermaine Jones agrees to let you search the place.

Approach the Scott Phantom floor radio in the corner, next to the piano. Remember your radio station note, the clue you found in Tyree's wallet? It read, "JJ always

listens to 275 FM." So twist the VOL dial to turn on the radio, switch the BAND dial from AM to FM, then turn the TUNE dial until 275 is selected. This trips a hidden switch and the radio's top pops open, revealing a very interesting stash of items.

SUBDUE THE GOONS.

Jones immediately calls in his two thugs to take you apart. KO the fellows, then take Earle's advice and inspect the stuff in the radio.

SEARCH THE RADIO.

You find a stack of cash, plenty of **morphine syrettes**, another numbers slip from Ottie's, and a big bag of cannabis. Don't forget to inspect the sticker on the underside of the lid; it gives you a new location, Ramez Removals, but you still need the address.

INTERROGATE JERMAINE JONES.

Now approach Jermaine Jones and press Talk to start the interview process. After Roy Earle lays out the unpleasant options for non-cooperation, Jones is more than willing to talk.

Key Clue Checklist: Jermaine Jones
Musical Booking Agency

✓ Morphine syrettes (updated)

INTERVIEW: JERMAINE JONES

TOPIC: *ARMY SURPLUS MORPHINE*

Jones says he knows nothing about who supplies the morphine. Doesn't seem like a good business model, does it? Nor does it sound plausible. But you have no proof otherwise yet.

CORRECT ASSESSMENT: *DOUBT*

Jones explains that he gets his cut, but that Lenny Finkelstein draws the action. Earle explains that Lenny is head mobster Mickey Cohen's brother-in-law. This gives you a new P.O.I.

TOPIC: *INVOLVEMENT OF "OTTIE"*

When Phelps asks about the connection between the morphine ring and the numbers slips, Jones scoffs and claims there is no link, and he doesn't know anyone named Merlon. But you have a statement from Fleetwood Morgan that contradicts this assertion. Let's wipe that overconfident grin off his face.

CORRECT ASSESSMENT: *LIE*
EVIDENCE: *DISTRIBUTOR IDENTIFIED*

Jones admits in a good-natured sort of way that Merlon Ottie runs the lottery for "the Jew-boy": this gives you **Finkelstein identified**. Jones also reports that Ottie is a gambler by nature, who bets on almost anything.

TOPIC: *LINK TO RAMEZ REMOVALS*

When Phelps asks about Ramez Removals, Jones will only admit to buying a radio from there. But watch his face to see twitches that belie some level of prevarication.

CORRECT ASSESSMENT: *DOUBT*

Jones will say only that Ramez is a good friend of Lenny the Fink. That's good enough to warrant an investigation of the Ramez operation, certainly.

CALL IN FOR THE RAMEZ REMOVALS ADDRESS.

Afterwards, the paddy wagon hauls off Jones and his men. Find the nearest gamewell to call KGPL for an address on Ramez Removals. You also get the owner's name, José Ramez. This gives you a new place to investigate.

LOCATION: OTTIE'S NUMBERS OPERATION

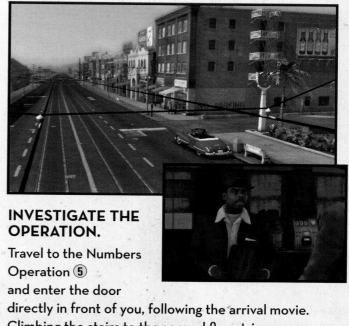

INVESTIGATE THE OPERATION.

Travel to the Numbers Operation ⑤ and enter the door directly in front of you, following the arrival movie. Climbing the stairs to the second floor triggers a scene: the detectives arrive and meet Merlon Ottie, who claims he runs a legitimate operation.

Key Clue Checklist:
Jermaine Jones Interview
✓ Finkelstein identified

Take a look around. A bank of telephones near Ottie's desk suggests a possible wire operation. Next, approach the two slot machines at the back of the room, behind Ottie. Examine the red slot machine.

Your task here is to match the three symbols in the order of the "strange doodle" you found at the overdose crime scene on Yucca Street: cherries, bell, WIN.

Press the button indicated onscreen to pull the slot machine's lever.

When you get one of the three slot symbols correct, follow the onscreen instructions to press the Hold button underneath the correct symbol. Keep pulling the lever and locking symbols until you have all three correct as shown in our screenshot. This opens the machine, revealing its secret compartment.

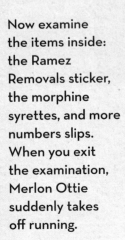

Now examine the items inside: the Ramez Removals sticker, the morphine syrettes, and more numbers slips. When you exit the examination, Merlon Ottie suddenly takes off running.

APPREHEND AND INTERVIEW OTTIE.

Chase Ottie downstairs, across the parking lot, and down Sunset Boulevard. (Tip: When Ottie crosses the lot he runs around the right side of the restaurant; circle around the left side to cut him off and he'll surrender.) Tackle him when you can; Phelps marches him back for an interview.

In Ottie's office, Roy Earle hands Ottie's cane to Phelps for a look. Examine it to flip open the top and find an **IOU note** from José Ramez to Ottie. Then Phelps orders Ottie to sit and answer some questions.

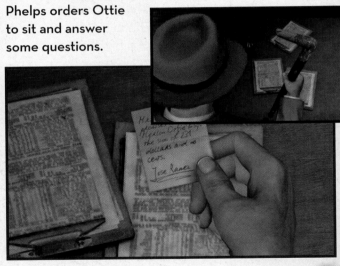

Key Clue Checklist:
Ottie's Numbers Operation

✓ IOU note

INTERVIEW: MERLON OTTIE

TOPIC: *ARMY SURPLUS MORPHINE*

Phelps asks about the Army-issue morphine, but Ottie insists it's not his line of work—he prefers sports betting. But his suddenly dry lips and shifty looks don't look very convincing, and you have a statement from Jermaine Jones, as well.

CORRECT ASSESSMENT: LIE
EVIDENCE: FINKELSTEIN IDENTIFIED

When Roy Earle presents the evidence, an angry Ottie admits he moves the dope that José Ramez brings him, but he doesn't like it. He seems frank about this, anyway.

TOPIC: *IOU NOTE FROM JOSÉ RAMEZ*

When Phelps points out that Ramez seems to owe Ottie a lot of money, Merlon responds, "We all owe somebody." Hard to argue with that.

CORRECT ASSESSMENT: TRUTH

Ottie explains that the money has nothing to do with the morphine shipment; it's just a gambling debt. This ends the short interview, and a uniform takes Ottie off to jail.

LOCATION: RAMEZ REMOVALS

PURSUE THE REMOVALS TRUCK.

Travel to Ramez Removals warehouse ⑥. As you arrive, Ramez is just leaving in a truck. Hop in your car and give chase. Get close so your partner can shoot out the truck tires, or try to nudge the truck off the road.

Soon the truck's back doors swing open and the guy in the back starts pushing out crates and furniture at your car.

After you finally halt the fleeing truck, the detectives bring Ramez back to his warehouse. He tries to play cute, so Phelps and Earle decide to explore the warehouse.

SEARCH THE WAREHOUSE.

Turn left and find the Ramez Removals ledger on the desk. (Note the newspaper on the opposite desk, as well. See our Tip on the next page.) Open it to find a number of deliveries to both Merlon Ottie and an entity known as the Polar Bear Ice Company.

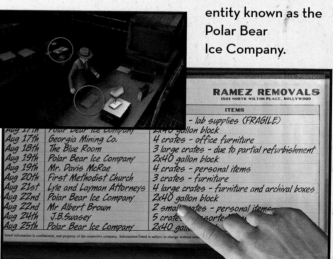

RAMEZ REMOVALS
1501 NORTH WILTON PLACE, HOLLYWOOD

	ITEMS	
		– lab supplies (FRAGILE)
Aug 17th	Polar Bear Ice Company	2x40 gallon block
Aug 17th	Georgia Mining Co.	4 crates – office furniture
Aug 18th	The Blue Room	3 large crates – due to partial refurbishment
Aug 19th	Polar Bear Ice Company	2x40 gallon block
Aug 19th	Mr. Davis McRae	4 crates – personal items
Aug 20th	First Methodist Church	3 crates – furniture
Aug 21st	Lyle and Layman Attorneys	4 large crates – furniture and archival boxes
Aug 22nd	Polar Bear Ice Company	2x40 gallon block
Aug 22nd	Mr Albert Brown	2 small crates – personal items
Aug 24th	J.B.Swasey	5 crates – assorted
Aug 25th	Polar Bear Ice Company	2x40 gall...

Listed information is confidential, and property of the respective company. Information listed is subject to change without...

Earle notices a trail of water puddles running through the furniture stacks. If you follow the trail, it leads you to a stack of tall crates—one is blocking the entrance to a well-lit room. Find the ladder just to the right of the crates and climb up to the catwalk high above the warehouse floor.

USE THE CRANE TO MOVE THE CRATE.

Follow the signs to the cargo crane operator's post and press the button indicated to take control. Your goal is to use the crane to move the crate that sits directly in front of the door below. Use the controls to center the lighted crosshairs directly over the target crate as shown in our screenshot. Then lower the crane to snag the crate and lift it out of your way.

Now you can go back down the ladder and enter the cold room with Roy Earle. It's filled with ice blocks that have something frozen inside. Shoot at the ice block sitting alone to shatter the ice and reveal what's inside: boxes of morphine syrettes. As Earle says, "It's like Santa's grotto for hopheads in here." Take a closer look at one of the syrettes to trigger a scene outside.

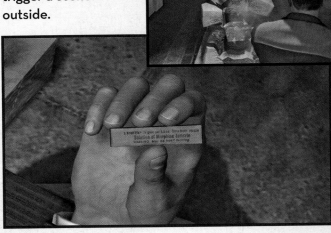

A truck from the Polar Bear Ice Company pulls up in front of warehouse and starts unloading a big block of ice. Phelps and Earle emerge, spot the object in the ice, and put the truckers under arrest. But Ramez takes their shift in focus as an opportunity to escape!

CHASE DOWN JOSÉ RAMEZ.

Chase him up and down the aisles of furniture in the darkened warehouse, then gun him down. Careful—he's armed with a shotgun. Now, as Phelps says, it's time to hunt some polar bear.

LOCATION: POLAR BEAR ICE COMPANY

APPREHEND LENNY FINKELSTEIN.

Travel to the Polar Bear Ice Company ⑦. Outside, a "janitor" tries to tell you the factory is closed, but Earle sees through the ruse. Inside, Lenny Finkelstein lets two of his thugs absorb your opening shots while he takes off running. Chase him down!

Unfortunately, Lenny has a small army at his disposal and they're determined to block your path. Fight your way across the Delivery & Loading Area to a room with a bar and dart board. Watch out for the shooter in the window directly behind the bar! Remember to check your mini-map for the red blips that mark enemy positions.

Continue down the hallway into the Machine Room. Fight your way around the pumping machine in the center of the room and approach the doorway leading into the Cold Room, a huge freezer filled with ice blocks—many of which encase boxes of Army surplus morphine. First, fight your way across the ground floor level. Then climb the stairs to the upper level.

Reaching the top of the staircase in the Cold Room triggers a quick scene: Phelps and Earle hold Finkelstein at gunpoint, but he refuses to go quietly. When the scene ends, immediately gun him down. Then follow Earle to the crates from the USS *Coolridge* and examine them. That wraps up the case.

THE SET UP

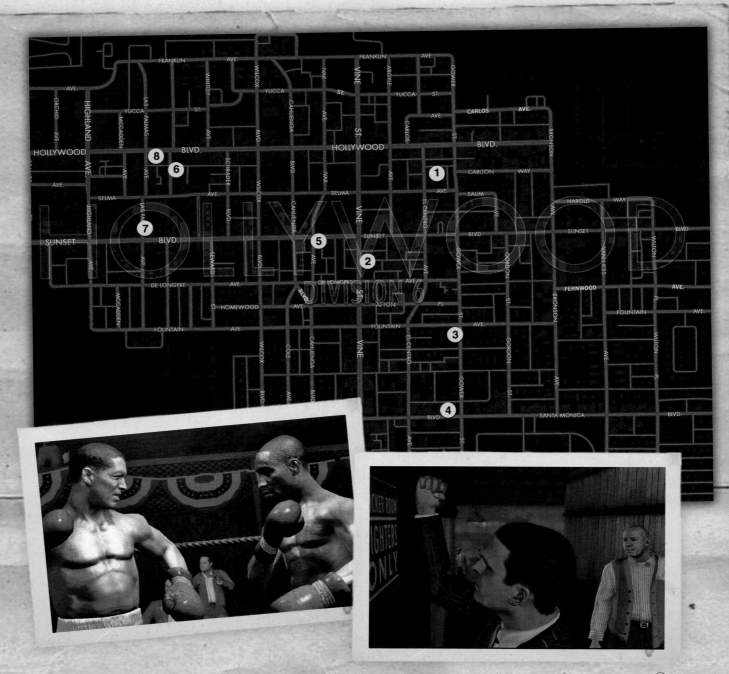

Roy Earle convinces his partner Cole Phelps to attend a boxing match at the American Legion Stadium ①.
An older British pugilist named Albert Hammond is supposed to take a dive with big money on the line, but he
disappoints a lot of gamblers by knocking out his opponent. Earle bet 50 bucks on Hammond's foe, so he has
a personal stake in finding out what happened. When the detectives reach the locker room, they find an angry
Carlo Arquero, the boxer's manager, pounding on the jammed door.

Objectives

* Search Locker Room.
* Investigate Hotel El Mar.
* Investigate Aleve Motel.
* Subdue Carlo Arquero & Interview Candy Edwards.
* Tail Candy to Thrifty Liquor & Investigate.
* Investigate Examiner Drugstore.
* Investigate Ray's Bookmakers.
* Tail Candy's Yellow Cab.
* Investigate Bus Depot.
* Investigate Egyptian Theatre.
* Eliminate Gunmen.

CASE REPORT

TOTAL NUMBER OF KEY CLUES	11
TOTAL NUMBER OF INTERVIEW QUESTIONS	3

Fail Conditions

* Phelps dies.
* Candy spots you tailing her.

NEWSPAPER CINEMATIC

Check out the newspaper on the training table with the headline "Alienist Fontaine." You see another meeting between Dr. Fontaine and Courtney Sheldon, the medical student at USC. Once again, the "story behind the headlines" gives you a critical piece of the larger story.

LOCATION: AMERICAN LEGION STADIUM

INVESTIGATE THE LOCKER ROOM.

After Phelps kicks in the locker room door, search the room. Earle explains that you need to find Hammond before he gets "clipped" for breaking his deal. Open Hammond's locker, the second one over from the pin board. Examine the pad of paper with **bookmakers' odds** and a telephone number jotted on it. There's a newspaper on one of the training tables that you might find interesting, too.

Exit the locker room to trigger a scene: Mickey Cohen, the kingpin himself, is in the hall putting heat on Hammond's manager, Arquero. You see that Cohen and Detective Earle are well acquainted. Phelps demands that Cohen keep his men away from Hammond or else.

CALL KGPL TO TRACE THE PHONE NUMBER.

Follow the hallway and use the phone near the exit door. Phelps gets an address for the phone number he found in Hammond's locker: it's the Hotel El Mar in Hollywood. Now return to your car and head for this new location.

Key Clue Checklist:
American Legion Stadium
✓ Bookmakers' odds

LOCATION: HOTEL EL MAR

FIND HAMMOND'S ROOM.

Travel to the Hotel El Mar ②. Enter and approach the deskman to trigger a scene: He says nobody named Hammond is at the hotel, but then it's not the sort of place where people use real names. He gives you the hotel register to check. Open it and take Earle's advice: Look for prominent Englishmen. Select the guest entry for "Winston Churchill" in Room 207. Then head upstairs to the second floor and find 207, just opposite the stairs.

SEARCH THE ROOM.

Enter Room 207 via the unlocked door and pluck the copy of the Western Union **telegram** from the refuse dumped on the floor from the tipped-over trashcan. It suggests that Albert Hammond is on his way home to England.

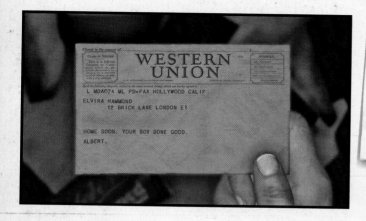

Key Clue Checklist: Hotel El Mar
- ✓ Telegram
- ✓ Movie ticket stub
- ✓ Magazine Coupon
- ✓ Bookmakers' payouts

LOCATION: ALEVE MOTEL
FIND CANDY'S ROOM.

Inspect the dresser top to find the **movie ticket stub** and some chocolates in a heart-shaped box, which indicates Hammond has a female companion. Then move to the table and examine the magazine. Scan the close-up and select (i.e., tap Phelps' finger on) the

magazine coupon to pick up a new P.O.I., Candy Edwards, and get her address. Could this be Hammond's love interest?

Travel to the Aleve Motel ③ and enter the motel office to trigger a scene: when Phelps asks about Candy Edwards, the blasé desk clerk sends the detectives up to apartment 7 via the outside staircase. She also mentions that some sleazy guy named Carlo was looking for Candy, too. Exit the office and go upstairs to apartment 7.

KNOCK OUT CARLO.

As you approach the door, you hear Carlo Arquero yelling at somebody. When Phelps kicks the door open, you see Carlo punching a blonde woman in the face. KO the goon!

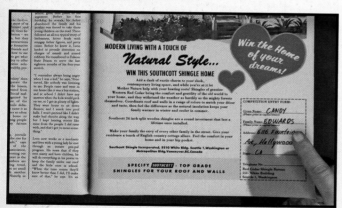

Finally, pick up the sheet of paper listing the **bookmakers' payouts** from the nightstand on the left side of the bed. Looks like Hammond stood to make a killing by betting the long odds on himself and then winning the fight. Now you can exit the hotel and go to the Candy Edwards address listed in the magazine coupon. It happens to be the Aleve Motel.

After knocking out Carlo, examine his unconscious body. You find a switchblade in his left breast pocket and a list of bookmakers in his right breast pocket—some of the names match up with Hammond's list.

INTERVIEW CANDY EDWARDS.

After close inspection of the key clues, a scene is triggered: Miss Edwards awakens and Phelps helps her to the chair. She agrees to answer some questions.

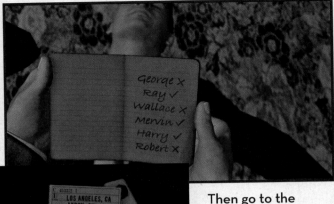

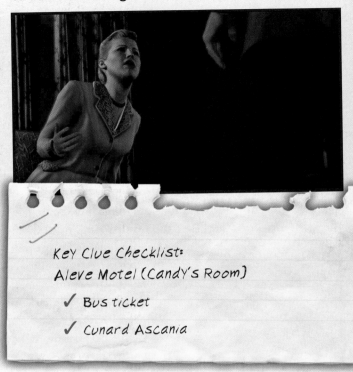

Then go to the vanity dresser and examine the one-way **bus ticket** to Akron, Ohio, and the card for the transoceanic passenger ship **Cunard Ascania**— which, as Phelps points out, sails from New York.

Key Clue Checklist:
Aleve Motel (Candy's Room)
✓ Bus ticket
✓ Cunard Ascania

INTERVIEW: CANDY EDWARDS

TOPIC: *WHEREABOUTS OF HAMMOND*

When Phelps asks where Albert Hammond might be, Candy claims their relationship is over, and she hasn't seen him. Watch her face. She may be a tough cookie, but she doesn't lie very convincingly. More importantly, you have a piece of physical evidence that undercuts her claim.

CORRECT ASSESSMENT: *LIE*
EVIDENCE: *MAGAZINE COUPON*

Candy admits she was in his room, but claims she left him before the fight because of his refusal to take a dive. This is plausible, so Phelps can't push the point further.

TOPIC: *LIST OF ODDS RECOVERED*

Phelps asks about the bookmakers' names (Harry, Mervin, Ray) on the list. Candy denies knowing them.

CORRECT ASSESSMENT: *LIE*
EVIDENCE: *BOOKMAKERS' ODDS*

When Phelps asks Candy for the betting slips, she suggests that Albert played dumb in order to make a killing and expresses amazement that Albert could "beat 'em all."

TOPIC: *PLANS TO LEAVE TOWN*

Phelps asks if Candy is leaving town, and she replies that she's going straight home to Akron. Her smile is a bit too smug, and she doesn't seem like the kind of girl to run home to Ohio.

CORRECT ASSESSMENT: *DOUBT*

Phelps gets tough and so does Earle, but Candy won't crack. She's tough, all right.

After the interview, the detectives run Carlo Arquero out of the room. Outside, Earle expresses amazement that Candy isn't running for the train station, considering all the dangerous types who probably think she's a partner in Hammond's scheme. Earle smells a payoff, and suggests you stake out Candy to see where she goes.

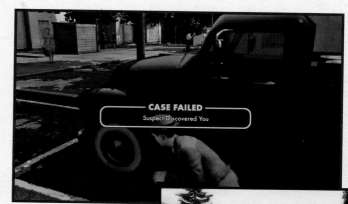

TAIL CANDY EDWARDS.

The scene shifts to the next morning, with Phelps and Earle patiently waiting in their car, parked near the Aleve Motel. Soon Candy emerges from her room with a big red suitcase and starts walking. Phelps tails her on foot while Earle follows with the car.

Phelps automatically sits on the nearby bench and picks up a newspaper to "go incognito." Wait until Candy rounds the corner of the motel building and reaches the parking lot, then begin your pursuit. Maintain a safe distance, and stay in cover as much as possible! Candy will stop and look around a number of times. If you're out in the open, she'll spot you and you get the "Case Failed: Suspect Discovered You" screen.

Hide behind cars, trees, building corners, fences, and so forth. You can also go incognito at telephone booths, sitting on shoeshine stands, or at window displays. Keep an eye on the red blip on your mini-map that marks Candy's location. If it starts to flash, you're either too close or she's getting too far away.

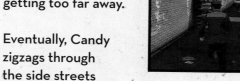

Eventually, Candy zigzags through the side streets of a residential area and veers down an alley past a Fireproof Warehouse sign—the alley leads out to Santa Monica Boulevard. When you reach the street, a cutscene plays: Candy enters Thrifty Liquor as your partner, Earle, pulls up in the car.

LOCATION: THRIFTY LIQUOR

INVESTIGATE THE FIRST BOOKMAKER'S OFFICE.

Get out of the car and enter Thrifty Liquor ④ to find no liquor whatsoever, but rather a busy bookmaker's business. This shop is run by Harry, the first name on the list of bookies you found in Hammond's locker. Your entrance triggers a scene: Harry says Candy ducked out the back after cleaning him out with her $3,600 in winnings. But before she left she made a phone call and wrote something on the notepad.

Approach the phone to bring up the notepad screen, then follow the onscreen instructions to lightly shade areas of the **bookie's notepad**. This reveals the note that Candy jotted on the pad just minutes earlier: Examiner Drugstore, plus its address on Ivar Avenue in Hollywood.

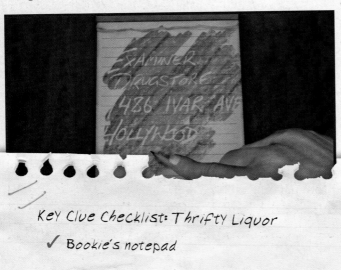

Key Clue Checklist: Thrifty Liquor
✓ Bookie's notepad

LOCATION: EXAMINER DRUGSTORE

INVESTIGATE THE SECOND BOOKMAKER'S OFFICE.

Travel to the Examiner Drugstore ⑤. En route you get a call from KGPL with a list of all known bookmakers operating out of storefronts in the Hollywood area. You already know about the first two, Thrifty Liquor and the Examiner Drugstore; the third one is at Mac's Spirits on North Cherokee and gets added to your location list as "Ray's Bookmakers." Ray is the third name on Hammond's list of bookies.

When you reach the Examiner Drugstore, enter to trigger a scene. The proprietor, Mervin—the second name on Hammond's list of bookies—has a voice for the ages, doesn't he? He says Candy took him for "four thousand clams and change" and just left via taxi. To call the cab, she consulted a card Mervin keeps by his phone.

Go to Mervin's phone and pick up the **Yellow Cab Company card**. Then use the phone: Phelps gets connected to Yellow Cab and picks up the cab number of the vehicle dispatched to pick up Candy at the Ivar Avenue address: 179.

Now go back to Mervin and talk to him. He verifies that Ray runs a bookie shop on North Cherokee, just south of Hollywood Boulevard. Return to your car.

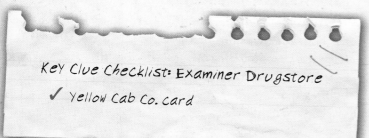

Key Clue Checklist: Examiner Drugstore
✓ Yellow Cab Co. card

LOCATION: RAY'S BOOKMAKERS

INVESTIGATE THE THIRD BOOKMAKER'S OFFICE.

Travel to Ray's Bookmakers ⑥. Your arrival triggers a scene: Yellow Cab 179 is parked out front, waiting. Phelps and Earle decide to tail the cab. Candy soon exits the office and hops back in her taxi.

TAIL YELLOW CAB 179.

Follow the cab as it zigzags around town and takes a very circuitous route to its destination. Remain at a safe distance and drive carefully. Remember that the target cab is marked as a red blip on your mini-map, so you can keep tabs even if it turns out of your sight.

When the taxi finally stops to drop off the passenger, it's at the Interstate Bus Depot ⑦, just a few blocks from where you started at Ray's bookie shop!

LOCATION: INTERSTATE BUS DEPOT
TAIL CANDY ACROSS THE DEPOT.

Inside the depot, Earle spots Hammond and starts tailing him while you follow Candy. After regaining control, go directly forward to the bench with the newspaper and pick it up; Phelps sits and holds up the paper to go incognito. Wait until Candy enters the ladies room to your left, then approach the door. You hear Candy scream and then a gunshot!

Reaching the door triggers a scene: Phelps enters to find Candy in a stall. The red suitcase is gone. When Earle arrives, he assumes Hammond is the perpetrator of this deed. But Phelps isn't so sure.

SEARCH THE CRIME SCENE.

Before you go, search the stall. Examine the **revolver** on the ground to view its chamber: .32 caliber, one shot fired. More importantly, pick up Candy's purse and open it. Examine the **movie ticket** to add the Egyptian Theatre location and address on Hollywood Boulevard. Now you've got a new place to visit. As Phelps says, "Not much else to go on."

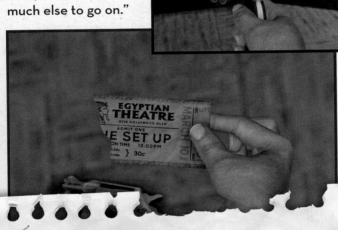

Key Clue Checklist: Interstate Bus Depot

✓ Revolver

✓ Movie ticket

LOCATION: EGYPTIAN THEATRE

INVESTIGATE THE THEATRE.

Travel to the Egyptian Theatre ⑧. Your arrival triggers a scene: a radio call from KGPL reports a message from the coroner. The revolver you found in the bus depot stall belonged to the victim. The cause of Candy Edwards' death wasn't a bullet, but a knife wound! And that fact points a finger squarely at Carlo Arquero. Now enter the theatre.

Step inside and you hear the voices of Albert Hammond and Carlo Arquero. Listen to the conversation, especially Carlo's incriminating statements. Up in a box seat, Carlo takes a few wild shots in the direction of Hammond's voice and shadow.

TAKE OUT ARQUERO AND HIS MEN.

Phelps and Earle make their move, and the gunfight begins. Shoot at Arquero until he runs from the high box on the left, and then start gunning down the goons who enter at the front of the theater, including one armed with a Tommy gun. (Check those red blips on the mini-map!) Another goon opens fire from the box on the right, too. Take them all out, then nail Arquero when he enters the main floor.

When Arquero drops, you've completed the case. Watch the final movie to see what happens to Albert Hammond, the guy who wouldn't take a dive.

MANIFEST DESTINY

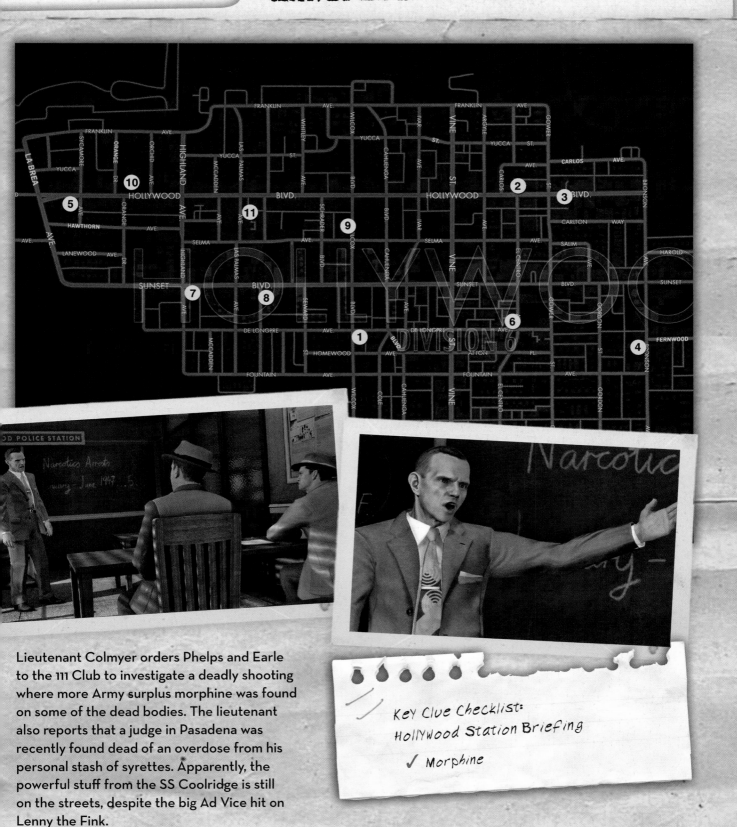

Lieutenant Colmyer orders Phelps and Earle to the 111 Club to investigate a deadly shooting where more Army surplus morphine was found on some of the dead bodies. The lieutenant also reports that a judge in Pasadena was recently found dead of an overdose from his personal stash of syrettes. Apparently, the powerful stuff from the SS Coolridge is still on the streets, despite the big Ad Vice hit on Lenny the Fink.

Key Clue Checklist:
Hollywood Station Briefing
✓ Morphine

Objectives

* Investigate 111 Club Shooting & Interview Hostess.
* Travel to The Blue Room & Interview Elsa Lichtmann.
* Interview Mickey Cohen at Mocambo Club.
* Talk to Det. Caldwell at Hollywood Station.
* Travel to Bus Shooting.
* Kill & Search Shooter.
* Interview Bus Driver.
* Travel to Kelso's Apartment & Interview Kelso.
* Travel to Robert's Diner & Chase Gunmen.
* Kill & Search Gunmen.
* Travel to Hollywood Post Office.
* Eliminate Shooters & Search Victims.
* Travel to Chinese Theater & Chase Gunmen.
* Travel to Alleyway Meeting & Eliminate Cohen's Goons.
* Return to Hollywood Station & Interview Courtney Sheldon.

CASE REPORT

TOTAL NUMBER OF KEY CLUES	15
TOTAL NUMBER OF INTERVIEW QUESTIONS	14

Fail Conditions

* Phelps dies.
* Any chased suspects escape.

LOCATION: 111 CLUB

INVESTIGATE THE 111 CLUB.

Travel from the Hollywood Police Station ① to the 111 Club ②. Your arrival triggers a scene: The Homicide team already there includes one of Phelps' old partners, Stefan Bekowsky. Phelps is surprised to learn that the dead club owner is a former member of his Marine unit, Eddie McGoldrick. Bekowsky reports that the other victims were a pair of musicians named Bowe and Bittleston, who once played in a band

with Lamont and Tyree, the two overdose victims from The Black Caesar case. Looks like interesting connections, all around.

Examine the body of Bowe, the fellow sitting against the bar at evidence marker A. Phelps notes that the killers pumped numerous rounds into him.

Find the instrument case marked by evidence marker B, on the floor near the bandstand. Open it to see a trumpet and three trumpet keys. Take out then put back each of the three keys in any order—you hear a click each time, then a secret compartment opens.

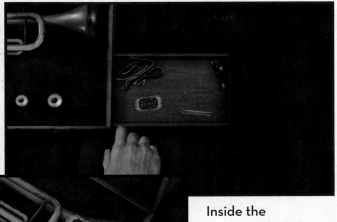

Walk through the open door just beyond Bittleston's body to examine the open crate filled with cartons of **Valor cigarettes**. Where would someone get cigarettes in such bulk?

Inside the compartment you find a **Blue Room pass** and a syringe. The syringe updates your **morphine** clue. This adds a new objective to investigate the Blue Room.

Now search the body of Bittleston at evidence marker C. Examine his right breast pocket to find a syrette, which updates your **morphine** clue again.

Nearby you find a gun rack holding three military **BARs** (Browning Automatic Rifles). Phelps notes that they look brand new, never fired; he suggests checking out the serial numbers. He also notes the pattern: morphine, cigarettes, weapons, all Army surplus. Earle suggests checking in at the Hollywood station to get details of the items stolen in the **Coolridge heist**.

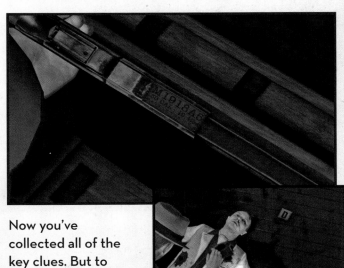

Now you've collected all of the key clues. But to be thorough, go into the back room to the body at evidence marker D. This victim is your fellow Marine, the club owner Eddie McGoldrick. Check out the nearby safe to find that it's still full of money. The killers clearly had no interest in robbery. This hit was meant to send a message.

INTERVIEW THE HOSTESS.

Join Bekowsky with the hostess near the bar. She's ready to talk.

Key Clue Checklist: 111 Club
- ✓ Blue Room pass
- ✓ Morphine (updated twice)
- ✓ Valor cigarettes
- ✓ BARs
- ✓ Coolridge heist

INTERVIEW: THE HOSTESS

TOPIC: *111 CLUB SHOOTING INCIDENT*

Phelps asks the hostess if she knows who might have done the shooting. She claims to have no idea; it was her day off. But she answers a little too quickly and seems a bit uneasy.

CORRECT ASSESSMENT: *DOUBT*

When Phelps puts on a little pressure, she points out that ever since Eddie McGoldrick bought the club, it's gotten regular visits from "tough guys"—i.e., mobsters.

TOPIC: *KNOWLEDGE OF MCGOLDRICK*

Phelps asks about Eddie. She says he knew nothing about running a club, but came into money somehow and bought the place recently.

CORRECT ASSESSMENT: *TRUTH*

When Phelps asks where she thinks Eddie got this money, she suggests he was selling something... and hints that it was illegal.

Now you have a choice of two locations to visit, the Blue Room or the Hollywood Police Station. Let's hit the jazz club first.

LOCATION: THE BLUE ROOM

INTERVIEW ELSA LICHTMANN.

Travel to The Blue Room ③, just down the street. Enter both sets of doors to trigger a scene: the detectives approach the bandstand as the singer, Elsa, and her band members rehearse. Her response to their interruption angers Roy Earle, but Phelps intercedes and the interview begins.

INTERVIEW: ELSA LICHTMANN

TOPIC: *ARMY SURPLUS MORPHINE*

Phelps points out the growing number of overdose cases and asks Elsa for any information she might have on the two tons of Army surplus morphine on the streets. She offers nothing. Given her known association with the recently departed musicians, her proclamation of ignorance seems dubious.

CORRECT ASSESSMENT: *DOUBT*

Phelps tries to pressure her by threatening to bring Earle back into the interrogation. The threat riles up Elsa's musicians, who resent the implication that their community is involved in the drug supply. As one of them puts it, "White man supplies, black man buys."

TOPIC: *MORPHINE OVERDOSE VICTIMS*

Elsa also denies any knowledge of the recent overdose victims. She remains unflappable, but clearly she knows more than she's telling.

CORRECT ASSESSMENT: *DOUBT*

When Phelps asserts that he's not going away, Elsa admits knowing the horn player, Cornell, and notes that he wasn't very good. One of the musicians calls Cornell "a sad, lonely cat." At this point, the interview is over: Elsa sends her band on break so she can speak privately with Phelps.

Elsa begins questioning Phelps' zeal in prosecuting a war on narcotics that she believes he can't win. Why is he questioning her instead of the man everyone knows is behind the supply pipeline in L.A.?

Even Earle agrees with Elsa on this point: it's time to see Mickey Cohen at his usual hangout, the Mocambo Club. But Phelps asks Earle to give him until morning to check out a few things first.

TAIL ELSA LICHTMANN.

The scene shifts to later that night: Phelps waits alone outside The Blue Room as Elsa exits the club to a taxicab. Follow her yellow cab; it's easy to spot in traffic. Be careful, as usual, to avoid getting too close or let her get too far away, and keep an eye on the red automobile icon on the mini-map.

When you reach Elsa's residence, watch the cutscene as Phelps follows her to her apartment. Outside, his partner keeps an eye on things.

LOCATION: THE MOCAMBO CLUB

INTERVIEW MICKEY COHEN.

The scene shifts again: the next day, close to noon, Phelps arrives at the Mocambo Club ⑤, where Earle waits for him outside. Follow the maitre d' to meet crime boss Mickey Cohen and his chief bodyguard and enforcer, Johnny Stompanato. It turns out Johnny was a Marine on Okinawa, too, and he admires Phelps for his exploits on Sugar Loaf. But Cohen is in no mood for pleasantries, and the interview sequence begins.

INTERVIEW: MEYER HARRIS "MICKEY" COHEN

TOPIC: *FINKELSTEIN DRUG OPERATION*

Phelps asks about Cohen's brother-in-law, Lenny Finkelstein, from whom the LAPD recovered a third of the stolen morphine shipment. Cohen flatly answers that he knows nothing about it, and levels a stare right at Phelps. Cohen didn't become a crime boss by cracking under simple questioning.

CORRECT ASSESSMENT: *DOUBT*

Phelps finds it hard to believe that Mickey doesn't know where Lenny got the dope or where the rest of the shipment is located. But as the mobster replies, "Kid, ask a question you might get an answer to."

TOPIC: *111 CLUB SHOOTING INCIDENT*

Phelps mentions the group of Marines suspected of stealing the morphine from the SS Coolridge, and suggests a further link to the killing of one of those Marines, Eddie McGoldrick, at the 111 Club. Again, with a mocking smile, Cohen coolly denies any knowledge of such things.

CORRECT ASSESSMENT: *DOUBT*

Afterwards, Cohen expresses shock that veterans would be getting involved in crime, and tells Earle that dope is not his thing. But the mobster promises to make inquiries, and the detectives make their exit. After an ominous exchange between the two mobsters, the scene automatically switches to the Hollywood Station.

LOCATION: HOLLYWOOD POLICE STATION

TALK TO THE DETECTIVES ON THE COOLRIDGE THEFT.

A mob of another kind, the media, clusters around the entrance to the police station. Listen to Earle describe the latest political wrangling. The partners visit Lieutenant Colmyer to ask who's on the Coolridge case. He sends them to the Burglary/Robbery Squad Room to meet with Detective Caldwell. Follow Earle to the squad room.

Your entrance triggers another scene: Caldwell reports that the Coolridge theft was an inside job, and he lists the stolen items, now familiar to you: BARs and cigarettes, as well as the morphine. Phelps tells Caldwell about the goods found at the 111 Club shootings. Then Caldwell shows the Vice detectives the ship's **manifest** listing all passengers and cargo.

The stolen items are circled in red; tap on them to get comments and update your clues for **stolen BARs** and **stolen Valors**. Phelps also notices the names of his former unit mates... including Eddie McGoldrick.

LOCATION: BUS SHOOTING

GUN DOWN THE ROOFTOP SNIPER.

Travel to the bus shooting ④. Your arrival triggers a wild scene: a rooftop gunman unloads withering automatic rifle fire on a city bus filled with passengers. His firepower easily outguns the cops currently on the scene!

No. on List	SHIP MANIFEST OF PASSENGERS & GOODS FOR THE UNITED STATES AT PORT OF ARR REFERENCE NO.	NO. OF UNITS	WEIGHT	ITEM(S)
A 1.	F2008L01-L176	175	1165 lbs	Medical pouch
A 2.	M1924A-FEB498216	850	4.2T	M1 Garand .30 Cal rifle
A 3.	M1928A1- AUG3114434	400	2.1T	M1928A1 .45 Cal Thompson Submach
A 4.	F5560L77-G150	1500	750 lbs	1 gallon hydration carrier
A 5.	M1918A5-JAN3450503	300	2.64T	M1918 .30 calibre Browning Auto
A 6.	P2059L05-P330	2100	2.5T	A.L.I.C.E. pack
A 7.	P2051L00-L600	600	320 lbs	M1 Combat Helmet with liner and
A 8.	W9890B33-B493	460	245 lbs	M3 Trench Knife
A 9.	CR99822V4-CR99824P1	8800	960 lbs	Valor cigarette carton
A 10.	CR99833V16-W99	3600	820	.30 calibre ammunition strippe
A 11.	F2215L00-F2219B66	500000	2T	Morphine Tartrate 1.5cc syrett
A 12.	F2006L02-L57	55	176	Zip rubber body bag
A 13.	F5509L11-L71	60	14 lbs	Heavy duty canvas stretcher

LOS ANGELES PORT AUTHORITY

But before they can discuss the cases any further, an officer rushes in with news of an attack on a city bus by a shooter with an automatic rifle. KGPL is calling for all units to the site for backup. Hurry out to your vehicle!

When you regain control, go left to the end of the building and take the first right up the alley. Continue past the parked truck and around the next corner to the fire escape ladder. Climb the fire escape to the roof.

Key Clue Checklist: Hollywood Police Station
✓ Manifest
✓ Stolen BARs (updated)
✓ Stolen Valors (updated)

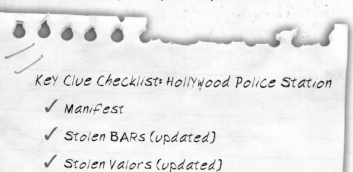

You emerge behind a stairwell exit structure. The gunman is directly across the roof, hiding behind another structure. Take cover at the left corner and gun him down!

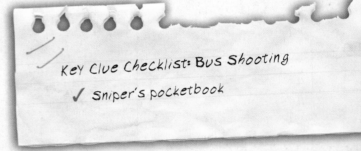

SEARCH THE SNIPER'S BODY.

Approach the fallen sniper. First, pick up his rifle and examine it to verify that it's one of the stolen BARs.

Then search the body to find the **sniper's pocketbook** in his right breast pocket. It lists a phone number and a restaurant table number at the Mocambo Club.

INTERVIEW FELIX ALVARRO.

After the search, you trigger one more scene: Phelps recognizes the transit bus driver as Felix Alvarro, another former soldier from the 6th Marines. After their greeting, the interview begins.

Key Clue Checklist: Bus Shooting

✓ Sniper's pocketbook

INTERVIEW: FELIX ALVARRO

TOPIC: *INFORMED OF COOLRIDGE HEIST*

Phelps asks about the dock heist, and Felix only admits that the police questioned him. He makes eye contact, but blinks repeatedly.

CORRECT ASSESSMENT: *DOUBT*

Phelps tells him about Eddie's fate at the 111 Club, trying to scare him into spilling more info. Felix only says that he heard Eddie came into some cash... and suggests Eddie should have kept a lower profile.

TOPIC: *MOTIVE FOR SHOOTING*

Phelps asks straight out who's shooting at Felix. Again, Felix claims to have no idea, folding his arms defiantly.

CORRECT ASSESSMENT: *LIE*
EVIDENCE: *SNIPER'S POCKETBOOK*

When Phelps tells Felix that his name was in the shooter's notebook, Felix finally admits the obvious: Mickey Cohen thinks that members of the **6th Marines** have the stolen morphine because they were on the Coolridge. Then Felix says Courtney Sheldon is meeting with Cohen to sort it out. He also tells Phelps that Jack Kelso is in Los Angeles now, too.

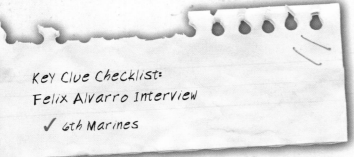

Key Clue Checklist:
Felix Alvarro Interview

✓ 6th Marines

CALL IN FOR KELSO'S ADDRESS.

Go to the nearby gamewell (just behind where the ambulance is parked) and use it to get Jack Kelso's address, which puts it on your map.

LOCATION: JACK KELSO'S APARTMENT

PICK UP JACK KELSO.

Travel to Kelso's apartment ⑥. En route, Phelps praises Kelso as a "tough customer," who would never get involved in something like the morphine theft. Earle wants to haul Kelso downtown to rattle him. But Phelps just says, "It won't work."

Your arrival triggers a scene: Kelso arrives at his building just after the detectives do. He agrees to talk and invites them inside. But Phelps insists that they go to the station. Kelso isn't happy about it, but Earle makes it clear that he has no choice in the matter.

Your trip back to the Hollywood Police Station ① happens automatically. Phelps makes an attempt at small talk that doesn't go very well.

LOCATION: HOLLYWOOD POLICE STATION
INTERVIEW JACK KELSO.

Upon arrival, Phelps leads Kelso into an interview room and Earle follows them in. The interview session begins immediately.

INTERVIEW: JACK KELSO

TOPIC: *ARMY SURPLUS MORPHINE*

Phelps brings up the gang war over the stolen morphine. Kelso says it has nothing to do with him. You have no proof that he's involved, but you know Kelso was on the Coolridge.

CORRECT ASSESSMENT: *DOUBT*

Earle plays the bad cop and vigorously points out this fact. But Kelso's comeback zinger about the city's dope rackets shows that he is, indeed, a tough customer.

TOPIC: *EX-MARINE MCGOLDRICK*

When Phelps asks if Kelso knew about Eddie McGoldrick's financial windfall and nightclub purchase, Kelso seems honest in his answer.

CORRECT ASSESSMENT: *TRUTH*

Kelso also hadn't heard about the 111 Club shooting, and seems genuinely sad to hear the news about Eddie.

TOPIC: *ARMS STOLEN FROM COOLRIDGE*

Kelso also claims to have no knowledge of the missing crate of BARs. His look is direct and steady.

CORRECT ASSESSMENT: *TRUTH*

Phelps follows up with the news about the bus shooting and presses Kelso to give up any information or innocent people will die. But Kelso turns it right back on Phelps with disparaging remarks about his motives and the medal he won "at the expense of men who fought for their country."

TOPIC: *SS COOLRIDGE ROBBERY*

Once again, Phelps asks directly what Kelso knows about the theft of Army surplus morphine from the Coolridge. Kelso deflects the question by reminding Phelps of their war experience.

CORRECT ASSESSMENT: *DOUBT*

The blood seems bad between the two ex-Marines, and then Kelso and Earle have a tense exchange, as well.

Earle tells Kelso he can go, but suddenly another cop pops into the room with a report of another shooting victim, Chris Majewski—another former Marine, another name from the Coolridge manifest.

LOCATION: ROBERT'S DINER

CHASE DOWN THE GREEN PACKARD.

Travel to Robert's Diner ⑦ to trigger a scene: a young man rushes out and points out the shooters, who exit the back of the diner and drive away in a green Packard.

Chase the car. You can't stop them until they reach a specific alleyway ⑧, but don't lose them. When it reaches the alley, the green Packard turns left next to Haskell's Menswear, and the two gunmen hop out and start shooting from the back of the alley.

LOCATION:
ALLEYWAY CRIME SCENE

KILL THE GUNMEN AND SEARCH THEM.

Gun down both shooters to trigger a quick scene: Phelps and Earle approach the first body to search it. This shooter is the only one you can search here; the other fellow has nothing of interest on him.

Check his right breast pocket to find the **shooter's notebook** with a note about a 9 PM meeting that night between Mickey Cohen and Courtney Sheldon. This adds Courtney Sheldon to your P.O.I. list.

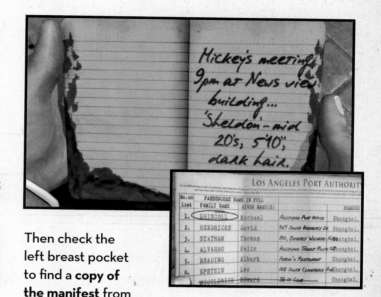

Then check the left breast pocket to find a **copy of the manifest** from the Coolridge with some disturbing notations in red. It looks like a hit list, with the dead men McGoldrick and Majewski crossed out. Two others, Driscoll and Beckett, are circled and associated with the Hollywood Post Office, with the last two circled, Higgins and Connolly, associated with Grauman's Chinese Theater. All of these names and locations are now listed in your notebook. You have two new places to investigate.

NEWSPAPER CINEMATIC

Don't miss the newspaper in the alley with the headline "LAPD Vice Scandal" near the first fallen shooter. It triggers a peek behind the scenes at some of the city's most powerful men, including the mayor, the district attorney, and the police chief. The Vice squad's Chief Detective also makes an appearance.

Key Clue Checklist: Alleyway Crime Scene
- ✓ Shooter's notebook
- ✓ Copy of manifest

LOCATION: HOLLYWOOD POST OFFICE

TAKE OUT THE GUNMEN.

Travel to the Hollywood Post Office ⑨ where you arrive in the middle of a wild gun battle. Wise guys are holed up in the post office, exchanging pleasantries with several police units in the street.

Use the parked squad cars for cover and start picking off the gunmen through the windows. Remember that you can open the trunk of any police car and pick up some better firepower. That can help a lot for this fight.

SEARCH THE VICTIMS' BODIES.

After taking out the shooters, you end up inside the post office near one of their victims. It's Beckett, another of the former Marines. Approach and search him to discover he's still alive. Listen to **Beckett's confession:** "Tell Courtney... bad luck. It was worth a try." Then find and examine the **business card** for Lenny Finkelstein of the Polar Bear Ice Company in his left hand.

You can find the other victim of the mob assassins, Driscoll, in an alcove of postal boxes. Search his left breast pocket to find a **note** that lists the address where the Sheldon/Cohen meeting is taking place that night. It appears that Courtney Sheldon was planning to bring his former squad mates to the meeting as backup—"his own fire team," as Phelps puts it.

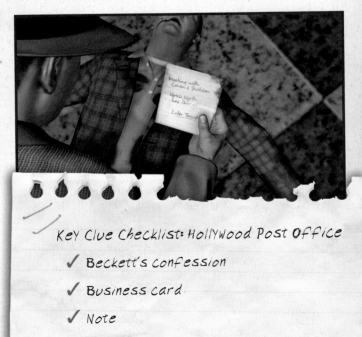

Key Clue Checklist: Hollywood Post Office
- ✓ Beckett's confession
- ✓ Business card
- ✓ Note

LOCATION: GRAUMAN'S CHINESE THEATER

CHASE DOWN THE GUNMEN'S RED CAR.

Travel to Grauman's Chinese Theater ⑩. Your arrival triggers a scene: Higgins and Connolly walk away from the theater entrance. Suddenly, a red car pulls up and disgorges a masked assassin, who Tommy-guns them down. The vehicle speeds off just as Phelps and Earle arrive.

Chase the shooters in the red car. Stay on the vehicle's tail as it zigzags through backstreets and backyards, and even veers across a high school football field. Pull up beside it when you can so that Earle can shoot out the tires, or just ram the car until you knock it out of commission. Then gun down the masked gunmen.

LOCATION: MEETING PLACE

TAKE OUT COHEN'S GOONS.

Travel to the designated Cohen-Sheldon meeting place ⑪ on North Las Palmas. Your arrival triggers a gunfight as Mickey Cohen speeds away in a car and his men open fire on Phelps and Earle. Start taking out the goons. Watch for a shooter up on the roof to the right.

More gunmen are posted down the first alley to the right. A pair of shooters makes a run at you in their car. Nail them as they try to get out. Then fight your way up the alleyway using dumpsters for cover. Keep watching for gunmen high and low. A good tactic is to climb a drainpipe onto the roof where the alley jags to the left; it provides a better vantage point on the thugs up ahead.

When the last gangster falls, a short scene plays: Detective Earle takes a call from KGPL with news that Courtney Sheldon is at Hollywood Station requesting an interview with Detective Phelps.

LOCATION: HOLLYWOOD POLICE STATION
INTERVIEW COURTNEY SHELDON.

Return to Hollywood Station ① to trigger a scene: Captain Donelly calls Earle into his office, letting Phelps handle the interview alone. Earle goes reluctantly. Approach the watch desk to learn your man is in Interview Room 2, the first door to the right of the watch desk.

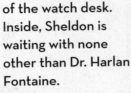

Inside, Sheldon is waiting with none other than Dr. Harlan Fontaine.

INTERVIEW: COURTNEY SHELDON

TOPIC: *6TH MARINES BEING TARGETED*

When Phelps mentions all the dead ex-Marines, Sheldon replies that he can't be blamed for their deaths. Of course, you've got evidence that suggests otherwise.

CORRECT ASSESSMENT: *LIE*
EVIDENCE: *NOTE*

Sheldon insists that he and his crew don't have the morphine, and turns to Dr. Fontaine for validation. Fontaine says he believes Sheldon.

TOPIC: *SS COOLRIDGE ROBBERY*

Phelps points out that Sheldon was on the Coolridge and had the opportunity. Sheldon lamely replies, "But that doesn't mean I was involved."

CORRECT ASSESSMENT: *LIE*
EVIDENCE: *BECKETT'S CONFESSION*

Sheldon expresses sorrow about Beckett and the others, but claims their actions cannot be pinned on him. When Phelps says he's going for Jack Kelso next, Sheldon vigorously defends Kelso, saying he's not involved. But then he makes a startling decision: He asks what kind of deal Phelps is willing to offer.

But just as it appears that Phelps and Sheldon are reaching an agreement, the Chief of Police Worrell and Captain Donelly burst in to interrupt. They send Phelps up to the chief's office. Note that the chief greets Dr. Fontaine warmly.

Watch the dramatic conclusion of Cole Phelps' run at the LAPD Administrative Vice desk as he suffers the consequences, professionally and personally, of his choices.

THE ARSON CASES

THE GAS MAN

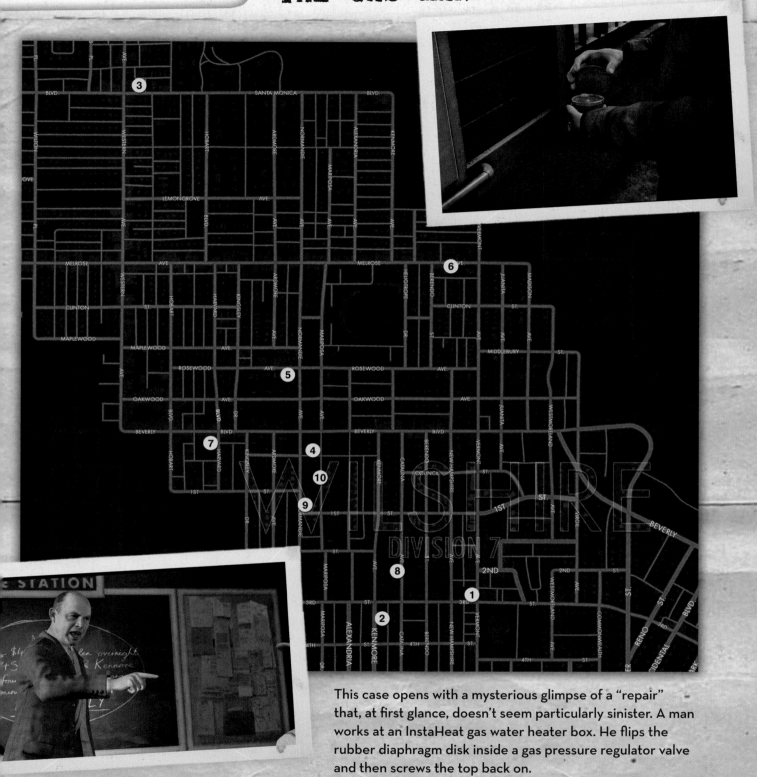

This case opens with a mysterious glimpse of a "repair" that, at first glance, doesn't seem particularly sinister. A man works at an InstaHeat gas water heater box. He flips the rubber diaphragm disk inside a gas pressure regulator valve and then screws the top back on.

The scene switches to the briefing room of the Wilshire Police Station. A disgraced Cole Phelps has been reassigned (i.e., demoted) to the Arson desk in the Wilshire Division until his case comes up before the review board. Captain Lachlan McKelty makes the announcement and then pairs Phelps with a new partner, the veteran Herschel Biggs. Their first assignment: two house fires, possibly suspicious.

Objectives

* Investigate Steffens Fire & Interview Don Steffens.
* Investigate Gulliver's Travel Agency & Interview John Cunningham.
* Investigate Elysian Field Development Site.
* Investigate Sawyer Fire.
* Complete Lynch's Gas Puzzle at Fire Station No. 32.
* Interview Ivan Rasic at InstaHeat.
* Inspect InstaHeat Lockers.
* Go to Clemens Worksite & Interview Clemens.
* Go to Ryan Worksite & Apprehend Ryan.
* Go to Varley Worksite & Apprehend Varley.
* Interview Varley & Ryan at Wilshire Station.
* Charge Suspect.

CASE REPORT

TOTAL NUMBER OF KEY CLUES	16
TOTAL NUMBER OF INTERVIEW QUESTIONS	16

Fail Conditions

* Phelps dies.
* Chapman, Ryan, or Varley escape.
* Injure Varley.
* Fail to charge suspect in final interrogations.

LOCATION: STEFFENS HOUSE FIRE

GO TO THE STEFFENS FIRE.

Travel from the Wilshire Police Station ① to the Steffens house fire ②. Nothing is left but smoldering ruins, and Biggs points out the "real pain" in the reactions of the Steffens couple, which suggests the fire wasn't an insurance scam. In fact, the officer on the scene reports that the Steffens have no insurance; the fire occurred the previous night while the family was on Catalina Island, enjoying a vacation they'd won.

INTERVIEW MR. STEFFENS.

Approach the man in the green shirt standing next to the woman grieving near the ruins. He introduces himself as Don Steffens and gives Phelps the **competition ticket** for the prize trip he won. They were issued from Gulliver's Travel Agency, a new place to investigate. Then the interview sequence begins.

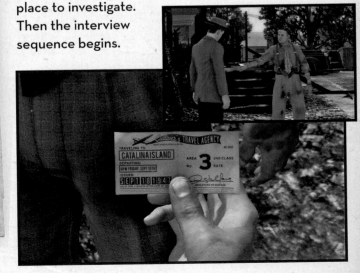

INTERVIEW: DON STEFFENS

TOPIC: *TRAVEL COMPETITION*

Steffens says the prize was a weekend on Catalina Island. The flyer for the competition came from a group called the **Suburban Redevelopment** fund. This adds another topic to your Questions list.

CORRECT ASSESSMENT: *TRUTH*

Steffens says his wife simply filled out the flyer and sent it in. That was the extent of the "competition": a woman later called to tell them they had won.

TOPIC: *SUBURBAN REDEVELOPMENT*

Steffens says the redevelopment group is buying out homes in the neighborhood. Most neighbors just took the cash and moved; Steffens says he never bargained with the buyers. But he folds his arms and sucks in his lower lip, looking a bit uncomfortable. Perhaps there's more to the story.

CORRECT ASSESSMENT: *DOUBT*

When Phelps points out that Steffens is the lone holdout in the neighborhood, the homeowner admits he was waiting for a better price because his house is the center lot. Now he has no choice but to take the price offered.

Key Clue Checklist:
Don Steffens Interview

✓ *Competition ticket*

✓ *Suburban Redevelopment*

SEARCH THE SITE.

Go around to the opposite side of the house and find the InstaHeat water heater unit on the ground. Inspect it to open the case and see the service log. The heater was recently serviced by Matthew Ryan; this adds **heater serviced by Ryan** to your Clue list and adds Matthew Ryan to your P.O.I. list.

USE A GAMEWELL.

Before you leave, jog up the street to the gamewell on the corner (next to the big "Building a Better California" sign) and call in for information and an address for the Suburban Redevelopment fund. You learn that it's a fund with both private investors and a government endowment, designed to speed up the building of homes for GIs. The address is at the corner of Beverly and Mariposa.

Key Clue Checklist: Steffens House Fire

✓ *Heater serviced by Ryan*

LOCATION: GULLIVER'S TRAVEL AGENCY

INTERVIEW JOHN CUNNINGHAM.

Travel to the Gulliver's Travel Agency ③. Phelps and Biggs enter and meet a sales rep named John Cunningham, who finds the Steffens entry in a ledger and shows it to the detectives. In the close-up of the ledger, examine the first page and tap on the

entries for both the Steffens and the Sawyer families. When you exit the ledger screen, the interview sequence begins.

INTERVIEW: JOHN CUNNINGHAM

TOPIC: *SUBURBAN REDEVELOPMENT*

Cunningham says the Suburban Redevelopment group runs the travel promotion and his list covers half of Los Angeles.

CORRECT ASSESSMENT: *TRUTH*

Cunningham chuckles when Phelps asks if the fund is a government agency. The sales rep says the government doesn't get involved with promotional activity like this.

TOPIC: *PROMOTIONAL TRAVEL CONTEST*

When Phelps asks about the prizes, Cunningham gets a little nervous. He suggests that the lucky winners get their names "pulled out of a hat." But he doesn't look very convincing.

CORRECT ASSESSMENT: *DOUBT*

Phelps brings up the "unlucky" Steffens family and presses for information on who awards the prizes. Cunningham admits that he simply gets a call every few weeks from the Suburban Redevelopment fund that tells him exactly who has won.

Afterwards, watch as Cunningham expresses sympathy for the Steffens family and Detective Biggs quickly accepts his generous offer of help.

LOCATION: SUBURBAN REDEVELOPMENT (ELYSIAN FIELDS SITE)

VISIT THE SITE.

Travel to the Suburban Redevelopment address ④ to discover that it's actually the site of an Elysian Fields housing development. Your arrival triggers a short exchange with the site foreman. You can go inside the Elysian

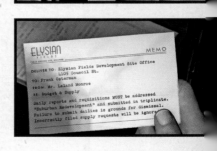

Fields subdivision office and find a memo on a desk from someone named Leland Monroe. Phelps notes that "Elysian Fields builds the houses and Suburban Redevelopment foots the bills."

LOCATION: SAWYER HOUSE FIRE

MEET ALBERT LYNCH.

Travel to the site of the Sawyer house fire ⑤. The coroner's wagon is there—not a good sign. Your arrival triggers a scene: Phelps and Biggs talk with Albert Lynch, chief investigator for the Los Angeles Fire Department, who welcomes Phelps to "the netherworld of arson." He reports a family of four found dead in their beds after a water heater explosion—another InstaHeat Model 70, like the one at the Steffens house.

TALK TO THE CORONER.

Enter the yard to trigger a scene: Coroner Mal Carruthers examines the bodies. He reports that the family died in bed around midnight from the carbon monoxide poisoning unleashed by the fire. They discuss the water heater problem and Phelps alludes to "another angle" that he can't elucidate yet.

FIND THE REGULATOR VALVE.

Turn and walk toward the fire truck to trigger a chime and find the InstaHeat **regulator valve** (circled in our screenshot) on the ground amongst the debris.

Finding the valve triggers a sequence of events: First, Lynch praises the find as significant. Then a patrol officer brings up a neighbor, Joanna Alford, with information. She tells Phelps that the family was supposed to be gone after winning a trip to Catalina Island from Guliver's Travel Agency. But the young son got sick, so they stayed home instead.

APPREHEND THE FIREBUG.

After the conversation with the neighbor, chief investigator Lynch spots a known firebug across the street. Phelps takes off running after the suspect, who sprints up an alley and yanks open a red door to escape through a diner. Follow him through the diner and out into the street beyond. You should be able to catch the firebug after he hops the fence across the street. Press the Tackle button to bring him down. If you can't manage to tackle the firebug, he eventually hides behind a wall and clotheslines Phelps if you run past. Then you'll have to KO him in a fistfight.

Phelps and Lynch automatically bring him back to the Sawyer lot for questioning. His name is Herbert Chapman and he admits he likes fires. Phelps turns out Chapman's pockets and produces a matchbook enclosed over a cigarette; as Lynch explains, it's a favorite arsonist's device for time-delay fire ignition. "If you want more time, you use a mosquito coil," adds Lynch.

Lynch tells Phelps to stop by later at Fire Station No. 32 because he has a theory about the Sawyer fire. Then Phelps and Biggs debate the scope of the investigation as they prepare to move on.

Key Clue Checklist: Sawyer House Fire
✓ Regulator valve

LOCATION: FIRE STATION NO. 32
MEET LYNCH AT THE FIRE STATION.

Travel to Fire Station No. 32 ⑥ and approach Lynch to trigger a scene: Lynch suggests you take a look at the **InstaHeat Model 70** water heater housing from the Sawyer fire. Open it to see that a repairman named Reginald Varley

serviced it recently. This adds Varley to your P.O.I. list and adds **heater serviced by Varley** to your Clue list.

Now listen while Lynch presents the components of his theory. He shows you a gas supply on one end (with a red lever) and a lighted mosquito coil on the other. In between, you must arrange three items: a pilot light (represented as a Bunsen burner), a regulator valve with a blue dial, and a balloon (representing the gas expanding in the room). The gas must make contact with the coil to form an explosion. He invites Phelps to work out the chain of events with the devices arrayed before him.

ALIGN THE DEVICES TO CREATE AN EXPLOSION.

From left to right, place the devices in the following order (and use our screenshot for visual reference): Bunsen burner, regulator valve, balloon.

When you create the correct chain of events, pull the red lever to turn on the gas. Lynch lights the Bunsen burner. Then watch as the balloon expands large enough to touch the mosquito coil and explode.

When the experiment is finished, Lynch hands Phelps the regulator valve found at the Sawyer site. The chief fire investigator says the LAPD detectives should take the valve to the InstaHeat factory to get an opinion. He gives you the address and you're on your way.

LOCATION: INSTAHEAT FACTORY
TALK TO THE RECEPTIONIST.

Travel to the InstaHeat factory ⑦ and enter the reception area, the first door on the right just inside the main entrance. You can inspect the InstaHeat

poster along the left wall to see the new model. Approach the receptionist to trigger a scene: She directs the detectives to the duty manager for the day, Ivan Rasic.

INTERVIEW IVAN RASIC.

Exit the reception area, go straight across the hall, and follow the arrow on the "Manager" sign through the door on the left. This triggers a scene: Phelps hands Rasic the InstaHeat pressure regulator valve and the manager points out a serious tampering problem—the rubber diaphragm inside has been reversed, which would cause gas leakage because the gas never closes off properly. Now the interview session begins.

INTERVIEW: IVAN RASIC
TOPIC: *INSTAHEAT MODEL 70*

Phelps wants Rasic to verify that the reversed valve is not a manufacturing flaw or a service repair. Rasic glances away twice as he says there's nothing inherently wrong with the design, but hedges in his wording by starting with "I don't think...."

CORRECT ASSESSMENT: *DOUBT*

Phelps pushes Rasic to admit that InstaHeat has changed the design. But the company is still installing the old Model 70 units because of the L.A. construction boom and the intense demand for water heaters.

TOPIC: *HEATER SERVICE HISTORY*

Rasic also admits that the rubber diaphragms go bad after a while and need to be replaced. Phelps asks about the qualifications of the company's repairmen—the names he's been seeing on the service logs inside the heaters. Rasic assures him they're all licensed, but he looks uneasy.

CORRECT ASSESSMENT: *LIE*
EVIDENCE: *HEATER SERVICED BY RYAN/VARLEY*

If you choose "Heater serviced by Ryan" from your Evidence list, Phelps asks about Matthew Ryan, the name on the Steffens' heater service log, and Rasic admits that the repairman has been in trouble in the past. If you choose "Heater serviced by Varley" from your Evidence list, Phelps asks about Reginald Varley, the name on the Sawyers' heater service log; Rasic will describe Varley as having a troubled history, as well. In either case, Rasic's response adds **Ivan Rasic's statement** to your Clue list. Phelps asks for a **list of gas fitters** doing the InstaHeat installations, and Rasic hands it right over.

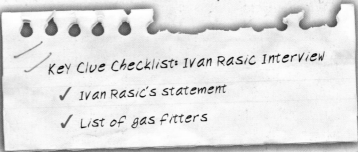

CALL IN THE GAS FITTER LIST TO R&I.

Phelps decides to check on the repairman list for arsonists or others with an arrest record. Use Rasic's phone over by the doorway to call in the list. You get a quick response: Walter Clemens is an arsonist; Matthew Ryan served time on assault charges; and Reginald Varley is wanted for murder in Detroit. Clemens is added to the other two repairmen on your P.O.I. list, and their criminal records become new clues.

TALK TO RASIC AGAIN.

Approach Rasic and press the Talk button to trigger another brief conversation. Phelps gets current worksite locations for all three suspects, then asks to see their lockers. Rasic reluctantly agrees to show you.

INSPECT THE SUSPECTS' LOCKERS.

Follow Rasic to the locker room. Walter Clemens' locker is the third from the far left. Open it to find **Clemens' anarchist pamphlet**.

Walk down a few more lockers to find Matthew Ryan's locker. Open it to find **Ryan's anarchist pamphlets**—boxes of them! Looks like he's the distributor.

Finally, find Reginald Varley's locker and open it to discover a box with **mosquito coils** inside. Examine the box further to remove a coil; this adds the clue to your Clue list. Biggs informs Rasic that mosquito coils are a favorite choice of ignition by arsonists.

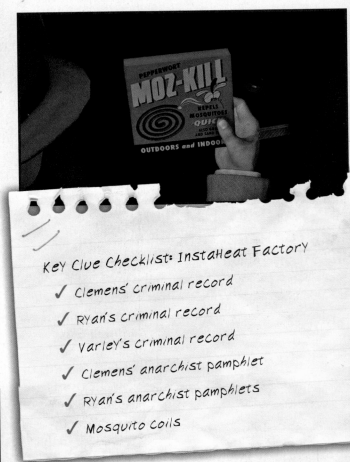

Key Clue Checklist: InstaHeat Factory

✓ Clemens' criminal record

✓ Ryan's criminal record

✓ Varley's criminal record

✓ Clemens' anarchist pamphlet

✓ Ryan's anarchist pamphlets

✓ Mosquito coils

WATCH THE SUSPICIOUS PERSON.

Exiting the InstaHeat factory triggers a short, ominous cutscene. Watch from behind as a man leans into a Chevrolet van and appears to tamper with a familiar looking pressure valve. Then the man gathers up tools in a toolbox and approaches a residential home.

LOCATION: CLEMENS' WORKSITE

INTERVIEW WALTER CLEMENS.

Travel to Clemens' worksite first ⑧. Your arrival triggers a scene: Phelps and Biggs get a little rough with Clemens and demand answers.

INTERVIEW: WALTER CLEMENS

TOPIC: *KNOWLEDGE OF VARLEY*

Phelps asks if Clemens knows Reginald Varley and, amazingly, he says no. This seems quite doubtful since their InstaHeat lockers are just a few feet away from each other. He also gives you a classic smirk.

CORRECT ASSESSMENT: *DOUBT*

A little heat from Phelps prompts Clemens to admit what he knows about Varley, who gets kickbacks from some developer to do their repair and installation work first. This bit of information is added to your Clue list as **Walter Clemens' statement.**

TOPIC: *KNOWLEDGE OF RYAN*

Asked if he knows Matthew Ryan, Clemens again claims no knowledge of the name despite the obvious proximity in the InstaHeat locker room. This time you have proof he's lying.

CORRECT ASSESSMENT: *LIE*
EVIDENCE: *CLEMENS' ANARCHIST PAMPHLET*

Confronted with the pamphlet, Clemens immediately turns on Ryan, saying he's the one pushing pamphlets on everybody. Clemens adds, "He's got it in for the company."

TOPIC: *EMPLOYMENT WITH INSTAHEAT*

When Phelps asks if the repairman is licensed and works for InstaHeat, Clemens looks nervous and says, "I contract for them. So what?" The way he screws up his face suggests extreme discomfort with the line of questioning.

CORRECT ASSESSMENT: *DOUBT*

Clemens admits that he burned down his own house. When he explains the reason he committed the arson, Biggs is sympathetic and apologizes for "the roust."

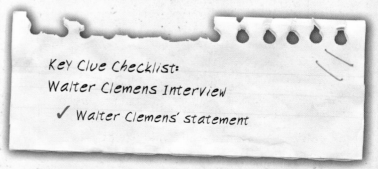

Key Clue Checklist:
Walter Clemens Interview
✓ Walter Clemens' statement

LOCATION: RYAN'S WORKSITE

APPREHEND MATTHEW RYAN.

Travel to Ryan's worksite ⑨ in the Elysian Fields housing development. Your arrival triggers a scene: as Phelps and Biggs approach Ryan, he suddenly hops into his work van and tries to escape, leading you directly through the housing sites. Careful! Construction workers scurry back and forth in your path. You might want to focus on getting through the construction without running down pedestrians, and wait to catch up with Ryan until he gets out on the streets.

Eventually, Ryan steers his van out onto Beverly Boulevard. You should be proficient at car chases by now. As always, try to pull up on the left side of Ryan's van so Biggs can shoot out its tires. Ram it when you can, as well. After finally disabling Ryan's van, hop out and approach the vehicle to arrest him. The paddy wagon hauls Ryan back to Wilshire Police Station for questioning.

LOCATION: VARLEY'S WORKSITE

APPREHEND REGINALD VARLEY.

Travel to Varley's worksite ⑩ on Mariposa. Your arrival triggers a scene similar to the last location: Phelps and Biggs approach, and Varley takes off. This time the suspect flees on foot. Like Ryan, he tries to escape by cutting through the housing development, running through half-built houses and empty lots. At one point, a bulldozer rolling a pipe section cuts off your view of Varley. When you get a clear shot, train your weapon

on him long enough to fill in the gauge and squeeze off a warning shot. Note that if you shoot Varley, you fail the case.

That halts him and Varley comes peacefully. He seems incredulous at the charge of arson Phelps levels at

him. A uniformed officer hauls Varley back to Wilshire Police Station. It's time to question your suspects.

LOCATION: WILSHIRE STATION
INTERVIEW REGINALD VARLEY.

Return to Wilshire Station ①. The watch commander, Hopkins, isn't particularly polite to Phelps, but Biggs sticks up for his new partner. Reginald Varley is in Interview Room 2, and Matthew Ryan is in Interview Room 1. Let's start with Varley in Room 2, who speaks with disdain about Ryan, "that pinko bastard."

INTERVIEW: REGINALD VARLEY

TOPIC: *WORK AT SAWYER RESIDENCE*

Phelps asks about the repairs on the Sawyer heater, and Varley replies he works at a lot of places and claims no memory of it. He adds that he doesn't do repairs, instead focusing on new installations. He fidgets a bit, but more importantly, you have the Sawyer service log.

CORRECT ASSESSMENT: *LIE*
EVIDENCE: *HEATER SERVICED BY VARLEY*

Varley has to admit that he worked at the Sawyer home, and reveals that Suburban Redevelopment wanted the Sawyers out. But he claims the service was free work offered by Suburban to entice the Sawyers to leave.

TOPIC: *SUBURBAN REDEVELOPMENT*

When Phelps accuses Varley of being in the pocket of the property developer, the suspect grins and denies it, saying, "Never. I've got principles." Even Phelps finds this lie amusing.

CORRECT ASSESSMENT: *LIE*
EVIDENCE: *WALTER CLEMENS STATEMENT*

Confronted with the evidence, Varley admits taking money to give Suburban Redevelopment jobs priority status. But he claims it's no big conspiracy—plenty of other construction workers were taking the money, too.

TOPIC: *INSTAHEAT MODEL 70*

Varley knows what happens if you reverse the regulator valve on an InstaHeat Model 70: "A big bang when you turn the pilot back on." But he vigorously denies purposely sabotaging the valve at the Sawyer's house.

CORRECT ASSESSMENT: *LIE*
EVIDENCE: *MOSQUITO COILS*

When Phelps brings up the mosquito coils found in his locker, Varley claims they belong to Ryan, who told him they were used for camping.

Now you can select either Charge Suspect or Leave Interrogation. You should talk to Ryan first, so leave for now.

INTERVIEW MATTHEW RYAN.

Head for Interview Room 1 to face Matthew Ryan, who scoffs at Phelps' opening gambit.

INTERVIEW: MATTHEW RYAN

TOPIC: *ANARCHIST LITERATURE*

Ryan admits that he wants to change the world. But when Phelps suggests he might be trying to sabotage water heaters to destroy the company, Ryan denies it.

CORRECT ASSESSMENT: *LIE*
EVIDENCE: *RYAN'S ANARCHIST PAMPHLETS*

Ryan does admit, however, that he passes out his pamphlets and has disgust for InstaHeat for cranking out poorly designed heaters.

TOPIC: *INSTAHEAT MODEL 70*

Ryan denies knowing how to reverse the diaphragm in the regulator valve of a Model 70 heater. Doesn't seem too plausible for a repairman, and you have the boss's statement about how easy it is to tamper with the pressure regulator.

CORRECT ASSESSMENT: *LIE*
EVIDENCE: *IVAN RASIC'S STATEMENT*

Phelps uses cool logic to make Ryan's lie obvious. When Phelps asks about the cause of the fire in Ryan's own home, the repairman refuses to say.

TOPIC: *SUBURBAN REDEVELOPMENT*

Phelps asks what Ryan can tell him about the Suburban Redevelopment fund. Ryan's one-word answer: "Nothing." But his lips purse and he looks nervous.

CORRECT ASSESSMENT: *DOUBT*

When Phelps suggests that Suburban Redevelopment might be behind Ryan's arson activities, Ryan responds plaintively that he has nothing to do with Suburban. He points the finger at Varley for his "cozy agreement with those fascists." This adds **Matthew Ryan's statement** to your Clue list.

TOPIC: *ATTEMPTED MURDER CHARGE*

Phelps suggests that Ryan has a history of violence, which the suspect strongly denies. But his folded arms and furrowed brow suggest some feelings of guilt.

CORRECT ASSESSMENT: *DOUBT*

Phelps brings up Ryan's attempted murder charge. Ryan points out that the court ruled no criminal liability. But he lost his family in the water heater explosion, and he blames the company that made the faulty heater—a company now wholly owned by InstaHeat.

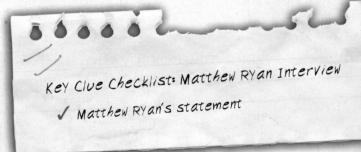

Key Clue Checklist: Matthew Ryan Interview
✓ Matthew Ryan's statement

CHARGE EITHER RYAN OR VARLEY WITH ARSON AND MURDER.

Take your pick. Either choice completes the case successfully, although Captain McKelty is more pleased with the results if you accuse the avowed anarchist, Ryan, and this is the only choice that earns you a five-star rating.

A WALK IN ELYSIAN FIELDS

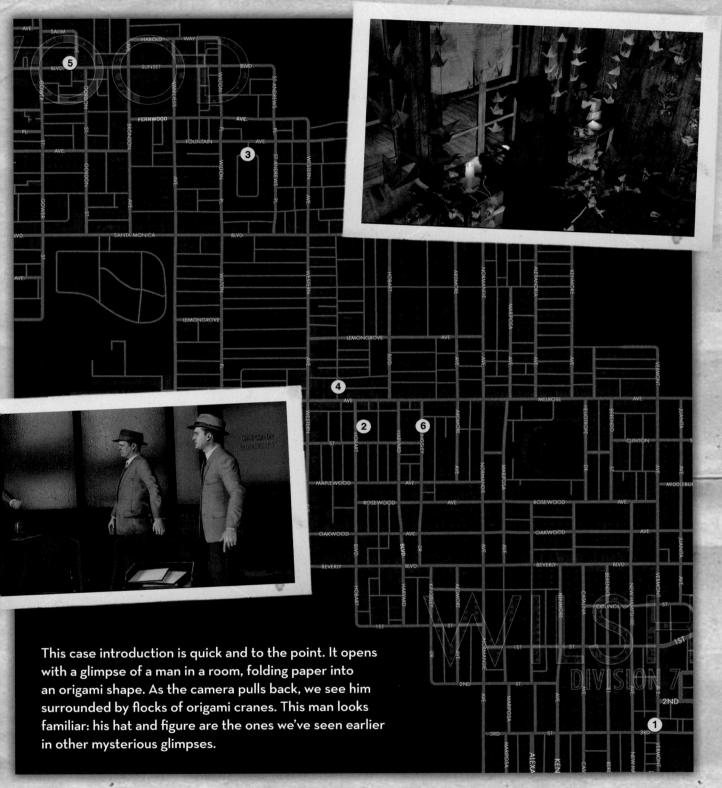

This case introduction is quick and to the point. It opens with a glimpse of a man in a room, folding paper into an origami shape. As the camera pulls back, we see him surrounded by flocks of origami cranes. This man looks familiar: his hat and figure are the ones we've seen earlier in other mysterious glimpses.

The scene switches to Captain McKelty's office at the Wilshire Police Station. Detectives Phelps and Biggs enter to grim news: another deadly house fire, with four more victims like the Sawyer family in the previous case.

Objectives

* Investigate the Morelli Fire.
* Interview Dudley Forman (Neighbor).
* Investigate Rancho Escondido.
* Interview Leland Monroe at Elysian Fields.
* Investigate Chapman's Apartment.
* Apprehend Herbert Chapman.

CASE REPORT

TOTAL NUMBER OF KEY CLUES	13
TOTAL NUMBER OF INTERVIEW QUESTIONS	8

Fail Conditions

* Phelps dies.
* Chapman escapes.

LOCATION: MORELLI HOUSE FIRE

TALK TO LYNCH.

Travel from Wilshire Station ① to the site of the house fire ② on North Hobart. Approach Coroner

Carruthers at the front door of the burned house and follow him inside to a disturbing sight: the charred remains of the Morelli family, burned black yet somehow kneeling on the living room floor.

Chief Investigator Albert Lynch believes they were moved to the spot after the explosion, but before the fire, adding **bodies moved** to your Clue list. He believes the cause of death was asphyxiation from gas inhalation—the Morellis died without feeling a thing. According to Lynch, the fire damage to the bodies was post-mortem.

INSPECT THE SITE.

Examine the bodies at evidence marker A for a close-up of the family. Then find the **family photograph** at evidence marker B. After examining both evidence markers, another scene is triggered: Phelps sees links between cases again. Biggs is skeptical, but both the coroner and the chief investigator find his theory plausible. Phelps thinks the arsonist feels guilt because he meant to burn houses, not families.

After Mr. Morelli's collapse, Biggs gets spooked and rushes out of the house. Carruthers suggests checking on Biggs, but there are a few more items of interest (no key clues) in the house if you're interested. Down in the cellar, for example, you can examine the hole blown out by the heater explosion.

Step outside the house to trigger a scene between the partners: Phelps learns that the ghosts of war and fire haunt Biggs, too. His service was at brutal Belleau Wood in World War I, 20 days of hell known as the deadliest battle in U.S. Marine Corps history. Then Phelps points out that the Morellis were also on the list of contest winners at Gulliver's Travel Agency. They decide to canvass the neighborhood.

FIND THE WATER HEATER.

Before checking with the neighbors, walk around the house to the debris near the hole blown in the foundation. Find and examine the **water heater** by evidence marker C to look at the service log. It's the same model you've seen at the other house fires: an InstaHeat Model 70.

SEARCH THE NEIGHBOR'S YARD.

Now step over the low wall on the left side of the Morelli yard. Walk to the front corner of the neighbor's yard near the tree to find Boondocker **boot prints** and a pile of Calderon **cigarette butts**. Phelps notes that someone was here keeping watch for quite a while.

INTERVIEW THE NEIGHBOR.

Approach the man standing near his front porch and press Talk to trigger a scene: Phelps asks about the fire. The neighbor mentions that the Morelli family

had just won a **weekend away**. He gives his name as Dudley Forman, and an interview sequence begins.

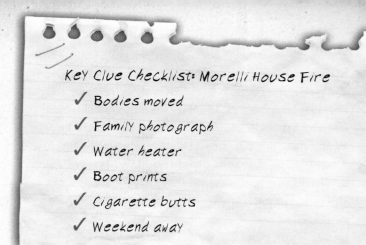

Key Clue Checklist: Morelli House Fire

- ✓ *Bodies moved*
- ✓ *Family photograph*
- ✓ *Water heater*
- ✓ *Boot prints*
- ✓ *Cigarette butts*
- ✓ *Weekend away*

INTERVIEW: DUDLEY FORMAN

TOPIC: *MORELLI FIRE WITNESS REPORT*

Phelps starts to ask a simple question, but Forman cuts him off, stating he was asleep when the explosion occurred. It's an odd reaction, and calls for a follow-up response.

CORRECT ASSESSMENT: DOUBT

Phelps suggests that Forman didn't like Morelli. Forman mentions that all the **houses** (are) **to be demolished** for a new subdivision, and admits that Morelli was being "difficult" about selling his property to the developer. This adds a pair of new topics to your Questions list.

TOPIC: SUSPICIOUS ACTIVITY

Phelps asks if anyone was hanging around before the explosion and Forman promptly answers, "Nope." But again, his reaction is strange: he glances off to the side as he answers, and then avoids eye contact.

CORRECT ASSESSMENT: DOUBT

When Phelps presses a bit and mentions signs of someone lurking by the fence, Forman suddenly remembers a guy hanging around and describes him in detail. He thought the fellow was the pest exterminator. This adds "Smoking Man" to your P.O.I. list.

TOPIC: PLANNED DEMOLITIONS

Phelps asks about the home demolitions. Forman says the housing developer is Elysian Fields, and is surprised that the detective hasn't seen the billboards of Leland Monroe, the owner, "beaming down" at him. But when Phelps asks if Morelli had taken an offer, Forman looks uncomfortable and says he doesn't know.

CORRECT ASSESSMENT: DOUBT

Phelps tries guilt and it works. Forman admits that Morelli built his own house and refused to sell to Elysian Fields, adding "Stubborn fool was ruining it for all of us."

TOPIC: PROMOTIONAL TRAVEL CONTEST

Forman says the Morelli family was supposed to be away for the weekend at Catalina Island as winners of a travel contest. But when Phelps asks who was running the competition, Forman says, "What? I don't know." The way he answers seems odd, but in this case it's just because Forman is an odd duck. He's actually telling the truth. Note the way he looks directly at Phelps.

CORRECT ASSESSMENT: TRUTH

Forman says the competition was an incentive for homeowners still thinking about selling.

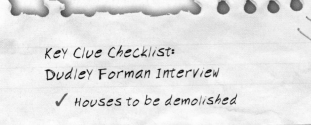

Key Clue Checklist:
Dudley Forman Interview

- ✓ *Houses to be demolished*

EXAMINE THE CLUE FROM BIGGS.

After your interview with Dudley Forman, he offers to give you one of the competition flyers; he has it in his kitchen. But Biggs finds one on the ground by the mailbox. It's been folded up into an **origami crane**. Examine it closer to unfold it and

see that it's one of the **Elysian Fields flyers**. This gives you a new objective and a new P.O.I., Leland Monroe. Forman returns with his flyer, which includes the "Win a Trip" attachment.

USE A GAMEWELL.

You need an address for the Elysian Fields development company, so use the gamewell just behind the coroner's wagon to call in for it. The KGPL operator also connects Phelps to Captain McKelty, who sternly warns against any inquiry into Leland Monroe. After Phelps hangs up, Biggs suggests checking out the big Rancho Escondido blaze. He knows the area, so it pops onto your Locations page.

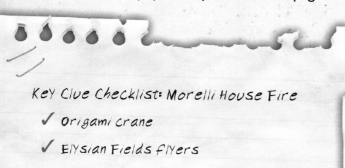

Key Clue Checklist: Morelli House Fire

✓ *Origami crane*

✓ *Elysian Fields flyers*

LOCATION: RANCHO ESCONDIDO

DISPERSE THE RIOT.

Travel to Rancho Escondido ③. You arrive in the middle of a tense situation: GI homeowners who lost houses in the huge blaze angrily confront police officers at the scene. Soon a riot breaks out. Step in and KO two rioters to bring the situation under control.

INSPECT THE NEARBY WALL.

After the fight, walk toward the brick chimney of the nearest burned house to get a chime; Phelps plucks a brick out of the wall. Examine it more closely to discover the **poor cement quality** between bricks. Biggs notices no wall ties either... and then the wall suddenly collapses! Not very well constructed. This discovery adds a topic to your Questions page when you interview Leland Monroe later. You've seen all you need to see here.

Key Clue Checklist: Rancho Escondido

✓ *Poor cement quality*

LOCATION: ELYSIAN FIELDS

INTERVIEW LELAND MONROE.

Travel to Elysian Fields ④ and enter via the front doors. Approach the lobby receptionist to trigger a scene: She sends you up to Monroe's secretary, who tries to put off the detectives. But when Phelps threatens to get a

warrant, Monroe himself steps out of his office and calls them inside.

You can examine the housing models and

posters in the office if you want. Then approach Monroe to trigger an interview sequence.

INTERVIEW: LELAND MONROE

TOPIC: *ELYSIAN LINKED TO ARSONS*

Phelps points out the fact that Elysian Fields flyers keep showing up at houses that subsequently burn down. Monroe says he advertises everywhere, so there's no explanation needed. Then he gives Phelps a wary look.

CORRECT ASSESSMENT: *DOUBT*

Phelps notes that each of the burned houses he's investigated has belonged to a family that wouldn't sell to Elysian Fields.

TOPIC: *PROMOTIONAL TRAVEL CONTEST*

Phelps asks about the Catalina Island promotion, but Monroe claims he's not familiar with it. His company runs many such promotions. Monroe's features are hard to read; his eyes seem to be permanently squinting, so they're difficult to see. Of course, you have flyers for the contest that feature his smiling face.

CORRECT ASSESSMENT: *LIE*
EVIDENCE: *ELYSIAN FIELDS FLYERS*

Again, Phelps points out that the prizes are given to holdouts—people who won't sell to Elysian. Monroe explains that his face is "the brand" on all advertising. He also pointedly mentions that the mayor and chief of police are members of the Suburban Redevelopment fund, as well.

TOPIC: *LOCAL LAND ACQUISITIONS*

Phelps asks what happens to development plans when a family like the Morellis holds out. Monroe says they work around the holdouts. "Business finds a way," he says.

CORRECT ASSESSMENT: *DOUBT*

When Phelps presses the point, Monroe claims he'd build around any holdout, but that "progress is an inexorable process" and eventually most people see sense.

TOPIC: *RANCHO ESCONDIDO FIRE*

This topic appears only if you found the "poor cement quality" clue at Rancho Escondido earlier. When Phelps asks if the new development that burned met building code regulations, Monroe replies, "Absolutely! Only the best for our returning heroes!"

CORRECT ASSESSMENT: *LIE*
EVIDENCE: *POOR CEMENT QUALITY*

Phelps and Biggs point out the shoddy workmanship at Rancho Escondido. Monroe responds that the buildings were fully inspected and insured by California Fire & Life. Then he offers to give you a list of the contractors he uses for waybills.

Monroe directs the detectives to his secretary. As Biggs exits, Monroe halts him... and delivers a little message about Monroe's position on the board of the police pension fund.

PICK UP THE CONTRACTOR LIST.

Approach the secretary and pick up the **list of contractors**. Notice anybody familiar? Tap on the name "Herbert Chapman," the firebug you chased down in your previous case, "The Gas Man." This adds him to your P.O.I. list and gives you the objective to find him.

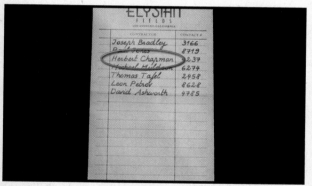

FIND A TELEPHONE.

Go downstairs to the lobby receptionist and turn right, going through the big green doors on the wall opposite her. Use one of the phones on an office worker's desk to call dispatch. Phelps learns that Chapman has been released, so

he puts out an APB (all points bulletin) on the firebug. The dispatcher says KGPL will get back to you on Chapman's last known address.

The end of the phone call triggers a fade to black, followed by a scene at The Blue Room later that evening.

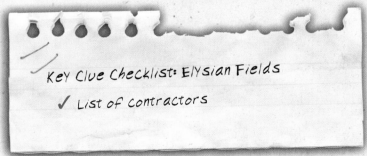

Key Clue Checklist: Elysian Fields
✓ List of contractors

LOCATION: THE BLUE ROOM

At the jazz club, Roy Earle stops by Phelps' table to deliver a warning to stay away from Elysian Fields. He says Homicide is taking over the Morelli case. Then the scene switches again, this time to outside Elsa's apartment the next morning.

LOCATION: ELSA'S APARTMENT

Detective Biggs waits for Phelps at their car outside Elsa's apartment building. When Phelps joins his partner, he learns that Biggs got the same hands-off message from Captain McKelty. When the scene ends, you get a KGPL radio call with Herbert Chapman's last known address. This puts the location on your map.

LOCATION: CHAPMAN'S APARTMENT

SEARCH CHAPMAN'S VAN.

Travel from Elsa's apartment ⑤ to Chapman's ⑥. Your arrival triggers a short scene: Phelps meets the landlord working on the lawn; he says Chapman isn't home. Chapman's van is parked on the lawn, however. Open the van's rear door and look inside.

Pick up and examine the box of **mosquito coils**; examine it further to open it and remove a coil. Inspect the box of **.45 caliber ammunition**; Phelps points out that Chapman is clearly armed. Finally, pick up and unfold the Elysian Fields flyer.

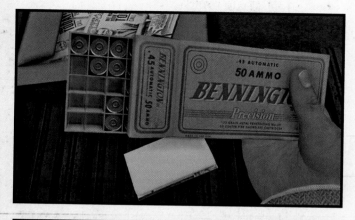

After setting down the third item, Biggs suddenly spots Chapman coming out of the Superior Laundry down the street. The suspect also spots the detectives, then pulls out his handgun and jumps aboard an electric trolley car. The chase is on!

Key Clue Checklist: Chapman's Apartment

✓ Mosquito coils

✓ .45 caliber ammunition

LOCATION: CITY STREETS

APPREHEND HERBERT CHAPMAN.

Follow that trolley! Chapman takes control of the car and starts plowing recklessly through traffic as he flees east on Melrose Avenue. Pull up alongside and slam into its middle section to knock off the side panel (at the word "Electric"), thus exposing the wheels.

Continue pulling up next to the exposed wheels until Biggs can

shoot them out. When the trolley finally halts, exit your vehicle. When you do, Chapman jumps out of the trolley and starts shooting. Take him out quickly!

LEARN ABOUT ELSA'S INSURANCE SETTLEMENT.

After Captain McKelty commends his detectives, watch the scene that sets up the next case. Elsa Lichtmann receives a generous insurance settlement for the death of her friend, Lou. But Phelps suggests that she should have an insurance investigator look into the matter: his old wartime rival, Jack Kelso.

HOUSE OF STICKS

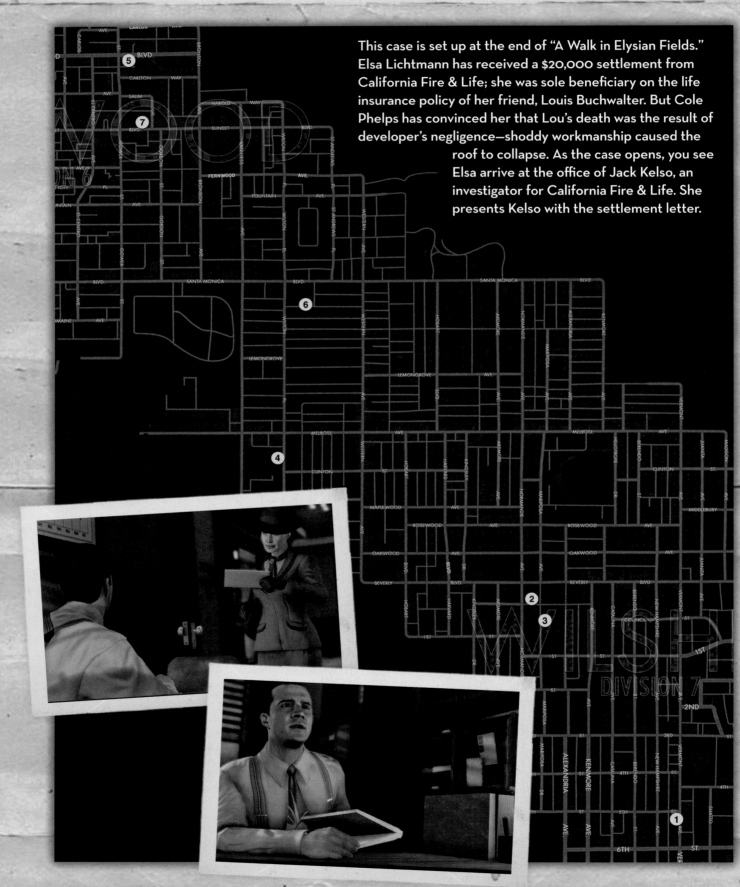

This case is set up at the end of "A Walk in Elysian Fields." Elsa Lichtmann has received a $20,000 settlement from California Fire & Life; she was sole beneficiary on the life insurance policy of her friend, Louis Buchwalter. But Cole Phelps has convinced her that Lou's death was the result of developer's negligence—shoddy workmanship caused the roof to collapse. As the case opens, you see Elsa arrive at the office of Jack Kelso, an investigator for California Fire & Life. She presents Kelso with the settlement letter.

Objectives

* Review Buchwalter Case Documents.
* Interview Elsa Lichtmann.
* Visit Curtis Benson's Office.
* Investigate Elysian Fields Office & Subdue Foreman.
* Investigate Demolished House & Escape Bulldozer.
* Investigate Keystone Film Studios.
* Investigate Elysian Fields Site 2.
* Escape Pursuers & Get to Elsa's Apartment.

CASE REPORT

TOTAL NUMBER OF KEY CLUES	11
TOTAL NUMBER OF INTERVIEW QUESTIONS	3

Fail Conditions

* Kelso dies.

LOCATION: CALIFORNIA FIRE & LIFE

REVIEW THE DOCUMENTS.

You now play as Jack Kelso, starting out in his office at California Fire & Life ①. Examine the **settlement letter** and check that Elsa gives you; Kelso calls it a "ridiculously generous settlement." But when Elsa says she believes her friend was a victim of foul play, she gets Kelso's attention and he pulls out the **Buchwalter case file**.

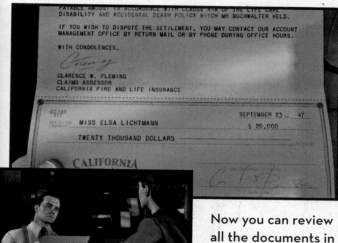

Now you can review all the documents in the file: blueprint, property details slip, and the accident report by the claims investigator. Read the report: a sagging ridge beam, a snapped ceiling rafter, and collapsing roof truss. Either Buchwalter was very unlucky or the building materials were substandard. But the insurance investigator absolves Elysian Fields of any fault.

RE: INSURANCE POLICY NUMBER 11901659

WHILE IN THE EMPLOY OF ELYSIAN FIELDS DEVELOPMENT, LOUIS JAN BUCHWALTER WAS KILLED WHEN THE ROOF OF THE PROPERTY ON WHICH HE WAS WORKING COLLAPSED.

ON TUESDAY 28TH JANUARY AT APPROXIMATELY 8.30 IN THE MORNING, MR BUCHWALTER WAS ASCENDING THE ROOF STRUCTURE OF A PROPERTY AT THE NORMANDIE AVENUE DEVELOPMENT WHEN A FAULT IN THE RIDGE BEAM CAUSED IT TO SAG. WITNESSES REPORT THAT MR BUCHWALTER SLIPPED AND ATTEMPTED TO RIGHT HIMSELF BY HOLDING ONTO A CEILING RAFTER, BUT THE RAFTER BROKE. MR BUCHWALTER FELL APPROXIMATELY 23 FEET TO THE GROUND. HIS FALLING WEIGHT CAUSED SEVERAL CEILING JOISTS TO SNAP, AND THESE FELL INWARD ALONG WITH PART OF A PREFABRICATED ROOF TRUSS.

AN AUTOPSY LATER REVEALED THAT MR BUCHWALTER'S CRANIUM WAS SHATTERED, PROBABLY WHEN HE STRUCK HIS HEAD ON ONE OF THE ROOF BEAMS. HE SUSTAINED SIGNIFICANT INTERNAL INJURIES AS A RESULT OF THE FALLING TIMBER, AND DIED OF INTERNAL HEMORRHAGE APPROXIMATELY TEN MINUTES AFTER THE INITIAL ROOF COLLAPSE.

INTERVIEW ELSA LICHTMANN.

After exiting the case file screen, talk to Elsa to trigger an interview sequence

INTERVIEW: ELSA LICHTMANN

TOPIC: *DISPUTED CLAIM PAYOUT*

Kelso asks about the basis for Elsa's claim. She replies that Lou Buchwalter was a craftsman and wouldn't build a faulty roof. Elsa is tough to read, but this reason seems a bit flimsy.

CORRECT ASSESSMENT: *DOUBT*

Kelso presses her to take the money, saying her intuition isn't enough to reopen an investigation. But Elsa insists that something was wrong with that house.

TOPIC: *CONNECTION TO BUCHWALTER*

When Kelso asks why Buchwalter named her as his beneficiary if they weren't married, Elsa hesitates... then replies that they were "family friends."

CORRECT ASSESSMENT: *DOUBT*

Kelso isn't buying her story, so Elsa levels with him: she was interned with Buchwalter on Ellis Island for four long years. Nazis had killed their parents, and yet they were confined to the island as "resident alien Germans" during the war.

TOPIC: *MOTIVE FOR DISPUTE*

Kelso rather roughly states that "accidents happen" and wonders what Elsa really wants. But she looks him directly in the eye and repeats that she wants the collapsed building thoroughly investigated.

CORRECT ASSESSMENT: *TRUTH*

Kelso finds her case intriguing, but adds that he needs more information. Then Elsa drops her bombshell: she believes there's a conspiracy afoot that includes Elysian Fields and Kelso's insurance company.

When the interview ends, Kelso asks Elsa for her address and phone number. She jots the number on a **slip of paper** and hands it over. Then a secretary appears with the message that Mr. Benson wants to see Kelso upstairs in his office.

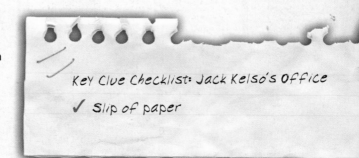

VISIT CURTIS BENSON'S OFFICE.

Follow the secretary upstairs to Benson's office. Your arrival triggers a scene: Benson works on his putting as Kelso tells him about Miss Lichtmann's refusal to take the payout. Benson orders him to forget about any investigation and get Elsa to take the payout.

LOCATION: ELYSIAN FIELDS SUBDIVISION OFFICE

SEARCH THE SUBDIVISION OFFICE.

Travel from California Fire & Life ① to the Elysian Fields site ②. Enter the subdivision office and find the **cement delivery receipt** on the leftmost desk. Kelso notes that it's an inferior way to mix cement; the ratio of cement to sand to aggregate is 1:4:8, not good for construction grade cement. Somebody's cutting corners.

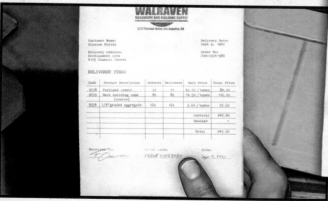

Now go to the rightmost desk to find a **demolition order**. It orders the destruction of all building work "associated with the incident of 01/28/1947"—the date that Lou Buchwalter was killed. The order also calls for all building material to be removed from the site. Could this be a sign of a cover-up? Then examine the **company memo** next to the order: Leland Monroe is putting heavy pressure on his construction crews to work fast.

SUBDUE FRANK OSTERMAN.

Exit the office to trigger a scene: the site foreman, Frank Osterman, aggressively confronts Kelso and starts a fistfight. Kelso is a tough fighter, however, so you can silence the loudmouth with just a

few punches. Afterwards, a defeated Osterman points out the demolished site where Lou Buchwalter died.

Key Clue Checklist:
Elysian Fields Subdivision Office

- ✓ *Cement delivery receipt*
- ✓ *Demolition order*
- ✓ *Company memo*

LOCATION: DEMOLISHED ELYSIAN FIELDS HOUSE

Kelso turns and starts sprinting down a steep-sided, pipe-filled trench. You can run full speed down the trench, hopping and climbing over pipes and platforms, until you reach the ladder at the far end. But you'll have to be proactive to make it; turn and shoot at Osterman to slow him down. Every time you try to shoot the foreman, he raises the bulldozer's blade to block your firing angle, so target and shoot fast.

SEARCH THE RUBBLE.

Travel the short distance to the demolished house ③ in the Normandie Avenue subdivision. Find the items marked by the red flags. At two flags you find pieces of wood with the words "Not For Construction Use" stenciled on them. At another flag, find the brick with almost no mortar on it. Go around to the back of the debris pile to find some **broken wood** that you must piece together like a puzzle to form the words: "Keystone Films." Kelso asks, "Who gets their lumber from a film studio?"

USE A GAMEWELL.

Now you need an address for Keystone Film Studios. Hop in your car and follow the blue phone icon on the map to find the gamewell just down the street at the corner. Use it to call in and get the address.

ESCAPE THE BULLDOZER!

Setting down the broken wood triggers an intense scene: Frank Osterman, angry at the ass-kicking he got, hops aboard a bulldozer and tries to run Kelso down.

Key Clue Checklist:
Demolished Elysian Fields House
✓ Broken wood

LOCATION: KEYSTONE FILM STUDIOS

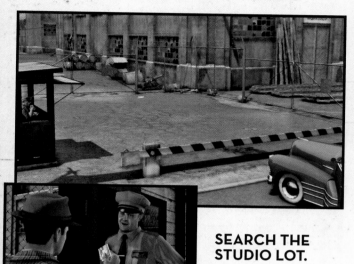

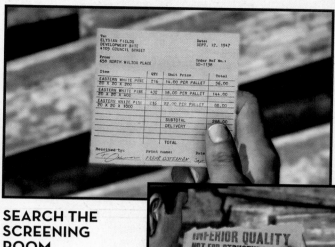

SEARCH THE STUDIO LOT.

Travel to the Keystone Film Studios ④. Your arrival triggers a scene: Kelso gives the gate guard a little incentive to let him snoop around for a while.

Start by hopping the gate to the right, near the building sign that reads "Construction Workshop." Then begin searching through the piles of lumber.

On the very first lumber pile to the left, after scaling the fence, you find the **lumber delivery receipt** for hundreds of pallets of Eastern White Pine. Then search the nearby lumber against the fence to find a sign that indicates **inferior quality lumber**, not for structural use. As Kelso points out, wood like this won't support a roof.

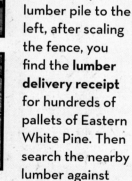

SEARCH THE SCREENING ROOM.

Now continue around the corner of the Construction Workshop and move along the fence to the next building, Stage 3. Turn left and proceed straight ahead to the doorway under the sign that reads "Screening Room."

Enter the screening room and examine the **film canister** on the table to the right, just inside the doorway. The title on the canister is "Suburban Redevelopment Fund." The canister is empty, but you'll find the missing film reel already loaded onto the projector. Examine the projector to open it.

The projector automatically starts up. In the close-up, turn the top dial to focus the picture; turn the middle dial to adjust the film speed. Once you get those set properly, flip the bottom switch to reverse the film direction, rewinding to the beginning.

Then watch the Suburban Redevelopment group meet at The Brown Derby to discuss their plans, and note all the powerful and familiar faces on the board... including Kelso's boss, Curtis Benson. You learn that the group is racing to put up houses fast enough to satisfy the federal government, which is threatening to meet demand with public housing—which Leland Monroe calls "tantamount to Communism." Now you see the reason for Monroe's big construction push, and perhaps the reason why holdouts are being bullied to sell. When the **film** ends, exit the building.

USE THE GUARD BOOTH TELEPHONE.

Head back to the guard's booth at the lot entrance and use the phone. Kelso calls his boss, Curtis Benson, and gets another stern warning. Then he calls Elsa Lichtmann, who arranges a meeting outside the stage door at The Blue Room to discuss the latest findings.

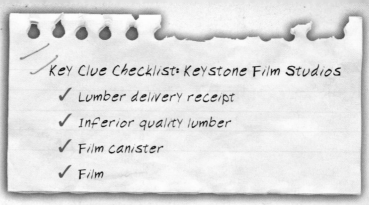

Key Clue Checklist: Keystone Film Studios
- ✓ Lumber delivery receipt
- ✓ Inferior quality lumber
- ✓ Film canister
- ✓ Film

LOCATION: THE BLUE ROOM

Watch the long scene as Cole Phelps catches a glimpse of the back alley meeting between Elsa and Jack Kelso.

LOCATION: ELYSIAN FIELDS SITE TWO

INVESTIGATE THE HOUSE.

Travel from the Blue Room club ⑤ to the second Elysian Fields building site ⑥ at the corner of Wilton and Santa Monica. Your arrival triggers a scene: Kelso spots an odd flickering light in the house across the street from the site office gate.

Enter the house and examine the light switch in the downstairs hallway. Kelso discovers that there's no wiring behind it! Then check out the kitchen sink and try to turn on one of the faucets. No plumbing!

Now go upstairs. When you enter the master bedroom (the big one just left of the upstairs bathroom), you trigger a scene: Three armed goons enter the room behind Kelso, who manages to talk them into holstering their weapons for a fistfight. Give it your best shot, but don't worry when Kelso goes down: there's no other alternative.

Kelso's knockout triggers another scene: the goons lean over Kelso and decide to toss him in the trunk of their car. After a fade to black, Kelso awakens in the trunk as the thugs enter the Elysian Fields site office.

Listen to the phone conversation in the office to see who's behind this attack. When the henchmen drive off to finish the job, watch as Kelso manages to escape the trunk.

COMMANDEER A VEHICLE AND ESCAPE THE PURSUERS.

When control returns, sprint to the Buick Coupe parked at the curb, across the street from the Elysian Fields headquarters building. Its owner has gotten out to visit the Fresh Fruit stand. Hop in and drive away.

Now you must lose the thugs. Several carloads of the angry fellows chase you. Note that Elsa's apartment appears as a yellow flag on your map when the chase begins, but you must lose the pursuers before heading there.

Take a zigzag route, using alleyways and back streets wherever possible. Keep an eye on your mini-map to keep track of your pursuers (marked as the red car icons) and to see them trying to cut you off up ahead. When all red blips disappear from the mini-map, Kelso says, "Where are they?" and you're in the clear.

LOCATION: ELSA'S APARTMENT
GET TO ELSA'S APARTMENT.

Travel to Elsa's apartment ⑦. Your arrival triggers the case-ending movie: Kelso staggers up to Elsa's apartment for a Marine reunion before passing out.

A POLITE INVITATION

Kelso awakens in a Medical Clinic with Elsa keeping watch at his bedside. She apologizes and tells him Cole Phelps needs his help. Kelso tells her she was right about Elysian Fields.

As Elsa exits, Assistant District Attorney Peterson drops in. He says he's running for DA and wants to start rooting out corruption rampant in the current administration. He offers Kelso a position as the DA's Special Investigator and says, "I'm going after the Vice Squad, Kelso." Then Kelso offers him something even better: Leland Monroe.

Key Clue Checklist: Medical Clinic
- ✓ Inferior Lumber
- ✓ Redevelopment Fund

Objectives

* Search Curtis Benson's Apartment & Interview Benson.
* Review Buchwalter Case File at Kelso's Office.
* Find Land Registry Office in Hall of Records.
* Find Lot Number and Land Value.
* Fight Your Way Out of Hall of Records.
* Take Monroe's Phone Call.
* Fight Into Monroe's Mansion.
* Fight to Monroe's Office.
* Search Monroe's Office.

CASE REPORT

TOTAL NUMBER OF KEY CLUES	7
TOTAL NUMBER OF INTERVIEW QUESTIONS	3

Fail Conditions

* Kelso dies.

LOCATION: MEDICAL CLINIC

EXIT THE CLINIC.

You begin at the Medical Clinic ① with a pair of clues on your Clue page, information carried over from the last case. Exit your room, go downstairs, and follow the blue car icon to Kelso's vehicle, a blue Chevrolet Fleetmaster.

LOCATION: CURTIS BENSON'S APARTMENT

SEARCH BENSON'S APARTMENT.

Travel to Curtis Benson's apartment ②. Approach the row of mailboxes under the street number 740 to find that Benson lives in Apartment 2. Climb the stairs, turn left, and follow the walkway sign to Apartment 2. Approach the door to knock; Benson answers.

This triggers a scene: Kelso demands to know everything about Benson's relationship with Leland Monroe. When Benson won't cooperate, Kelso helps his boss sit down and then announces that he's taking a look around.

Go past Benson to the table in the back-left corner of the room to find a California Fire & Life **insurance agreement** that insures the Rancho Escondido housing development for Elysian Fields. Then find the folder on the nearby dining table.

Open it to discover **share certificates** that show Curtis Benson owns stock in the Suburban Redevelopment fund.

INTERROGATE CURTIS BENSON.

After the girl leaves, approach Benson and press the Talk button to start the interview.

Key Clue Checklist:
Curtis Benson's Apartment
✓ Insurance agreement
✓ Share certificates

When you've found those items, approach the bedroom door on the left side of the big semicircular sofa. Kelso kicks open the door and triggers a scene: Benson's debauchery seems par for the Hollywood course. Kelso is furious, and more than ready to take Benson down. He enjoys flashing his new DA's badge.

INTERVIEW: CURTIS BENSON

TOPIC: *MOTIVE FOR FRAUD*

Kelso asks why a vice president of the company would take such a risk on a scam like Monroe's phony subdevelopment. Benson replies that it's "a simple business transaction."

CORRECT ASSESSMENT: *LIE*
EVIDENCE: *SHARE CERTIFICATES*

But when Kelso points out that the stock certificates are in Benson's name, not California Fire & Life, Benson unleashes pent-up anger at the company.

TOPIC: *SUBURBAN REDEVELOPMENT*

Kelso asks about the fund's real purpose. Gazing anywhere but at Kelso's eyes, Benson claims it's just business people meeting demand for new homes.

CORRECT ASSESSMENT: *LIE*
EVIDENCE: *INSURANCE AGREEMENT*

Kelso points out that California Fire & Life is carrying the paper on Rancho Escondido. Benson scoffs, saying that the best result from insurance would be replacement costs. He says, "The stakes are much, much higher."

TOPIC: *BUCHWALTER CASE SETTLEMENT*

Kelso brings up the cheap materials and shoddy workmanship that led to Lou Buchwalter's death. Benson suggests he knows nothing about Monroe's building materials.

CORRECT ASSESSMENT: *DOUBT*

When Kelso threatens to get rough, Benson just laughs and says everything the investigator needs to know is right there in the case file.

LOCATION: CALIFORNIA FIRE & LIFE

REVIEW THE BUCHWALTER CASE FILE.

Travel to the California Fire & Life ③ corporate offices and enter the building. Walk past the Enquiries desk

to the elevators on the back wall and automatically ride up one floor. Kelso's office is the first one on the right after you step off the elevator.

The **Buchwalter case file** is on Kelso's desk. Open it and examine the blueprints.

Tap on the map coordinates; Kelso notes them aloud. Then look at the pink slip listing property details. Tap on the Independent Valuation line. Kelso notes that while the current listed value of the house and land is $3500, the insured replacement value is only $900. The **improved land value** is significant.

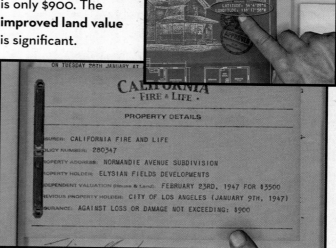

When you're done with the case file, a scene is triggered: Kelso's secretary ushers in a visitor, Detective Phelps of the LAPD. The two ex-Marines get right down to business in a lengthy conversation about present and past. Kelso suggests the next place to look: the Hall of Records.

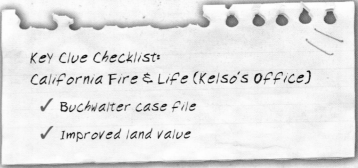

Key Clue Checklist:
California Fire & Life (Kelso's Office)
✓ Buchwalter case file
✓ Improved land value

LOCATION: HALL OF RECORDS

FIND THE LAND REGISTRY OFFICE.

You automatically travel to the Hall of Records ④. Enter the building and approach the desk guard to trigger a quick scene: Kelso asks about the land registry office, and the guard sends him upstairs. Climb to the top of the nearby staircase, follow the "Land Registry" sign to the office, and approach the clerk.

Kelso asks for the company details of the Suburban Redevelopment fund. The clerk leads you to a shelf marked "S" full of ledgers. Inspect the shelf to pull out the ledger you need and open it. Turn the page to find the listing for Suburban and its list of Directors. Be sure to tap on Courtney Sheldon's name to add it to your P.O.I. list.

FIND THE BUCHWALTER CASE'S LOT NUMBER.

After Kelso notes Sheldon's name, he asks for information on a plot of land. Since you only have the plot's coordinates, the clerk takes you to a coordinate plotting mechanism. Enter the latitude: 34 degrees, 04 minutes, 29 seconds. Then enter the longitude: 118 degrees, 17 minutes, 58 seconds. This gives you **Elysian lot number 1876988.**

FIND THE PLOT'S LAND VALUE.

Now you must do some calculating to find the lot information. As the clerk explains, you must convert your lot number to a letter to find the listing.

Here's how you get there: as the clerk explains, there are 90,000 lot numbers per book, so to find your letter, use the Hall of Records calculator to divide the lot number (1,876,988) by 90,000 then pull the gold handle to get 20.

Now sing your ABC's while counting on your fingers, starting at B because, as the clerk explains, A starts at zero. (Just our suggestion.) The twentieth letter of the alphabet is normally T, but since you skipped A, you end up at U. Go to the shelf marked "U."

Kelso takes out the correct land value record book. Open it and find the lot number 1876988. The listed owner is Randall Jones and the listed land value is $350. But as Kelso notes, with the new home in place the site is valued at $3,500, a tenfold increase in worth. "They can make a killing," he says. But how do they pull it off?

FIGHT YOUR WAY OUT OF THE HALL.

After viewing the land value, Kelso starts to leave but runs into his favorite goons, the fellows who beat him earlier. This time you have a weapon, too, so use the stacks as cover and gun down all of Monroe's hired henchman.

Remember to keep an eye on the mini-map's red blips marking the enemy locations. Watch out for the goon with the shotgun who tries to flank you on the right. Find him tucked against the "N" records shelf. After gunning him down, nab his shotgun and use it to dispatch his associates.

WATCH KELSO MEET SHELDON.

When the last thug falls at the Hall of Records, you trigger a long scene: Kelso stops by the USC School of Medicine to chat with young Courtney Sheldon, medical student and apparently a primary investor in the Suburban Redevelopment fund.

Kelso lays out what he just learned about the fund... and when Kelso mentions Dr. Fontaine, Sheldon looks mystified. He comes clean with the story, but it's colored by his naivety and faith in Fontaine. When Kelso tells him the truth about the "matchstick houses" and the insurance fraud, Sheldon is stunned—and continues to make a case for his mentor, Fontaine. But Kelso tells him the hard truth: "You're the fall guy."

Key Clue Checklist: Hall of Records

✓ Elysian lot number 1876988

LOCATION: KELSO'S APARTMENT

ANSWER THE TELEPHONE.

The scene automatically cuts to the hallway outside Kelso's apartment ⑤. Enter the first door on the right, Apartment 301. Kelso's phone is ringing; approach the phone to answer.

Guess who? It's Leland Monroe. He wants to meet Kelso at his mansion that night. Kelso says he might come. After hanging up on Monroe, Kelso picks up the phone again and starts dialing.

LOCATION: LELAND MONROE'S MANSION

FIGHT YOUR WAY INTO THE HOUSE.

Travel to Monroe's palatial estate ⑥ off Santa Monica Boulevard. Your arrival triggers a scene: Kelso has assembled a fire team of former 6th Marines to help him storm the palace. The battle starts in the estate gardens.

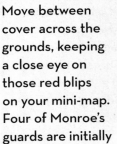

Move between cover across the grounds, keeping a close eye on those red blips on your mini-map. Four of Monroe's guards are initially deployed in the garden, but reinforcements from the house are plentiful, so stay sharp. Be sure to upgrade your weapon when you pass fallen foes, and be careful not to target your own guys. When you get close to the mansion, a full new squad of goons appears on your map and opens fire.

FIGHT YOUR WAY UP TO MONROE'S OFFICE.

After finally reaching the house, approach the front door to kick it open, then take cover immediately beside the doorway. Two gunmen are posted just inside, waiting for you. Eliminate them and step into the entry hall.

Use the same approach at the next doorway leading into the dining hall. Gun down the goon, then kick down the next door to trigger a scene: Kelso encounters Monroe's personal secretary. But when he lowers his gun, she raises hers—and despite her tough talk, she surprises herself when it goes off.

Kick through the next two doors to reach the central hall that leads to the main staircase. Two guards are posted on ground level, and two more are waiting up on the second level along the balustrade.

Climb the stairs and follow the hall to the open doorway that leads into the bathroom. Enter and go through the door to the left to reach Monroe's office and trigger a scene: Monroe is opening his safe as Kelso bursts in. Kelso puts a bullet into Monroe's thigh as his "opening negotiating position."

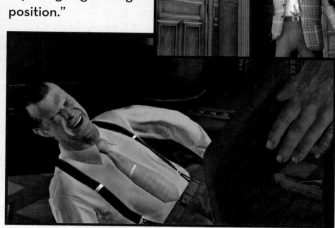

SEARCH MONROE'S OFFICE.

Open Monroe's safe and examine the items inside. You find some stock certificates for the Suburban Redevelopment fund and a green notebook that lists Monroe's payouts to cops and other officials. (Note your ex-partner, Roy Earle, listed three times!) You also find a police dossier on Dr. Harlan Fontaine.

Now find the folder on Monroe's desk and open it to see a list of homeowner holdouts, including family names you're familiar with from Phelps' arson cases: Steffens, Sawyer, and Morelli. Finally, look on the credenza behind Monroe's desk to find a newspaper and a framed photo of the directors of the Suburban Redevelopment fund.

NEWSPAPER CINEMATIC

On Monroe's credenza you find a newspaper with the headline "Suburban Redevelopment." Pick it up to see the final meeting between student and mentor.

After viewing all the evidence, Kelso uses Monroe's phone to call Detective Phelps, and he tells Detective Biggs to come pick up Monroe. But he also learns some news about Elsa, Dr. Fontaine... and a bug exterminator. You'll understand more once you watch the scene triggered after the case report screen for "A Polite Invitation."

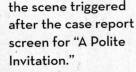

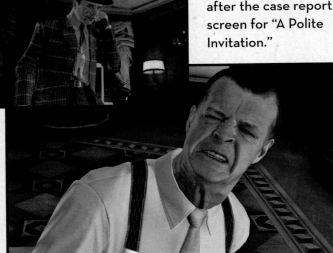

WATCH THE FLASHBACK.

After you close the case report for "A Polite Conversation," view a scene that actually happened prior to Kelso's assault on Leland Monroe's mansion. It's the incident Kelso learns about from Detective Biggs on Leland Monroe's office phone and then discusses with the wounded Monroe.

Elsa Lichtmann stops in for a psychotherapy session with Dr. Harlan Fontaine. After hearing some disturbing news from Elsa about an arson investigation, Dr. Fontaine finds himself forced to deliver some rather unconventional therapy to his patient, using a crystal ball.

Suddenly, another patient—Ira, the bug exterminator mentioned by Monroe at the end of the last case—breaks in to deliver some respiratory therapy of his own to Dr. Fontaine. Then he carries off the stricken Elsa.

A DIFFERENT KIND OF WAR

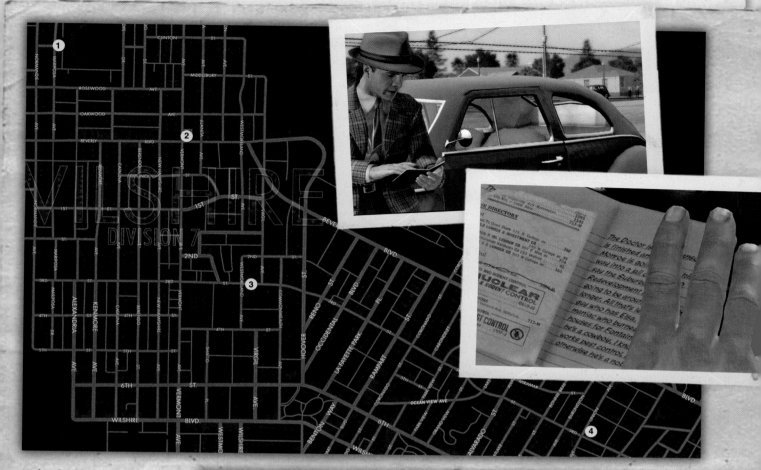

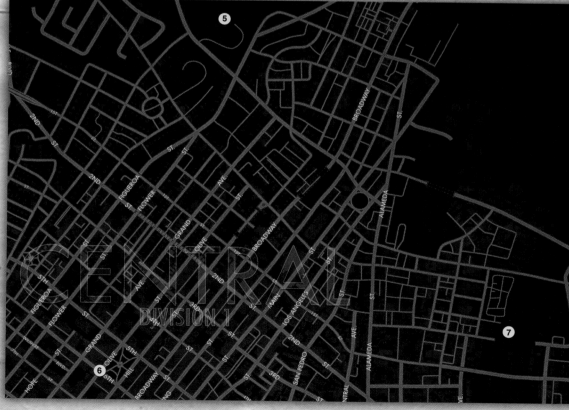

Kelso knows that the arsonist who killed Dr. Fontaine and then kidnapped Elsa is a bug sprayer and a big "cowboy" type. As your notebook explains, this suspect is the missing link between Elysian Fields, California Fire & Life, and the Suburban Redevelopment fund. To identify and track down the "bug sprayer arsonist," Kelso has torn the listings for L.A. area pest exterminators from a phonebook. This gives you three new locations to visit: Westlake Pest Control, Nuclear Bug & Rodent Control, and Rapid Exterminators.

Objectives

* Investigate Rapid Exterminators.
* Investigate Nuclear Bug & Rodent Control.
* Investigate Westlake Pest Control.
* Search Dr. Fontaine's Offices.
* Search Rancho Rincon Bunkhouse.
* Escort Kelso to L.A. River Tunnels Entrance.
* Fight Through Tunnels to Pump House.
* Watch L.A. Noire Finale.

CASE REPORT

TOTAL NUMBER OF KEY CLUES	7
TOTAL NUMBER OF INTERVIEW QUESTIONS	NONE

Fail Conditions

* Phelps dies.
* Kelso dies.

LOCATION: RAPID EXTERMINATORS

CHECK IN AT THE SERVICE DESK.

Travel from your starting point in the parking lot of the Los Angeles Speedway ① to Rapid Exterminators ②. Enter the building and approach the man at the desk, then press Talk to trigger a scene: Kelso asks the deskman if he's got a big cowboy working as a bug sprayer, and the answer is no. Be sure to check out the newspaper on the counter.

NEWSPAPER CINEMATIC

Pick up the newspaper with the headline "Crusade Against Corruption" from the service counter inside Rapid Exterminators. Watch the tense standoff between old partners as Cole Phelps uncovers the final blowback from Courtney Sheldon's actions on the SS Coolridge.

LOCATION: NUCLEAR BUG & RODENT CONTROL

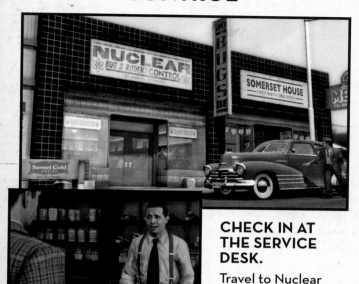

CHECK IN AT THE SERVICE DESK.

Travel to Nuclear Bug & Rodent Control ③.

Approach the service counter to trigger a scene: Kelso asks about a bug sprayer with a cowboy accent, but nobody matching that description works there either.

LOCATION: WESTLAKE PEST CONTROL

CHECK IN AT THE SERVICE DESK.

Travel to Westlake Pest Control ④. Once again,

approach the service desk to trigger a scene: Kelso finally gets information on the cowboy bug sprayer. The deskman says the fellow lives in a bunkhouse at the remains of the old Rancho Rincon. Then the scene automatically flashes back to Dr. Fontaine's surgery the previous day.

LOCATION: DR. FONTAINE'S SURGERY (THE DAY BEFORE)
SEARCH FONTAINE'S OFFICE.

Watch the introductory scene: Phelps and Biggs arrive at the scene, where Cole's ex-partner Rusty Galloway briefs them. Dr. Fontaine is dead, and a nurse saw one of his patients—"some big Boris Karloff type"—carry out Elsa Lichtmann.

Follow Galloway through the secretary's office into a small anteroom outside Fontaine's office. Open the cabinet and examine a morphine syrette box to see that this is Fontaine's **morphine cabinet**.

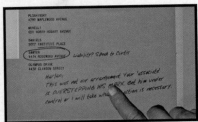

Continue into Fontaine's office. First, find the folder on the small table beside the entry door. Examine it to find **Fontaine's blackmail papers** that tie Leland Monroe to the arsons. Read Fontaine's note, but be sure to turn pages to see both the arson list (select the circled Sawyer name to get the key clue) and the psychiatric report on the cowboy arsonist; his name and other specifics are redacted. Doesn't look good....

Now turn and pick up the bloodstained **crystal ball** lying on the floor. You can also examine the shattered glass of the break-in. Finally, examine the body of Harlan Fontaine. The only item of interest is the lighter engraved with the initials "I.H." clutched in this left hand. Who is I.H.?

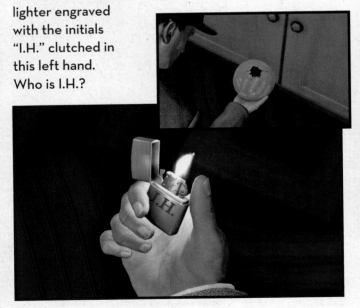

Finally, inspect Fontaine's desk. Examine the map on the left; Phelps notes that Fontaine has been marking the map, and moves it to reveal a blank pad of paper underneath. Use the charcoal marker to shade the blank paper and reveal the doctor's markings: he's placed Xs on a number of places along a curving line. The marked locations—Edgewood Grove, McCarthy Vista, Rancho Escondido, and Crescent Heights—are all new Elysian Fields housing developments. But what does it mean?

When you select the front page torn from the newspaper on the right, Phelps slides it underneath the shaded tracing you just made. It reveals that all of the new houses are being built directly in the path of the proposed new Whitnall Freeway! Now Phelps realizes the true nature of the Suburban Redevelopment scam.

Be sure to view the "story behind the headlines" via the newspaper on the desk, as well.

Key Clue Checklist: Dr. Fontaine's Office
- ✓ Morphine cabinet
- ✓ Fontaine's blackmail papers
- ✓ Crystal ball
- ✓ Freeway route

LOCATION: RANCHO RINCON BUNKHOUSE (TODAY)
SEARCH THE BUNKHOUSE.

Now you return to the game-time present as Kelso automatically arrives at the Rancho Rincon address ⑤. Approach the bunkhouse door to knock. Nobody answers, so kick in the door and enter. Just inside, search the worktable on the right to find a **flame thrower**. In the kitchen through the first passage on the right you find a familiar item: a pressure valve for an InstaHeat 70 water heater.

Enter the doorway on the right, just off the living room, to trigger a scene: Kelso enters to find a candlelit room hung with hundreds of folded paper birds. Pick up and examine an **origami crane** amidst the candles.

Examine the map of the Los Angeles River tunnels, hanging on the wall behind the candles, to add those to your New Locations page. As Kelso says, "This guy's a tunnel rat." Then examine the wall to the right to find some photographs of Okinawa; Kelso recognizes the soldiers' faces. Then it hits him: he knows the identity of the Okie cowboy with the flamethrower.

This realization triggers a scene: Kelso uses the bunkhouse phone to call his new boss, the Assistant DA, and reports his findings. He tells Peterson to meet him at the L.A. tunnel entrance , north of the 1st Street bridge. Then Kelso calls in an urgent radio message for Detective Cole Phelps.

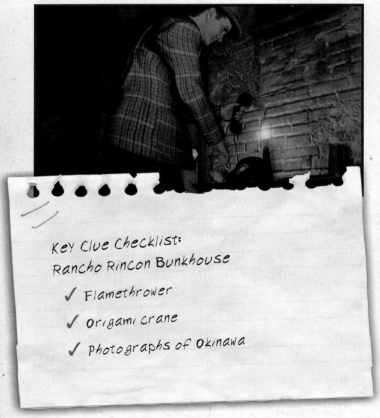

Key Clue Checklist:
Rancho Rincon Bunkhouse

✓ Flamethrower

✓ Origami Crane

✓ Photographs of Okinawa

LOCATION: WILSHIRE POLICE STATION

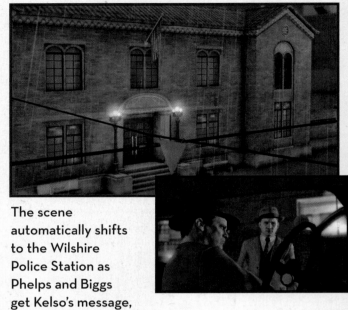

The scene automatically shifts to the Wilshire Police Station as Phelps and Biggs get Kelso's message, which directs them to the same tunnel entrance. An LAPD unit soon spots Kelso's vehicle on Sunset Boulevard, and Phelps decides Jack will need help to make it to the river—because plenty of crooked cops now want Kelso dead.

LOCATION: STREETS OF L.A.
ESCORT KELSO TO THE L.A. RIVER TUNNELS.

At the corner of 6th and Olive ⑥, Phelps and Biggs spot Kelso's car being hotly pursued by LAPD patrol units. Your new objective is to help Kelso reach the tunnel entrance in one piece. Catch up to the chase and start nudging police vehicles (marked as red car icons on your map) off the road.

Try to stay close to Kelso's tail and screen off attackers trying to pull up behind him. Soon police units target your car, too. Kelso eventually works his way to the tunnel entrance ⑦ where Phelps and Biggs join him along with Assistant DA Peterson. Kelso shows Phelps the map he found at the ranch house that marks Ira's tunnel routes.

LOCATION: L.A. RIVER TUNNELS

WATCH THE INTRO SCENE.

Kelso and Phelps split up and start searching. Chief Worrell arrives to lead the police team, and Asst. DA Peterson goes forward to meet them.

FIGHT YOUR WAY THROUGH THE TUNNELS.

Refer to our maze map made from the L.A. River tunnel blueprint you found in the Rancho Rincon bunkhouse. Kelso enters at the location Ⓐ marked on our map. Your goal is to work through the tunnels to the Jackson Street Pump Room Ⓗ, fighting past crooked cops trying to take you out. Note that you can find two caches of heavier weapons en route.

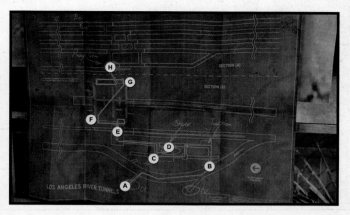

Check your mini-map for the red blips. Spot and take out the initial squad of enemy gunmen in the first tunnel. As you move past fallen foes, be sure to pick up dropped weapons for better firepower.

Enter the side tunnel on the left wall Ⓑ—it's marked as Almeda Outlet A2. Follow that passage to its end.

Around the next corner, there's a Caution sign at the head of a low, narrow tunnel with a closed gate at the end. Proceed to the spillway about halfway down the tunnel—the water runs from right to left—and hop in.

Follow spillway to the next tunnel, then turn right and follow the water flow to the ladder beside the gate. Nail the gunman crawling down the ladder as you approach!

FIND THE FIRST STOREROOM.

Climb the ladder (it's labeled "L2" at the top) and turn right, ready to shoot. Follow the walkway overlooking the water to find the small room marked as "Store" on Ira's blueprint map.

The room is stocked with weapons, including Thompson machineguns and military BARs stolen from the SS Coolridge. Grab a bigger gun, exit the storeroom, and go right, then right again to the next tunnel, labeled "Santa Fe Outlet."

This tunnel is lined with big pipes that you can use for cover; however, they also hide enemy gunmen. As you fight down to the far end, one of the crooked cops gets toasted, literally, by an unseen attacker on the other side of a closed gate. Apparently, Ira has another flamethrower in his personal arsenal.

Follow the bridge across the water to the doorway labeled "Santa Fe/Jackson St Vault Room." This leads to a walkway overlooking a cavernous central room.

GET ACROSS THE VAULT ROOM.

Immediately take cover behind the metal sheeting on the railing and start unleashing BAR fire at the numerous shooters deployed on the room's opposite side. Once again, you'll get help from Ira's flamethrower at the far right (see our shot). The shooters are on multiple levels, so keep an eye

on your mini-map to see which targets are below you.

When the coast is clear, turn right and go down the staircase to the lower level of the Vault Room. Be ready for another squad of shooters in the corridor at the bottom of the stairs.

Fight your way down the corridor and find another armory of SS Coolridge weapons in the room Ⓕ at the far end. Stock up on ammo or switch weapons if you want.

Take a step out of the weapon storeroom and turn left to descend the ladder down into the water. This triggers a quick cutscene: Water surges into the Vault Room from drainage pipes as the rain outside continues to swell the river.

Wade through the rising water to the opposite corner of the Vault Room Ⓖ and climb the ladder there. Hurry! Kelso will drown if you don't hustle directly to the ladder. Fight your way down the next corridor to the stairs at the end and climb them to the upper walkway.

FIND THE PUMP ROOM.

Take cover at the top of the stairs and gun down the shooters waiting on the upper walkways. Then slip around the corner and run down the walkway to the first passage on your left, labeled "Jackson St Pump Room." Here's your last move of the main story: Go down that corridor to enter the Pump Room Ⓗ and trigger the game-ending movie sequences.

Your gameplay is done. Now watch to see how the story plays out for Phelps, Kelso, and Elsa.

STREET CRIMES

Street Crimes (or unassigned cases) are desk specific and are unlocked based on the Assigned Cases you've completed. You can play any of the Street Crime cases during any case of a particular desk whenever entering its particular trigger radius on the map.

When a Street Crime is available, a request for help is broadcast over the police radio. A running man icon appears on the mini-map to display the location of the crime. Press the indicated button to accept the case.

You can also choose to replay a certain Street Crime by accessing the Cases option from the Main menu, then selecting a previously completed case from a department folder. You can also complete Street Crimes by entering Free Roam. Keep in mind that each Street Crime is available only at a certain time of the day.

UNLOCKED DURING ASSIGNED CASE	UNASSIGNED CASE NAME	TIME TRIGGERED	DESK
	01 BOXING CLEVER	21:00 – 04:00	TRAFFIC
	02 COSMIC RAYS	21:00 – 04:00	TRAFFIC
	03 MASKED GUNMAN	21:00 – 04:00	TRAFFIC
	04 SHOO-SHOO BANDITS	21:00 – 04:00	TRAFFIC
	05 GANGFIGHT	21:00 – 04:00	TRAFFIC
THE DRIVER'S SEAT	06 AMATEUR HOUR	20:00 – 04:00	TRAFFIC
	07 DEATH FROM ABOVE	20:00 – 04:00	TRAFFIC
	08 THEATER ROBBERY	19:15 – 21:00	TRAFFIC
	09 PAWNSHOP HOLDUP	08:00 – 16:00	TRAFFIC
	10 HOTEL BANDITS	08:00 – 16:00	TRAFFIC
THE CONSUL'S CAR (PS3-US ONLY)	11 ARMY SURPLUS	08:00 – 16:00	TRAFFIC
A MARRIAGE MADE IN HEAVEN	12 HUNG OUT TO DRY	20:00 – 04:00	TRAFFIC
	13 VENGEFUL EX	08:30 – 18:00	HOMICIDE
	14 DEATH PLUNGE	08:30 – 18:00	HOMICIDE
	15 CANNED FISH	19:00 – 06:30	HOMICIDE
THE RED LIPSTICK MURDER	16 WOULD BE ROBBER	08:30 – 18:00	HOMICIDE
	17 RUNNING BATTLE	08:00 – 19:00	HOMICIDE
	18 BANK JOB	08:00 – 16:00	HOMICIDE
	19 UNSUCCESSFUL HOLDUP	08:00 – 16:00	HOMICIDE
	20 COP KILLER SHOT	08:00 – 16:00	HOMICIDE
THE SILK STOCKING MURDER	21 HONEY BOY	08:00 – 16:00	HOMICIDE
THE STUDIO SECRETARY MURDER	22 MISUNDERSTANDING	08:00 – 16:00	HOMICIDE
	23 THICKER THAN WATER	07:00 – 19:00	HOMICIDE
THE QUARTER MOON MURDERS	24 KILLER BANDITS	08:00 – 16:00	HOMICIDE
	25 BOWLING LANE ROBBERY	08:00 – 16:00	HOMICIDE
	26 COMMIES	08:00 – 16:00	VICE
	27 FATAL PLUNGE	08:00 – 18:00	VICE
THE BLACK CAESAR	28 AGAINST THE ODDS	08:00 – 16:00	VICE
	29 DAYLIGHT ROBBERY	08:00 – 16:00	VICE
	30 THE BLUE LINE	08:00 – 16:00	VICE
	31 ZOOT SUIT RIOT	19:00 – 07:00	VICE
THE SET UP	32 THE BADGER GAME	19:00 – 07:00	VICE
	33 CAMERA OBSCURA	19:00 – 07:00	VICE
MANIFEST DESTINY	34 SECRET KEEPERS	08:30 – 17:40	VICE
	35 BAD DATE	21:00 – 05:00	VICE
	36 ACCIDENT PRONE	19:00 – 07:00	ARSON
THE GAS MAN	37 PAPER SACK HOLDUP	19:00 – 07:00	ARSON
	38 CAFÉ HOLDUP	08:00 – 18:00	ARSON
	39 BUS STOP SHOOTING	08:00 – 16:00	ARSON
A WALK IN ELYSIAN FIELDS	40 HOT PROPERTY	08:00 – 16:00	ARSON

TRAFFIC

1: BOXING CLEVER

Phelps takes a call from KGPL, directing him to a 459 (robbery) in progress at 267 South Main Street, Goldberg's Drug Store in Central LA.

Objectives

* Apprehend the burglary suspect.

Fail Conditions

* Phelps or Bekowsky die.
* Junkie escapes.

TIME AVAILABLE: 21:00—4:00

DRIVE TO THE CRIME SCENE.

When in the correct vicinity of this crime and after accepting the KGPL request, a red running man icon  appears on the map. Drive to 267 South Main Street to catch the burglar red-handed as he loots Goldberg's Drug Store ①.

APPREHEND THE BURGLARY SUSPECT.

The suspect takes off running when you enter the ransacked shop. Phelps chases him through the back hallway. The suspect runs through the back alley only to be cut off by a civilian vehicle. He then quickly diverts and jumps a wooden privacy fence on the left. After Phelps follows him over the fence, pursue the suspect up the ladder in the adjacent construction site.

If you get too close to a suspect while climbing a ladder, the criminal tries to fit the heel of his shoe into your eye socket. This undoubtedly impedes your progress up the ladder. Allow a little room on the ladder between you and the pursued. Once on the second floor of the structure, follow the suspect around to the left and up a second ladder.

FIGHT AND ARREST THE SUSPECT.

Follow the suspect to the edge of the platform to the right on the third level. The suspect is trapped. With

nowhere to go, he decides his fists are now his only means of escape. Remember to dodge thrown punches and to punch immediately following a dodge for the best opportunity to land a solid hit. Attempt to make the arrest when the opponent is on the floor. Just punch him a few times to trigger a finishing move and end the case.

2: COSMIC RAYS

Phelps accepts a 415 (disturbance) call, concerning the Alaco Gas Station at 7th and Flower—a possible mental case.

Objectives

* Apprehend the disturbed. suspect unharmed.

Fail Conditions

* Phelps or Bekowsky die.

* Suspect escapes.

TIME AVAILABLE: 21:00—4:00

DRIVE TO THE CRIME SCENE.

Follow the red running man icon to 7th and Flower to find the disturbed suspect beating on an unconscious man at the Alaco Gas Station ②. He beats on the bleeding body while uttering crazy words like, "You're the one who's been sending cosmic rays into my room!" and "You're not going to control my thoughts any more!" That's when you notice that Jamison is

wearing a metal pot wrapped with copper wiring on his head.

CHASE THE SUSPECT.

While trying to calm him down, he drops the bat and takes off running.

The suspect runs in the direction of the nearby Maybelle's Fried Chicken restaurant and takes a sharp right down the connecting sidewalk in front of the store. You'll see people pointing in the direction where he ran as you pass by.

SUICIDE PLUNGE.

The chase ends on a building rooftop across from the Alaco Gas Station. When you reach the rooftop, the disturbed suspect salutes and happily dives off the edge to his death.

3: MASKED GUNMAN

A 459 (burglary) has occurred at 6th and Ceres, and the suspect is at large—a male Caucasian believed to still be in the area.

Objectives

* Subdue the suspect.

Fail Conditions

* Phelps or Bekowsky die.
* Hostage is killed.
* Suspect is allowed to flee.

TIME AVAILABLE:
21:00—4:00

DRIVE TO THE CRIME SCENE.

Follow the red running man icon to the corner of 6th and Gladys ③. You'll automatically leave the vehicle and meet a witness at the corner of a building where she has sighted the suspect on a nearby rooftop. He's armed.

SUBDUE THE SUSPECT.

When the cinematic ends, climb the ladder to the rooftop where the gunman was spotted. Run directly across the width of the roof and quickly slide down the pipe, then climb the fence to your left.

DEADLY FORCE.

Run toward Ceres Ave and turn left around the building to chase the suspect along the crowded sidewalk. Avoid running into civilians; the collision slows you down. He veers left through the first gate opening. Follow him through the parking lot and over a brick wall. Now's your chance! Once you land on your feet, draw your weapon and shoot the fleeing gunman. The warning shot is not an option when a suspect has fired at you. Take him down to complete the case.

SAVE THE HOSTAGE.

If the suspect is allowed to reach a certain point, he will take a hostage to use as a human shield.

The trick to completing this challenge is to avoid adjusting your aim at all as the lead-in cinematic ends. During the first instant of the challenge, the gunman puts his head into view to the right (your left) of the hostage's. As soon as this happens, shoot. The gunman goes down and the case is closed.

4: SHOO-SHOO BANDITS

A 211 (holdup alarm) has occurred at Angel's Flight Railway, 3rd and Hill Street.

Objectives

* Locate the suspects.
* Subdue the suspects.

Fail Conditions

* Phelps or Bekowsky die.
* Suspects escape.

TIME AVAILABLE: 21:00–4:00

DRIVE TO THE CRIME SCENE.

Follow the red running man icon to Angel's Flight Railway ④. Here you and Bekowsky find a man on the sidewalk who's been robbed (they even took his shoes). The victim urges you to pursue the robbers.

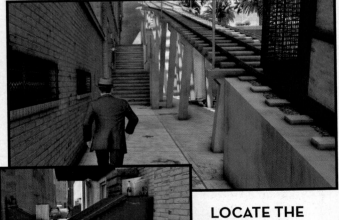

LOCATE THE SUSPECTS.

You face the last known direction of the escaping bandits from the beginning of the pursuit. There's an alleyway at the top of the second flight of stairs. Run left down the alley. You'll find the suspects a few building-lengths further down this path.

SUBDUE THE SUSPECTS.

Cover behind the first dumpster on the right and begin firing at the armed suspects. You must take them both down quickly or they'll escape in the nearby getaway vehicle. If they drive off, you have no chance of catching them on foot.

Use multiple automatic aims (if you have this option turned on) to take them out. To do this, while in cover (hugging the dumpster), shoot at the closest gunman. An automatic aim occurs on your first shot fired from cover. If you return to cover, the next shot fired from here will also have auto aim assistance. All is not lost if the second gunman actually enters the getaway vehicle; target his head through the back window and shoot repeatedly until you hear his skull hit the horn.

5: GANGFIGHT

An officer needs help with a, 415 (disturbance): gang fight in the alleyway of 1624 West 3rd Street.

Objectives

* Subdue the armed suspects.

Fail Conditions

* Phelps or Bekowsky die.

TIME AVAILABLE:
21:00—4:00
DRIVE TO THE CRIME SCENE.

Follow the red running man icon to 1624 West 3rd Street ⑤. When you arrive, a uniformed police officer briefs you on the situation. The Third Street Gang and the Diamond Street Gang are on the brink of an ugly rumble, but no bloodshed yet. Shots are fired just before the cinematic ends.

SUBDUE THE ARMED SUSPECTS.

You begin this gun battle crouched behind the hood of a police cruiser. Remain there and begin firing at the nearby gunmen hiding behind cars in the parking lot. For a much clearer and easier shot, wait a few moments without firing and a couple of the closest suspects leave cover and advance toward you. This is when you should pop up and gun them down.

Run toward the bodies you dropped and find cover behind a nearby vehicle. When you have an opportunity, pick up one of their dropped weapons. From this new position, you can take out the remaining four gunmen, who are covering behind vehicles further ahead in the same parking lot.

After gunning down the sixth thug, a car drives up in the distance to offer support. Now there are two more gunmen to subdue. Move forward safely while using the cars for cover. Fire your weapon to take the additional gunmen down quite easily from a safe distance.

6: AMATEUR HOUR

KGPL requests any unit to help with a 459 (burglary). Possible suspects are inside Sillman's Jewelry Store at 829 South Olive.

Objectives

* Subdue the armed suspects.
* Assist Detective Bekowsky.
* Apprehend the female suspect.

Fail Conditions

* Female robber is injured before she tries to escape.
* Phelps or Bekowsky die.

TIME AVAILABLE:
20:00—04:00

DRIVE TO THE CRIME SCENE.

When you reach Sillman's Jewelry Store ⑥, a cutscene shows crooks in the process of breaking into the store's safe. A woman stands over the nervous safecracker as if her hovering will speed the tedious job. You arrive on the scene as guards take positions inside the building. Just before the raid begins, the crooks spot your team and then scatter, and the female crook kneels on the floor before the large entry hole and surrenders.

SUBDUE THE ARMED SUSPECTS.

The store is dark, but your clip-on flashlight helps you find your way around (it turns on automatically in insufficient light). Step through the hole in the wall and ignore the surrendering woman. Do not shoot this suspect; she must live. Head toward the only red blip appearing on the mini-map and take cover behind the left side of the doorway. The first gunman takes cover behind a counter in the Jewelry showroom.

When he pops up to fire, gun him down. Or, when he goes back for cover, place a well-aimed bullet in his exposed cranium.

SECOND FLOOR TACTICS.

Enter the showroom and walk backwards up the stairs slowly while in the aiming stance. Look for two red blips to appear on the mini-map ahead of you on the second floor. Walk up the stairs slowly so you can cover from enemy fire by simply walking back down the stairs—using the actual second floor for cover. Shoot the two men behind the display cabinet at the front of the store on the second floor. If you don't see them, shoot the glass away until you do.

ASSIST DETECTIVE BEKOWSKY.

With the gunmen on the upper floor dead, return to the hole in the back wall on the first floor. You'll find the female prisoner stepping over Bekowsky's unconscious body while escaping back through the hole to the rear parking lot.

APPREHEND THE FEMALE SUSPECT.

Take a few shots at her as she tries to escape using the nearby vehicle. If you can't get a bead on her, don't worry; she collides with an alley wall a short distance away. Approach the wrecked vehicle and make your arrest.

CASE# UNASSIGNED

7: DEATH FROM ABOVE

KGPL reports shots fired and an officer needing help at Shatto and Valencia. Code Three (wants you to come in with sirens and lights), all other units Code Two (no sirens or lights).

Objectives

* Subdue the armed suspects.
* Incapacitate the suspect before he fires to save the hostage.

Fail Conditions

* Phelps or Bekowsky die.
* Hostage dies.

Trunk Weapons

There are weapons in the trunk of the police cruiser you're covering behind in the beginning of this case. Quickly grab one and return to cover. This will help with the long-range shooting required here.

TIME AVAILABLE:
20:00—04:00
DRIVE TO THE CRIME SCENE.

When you arrive on the scene at Shatto and Valencia ⑦ a uniformed officer briefs you on the situation. A routine traffic stop turns up loads of weapons in a trunk. Bullets start flying and the suspects snatch up the guns and one of the cops. They head to higher ground and make a stand on top of a building. The captive officer is alive, but who knows for how long.

SUBDUE THE ARMED SUSPECTS.

Remain where you start the mission, behind cover of the original police cruiser. Carefully pop up to shoot the two gunmen visible on the top of the tall building. A third gunman is also positioned on the lower rooftop to the right of the building. Once the two gunmen on the tallest building are down, quickly move and take cover behind the next car to your right. Pop up and shoot the third gunman on the lower rooftop, then sprint to his location.

Follow your partner, who's climbing up the pipe on the wall near the alley. On the next rooftop, you'll find the body of the gunman you killed and his weapon. You do not need his weapon. Climb the nearby ladder to the rooftop and prepare for some precision shooting.

CLIMB TO THE ROOFTOPS.

When you reach the rooftop, you find the last gunman with his pistol to an officer's head. There is no cover; just shoot the gunman before he kills the hostage. Failure results if you wait too long and the gunman shoots the hostage, or if you accidentally do this on your own.

INCAPACITATE THE SUSPECT BEFORE HE FIRES TO SAVE THE HOSTAGE.

The trick to completing this challenge is to avoid adjusting your aim at all as you exit the cinematic lead-in. In the first moment of the challenge, the gunman puts his head into view to the right (your left) of the hostage's head. As soon as this happens, shoot. The gunman goes down and the case is closed.

You could also aim and shoot the gunman's arm, which is an easier target. However, you have a narrow window of opportunity to put a couple more bullets in him as he releases the hostage. You must quickly pull off a few more deadly rounds before he shoots you or the hostage.

CASE# UNASSIGNED

8: THEATER ROBBERY

There's a 211 (holdup alarm) in progress at 933 South Broadway at the United Artists Theater.

Objectives
* Pursue the suspect.
* Apprehend the suspect.

Fail Conditions
* Phelps or Bekowsky die.
* Criminal escapes.

TIME AVAILABLE: 19:15–21:00
DRIVE TO THE CRIME SCENE.
When you arrive at the United Artists Theater ⑧, the armed gunman is seen threatening the employee in the ticket booth, vowing to hunt her down if she calls the cops. But it's too late; she tripped the silent alarm. The robber is on the verge of shooting her before running to his vehicle. You can spot his blue car driving away from the scene.

PURSUE THE SUSPECT.

Stay as close as possible to the suspect. If you lose sight of him, double-check his position on the mini-map (indicated by a red car icon). This icon begins to flash when the suspect gains too great a lead. You fail the mission if the icon flashes and fades from the map.

He takes you through some very sharp turns. The majority of the chase is through some very narrow alleyways with plenty of debris and objects to dodge, such as dumpsters, fences, and parking lot booths. Actually being able to catch up to the suspect enough to spin him out or to allow your partner to shoot out his tires is pretty much impossible.

APPREHEND THE SUSPECT.

If you follow him long enough, he eventually comes to a stop in a small parking lot on the corner of 6th and Broadway. Stop here and chase him up the pipe on the building at the back of the parking lot (behind the trash truck). He's armed, so a warning shot is not an option.

The suspect shoots at you as he crosses the metal catwalk over the large skylight window. Your best opportunity to gun him down is before he leaves the first rooftop and bolts around the next corner. Draw your weapon for a quick auto aim to get the reticle on him, then pull the trigger a few times to make sure he goes down. If you miss here, he stops to engage in a gunfight on the next rooftop after the billboard scaffold crossing.

CASE# UNASSIGNED

9: PAWNSHOP HOLDUP

KGPL reports a 211 (holdup alarm) and shots fired. The help call is at Globe Loan and Jewelry, 333 South Main Street.

Objectives

* Gain access to the premises.
* Subdue the armed robbery suspects.
* Incapacitate the suspect before he fires to save the hostage.

Fail Conditions

* Uniformed officer dies.
* Hostage dies.
* Phelps or Bekowsky die.

TIME AVAILABLE: 08:00 TO 16:00.

DRIVE TO THE CRIME SCENE.

When you arrive at Globe Loan and Jewelry ⑨, a single officer has the place held down and needs assistance. He says three gunmen locked themselves in with two hostages. He tried going in through the front, but the gunmen have it fortified. The plan is for you to go around to the back while the uniformed police officer keeps them distracted up front.

GAIN ACCESS TO THE PREMISES

Follow your partner into the nearby alley to circle around to the back of the pawnshop. Take a right out of the alley and continue to the

next to last dock opening on the right in the dead-end alleyway. Kick in the door to gain access to the pawnshop's back room.

SUBDUE THE ARMED ROBBERY SUSPECTS

Kick in the second door, then quickly advance a few feet and take cover behind a large filing cabinet to avoid being shot by the two gunmen in this back office. They are on the opposite side of the room, both using cover. One has a pistol and the other a shotgun. Swing out from cover and get your rounds off before the gunman on the left shoots. Get back to cover and repeat this process to take out the second gunman with a shotgun in the back-right corner.

There's one gunman remaining and he's on the rooftop with a hostage. Forget about picking up dropped weapons and just run up the stairs in the back-left corner of the room. On the next landing, you'll find a dead hostage. Continue up the next set of stairs to reach the rooftop.

INCAPACITATE THE SUSPECT BEFORE HE FIRES TO SAVE THE HOSTAGE.

The trick to completing this challenge is to avoid adjusting your aim at all as you exit the cinematic lead-in. In the first instant of the challenge, the gunman puts his head into view to the right (your left) of the hostage's head. As soon as this happens, shoot. The gunman goes down and the case is closed.

You could also aim and shoot the gunman's arm, which is an easier target. However, you have a narrow window of opportunity to

put a couple more bullets in him as he releases the hostage. You must quickly pull off a few more deadly rounds before he shoots you or the hostage.

10: HOTEL BANDITS

KGPL needs any unit able to handle a citizen's 211 report (holdup) in progress at 437 8th St at the Bristol Hotel. Suspects are linked to previous 211 calls.

Objectives

* Pursue the suspects.

* Subdue the suspects.

Fail Conditions

* Perpetrators escape.

* Phelps or Bekowsky die.

TIME AVAILABLE:
08:00—16:00

DRIVE TO THE CRIME SCENE.

When you arrive on the scene at the Bristol Hotel ⑩, the robbery is in progress. A gunman holds a shotgun on the hotel clerk as he fumbles with a moneybag. When the suspect sees you, he takes off running.

PURSUE THE SUSPECTS

Run through the hotel entrance and follow your partner into the back-right hallway. Once at the end of this long and winding passage, exit the building through the open doorway on the right. If you have trouble navigating up to this point, just follow your partner. Turn left through the

connecting alleyway and join your partner, who's watching the suspects jack a Buick Custom and escape onto Hill St. This is where the pursuit turns into a car chase.

You enter and unlock the Cord 810 Soft-top. Follow the suspect in the speeding vehicle as closely as possible. The chase continues with a left on 6th and an immediate right onto Olive.

There's a long stretch on Olive. Try to catch up to allow your partner to get a clear shot at the tires.

Just as you cross the intersection of 4th and Olive, the suspect veers into the narrow opening of a parking garage on the right. Exit the vehicle and look for the red blip on the map. Follow the suspect up two flights of stairs to reach the top deck of the parking garage.

Hot on their tail

If you are right on the suspects' tail as they enter the garage, there's time to exit your vehicle and gun them down on the stairs before they reach the second floor.

SUBDUE THE SUSPECTS

You're exposed to enemy gunfire as you crest the top of the stairs on the top deck of the parking garage. You must defeat two gunmen on this level. Draw and allow the first auto-aim to find one of the suspects. Gun him down quickly, then seek cover behind the nearest vehicle. Pop up and shoot the remaining suspect to complete the case.

11: ARMY SURPLUS

KGPL requests assistance for an officer at 540 West 9th St at Uncle Sam's Army Surplus.

Objectives

* Subdue the armed robbery suspect

Fail Conditions

* Phelps or Bekowsky die.

TIME AVAILABLE:
08:00—16:00
DRIVE TO THE CRIME SCENE.

When you arrive at Uncle Sam's Army Surplus ⑪, a scene unfolds in which the arresting officer is holding two robbers at gunpoint. The drunken storeowner then comes out waving a gun. This distraction gives the robbers just enough time to pull weapons out and gun down both the cop and the storeowner. All this happens as you make your way toward the scene through the store.

SUBDUE THE ARMED ROBBERY SUSPECTS.

As soon as the action starts, your partner runs out the back door and starts laying down suppressing fire. Remain in the building and take cover behind the open doorway. Swing out and shoot the robber on the right. Gun him down and swing back to cover behind the doorway.

The remaining gunman takes cover behind parked vehicles or the short wall. Swing out and use manual aim to pop him in the noggin when he reaches out to blind fire. Gunning down both men ends the case successfully.

CASE# UNASSIGNED

12: HUNG OUT TO DRY

Objectives

* Subdue the armed robbery suspects.

Fail Conditions

* Oswald Jacobs dies.
* Phelps or Bekowsky die.

All units in the vicinity of 536 South Figueroa have been requested to see the security guard at Hoelcher's Textiles, where a reported 459 (burglary) is in progress. Four male suspects are believed to still be in the building.

TIME AVAILABLE:

20:00—04:00
DRIVE TO THE CRIME SCENE.

When you arrive at Hoelcher's Textiles ⑫, you meet Oswald Jacobs, the security guard here at Hoelcher's Textiles.

SUBDUE THE ARMED ROBBERY SUSPECTS.

Your partner is covering to the right of the large warehouse entrance. Cover the left side. Look inside to see a group of gunmen talking. Five appear on the mini-map, indicated by red blips. Swing out from cover and shoot as many of them as you can before they settle into cover. Try to take down at least one before they scramble.

From this position, you should be able to take out the three closest gunmen. Try repositioning yourself at the front of the truck sticking out of the warehouse opening. From there, you can get a better angle on the third closest gunman.

When the opportunity presents itself, rush in and take cover behind the nearest structural column on the right. From this position, you should be able to take out the remaining two men. The hardest target is the one in the back room. However, it is possible to place the reticle on what little of his head he exposes while covered and performing blind fires.

As soon as all five gunmen on the map are dead, another one pops up. He appears to be in the same back room. On your way there, pick up a dropped machine gun. If the last enemy doesn't rush down the stairs immediately, enter the back room while in a manual aim stance and trace the reticle up the stairs. The final enemy is usually on the steps. Gun him down to complete the case.

HOMICIDE

CASE UNLOCKS
The unassigned cases described in this section are unlocked during the Assigned Case, "The Red Lipstick Murder."

13: VENGEFUL EX

A citizen reports a possible 415 (disturbance) at Olvera Street Plaza.

Objectives

* Subdue the armed suspect.

Fail Conditions

* Phelps or Galloway die.
* Suspect escapes.

TIME AVAILABLE: 08:30—18:00.

DRIVE TO THE CRIME SCENE.

You arrive at Olvera Street Plaza 13 to discover a domestic dispute between an old couple. The old man with the gun accuses the lady of cheating on him. She takes a swing at him and he quickly grabs her arm. A nearby police offer gets caught up in the dispute and gets shot.

SUBDUE THE ARMED SUSPECT.

After the opening cinematic, Phelps is in an alleyway facing the scene of the crime. Find the suspect on your map and move cautiously into the plaza while looking for available cover.

Ironically, an out of control pickup truck nails the lady in the dispute and knocks her unconscious on the ground. Sprint around the truck heading right through the main plaza pathway. Continue forward until you spook the old gunman from his hiding place behind a row of stacked pallets on your left.

He pauses at the end of the pallet row, then runs for more cover further down the street. This is your opportunity to gun him down as he flees and takes hurried potshots at you. If you miss, there are plenty more opportunities to shoot at the old boy from behind the many objects that can be used for cover in this plaza street.

14: DEATH PLUNGE

Car 16 Adam reports a possible jumper at the Methodist Church on the corner of 8th and Hope.

Objectives

* Reach the roof.
* Reach the suspect in time.

Fail Conditions

* Phelps or Galloway die.
* Jumper jumps.

TIME AVAILABLE: 08:30—18:00.

DRIVE TO THE CRIME SCENE.

When you arrive at First Methodist Church ⑭ at 8th and Hope, you discover the jumper threatening

to leap from the church's bell tower. While a uniformed police officer tries to "calm" him, you and your partner race to save the desperate fellow.

REACH THE ROOF.

This is a timed mission, but there's no clock that indicates exactly how you're doing. So be quick. After the opening

cinematic, run after your partner as he veers left into the nearest alleyway. Follow him as he runs alongside the church wall and veers left around a corner. Just beyond that turn is a pipe that leads to the roof. Take your partner's cue and begin climbing toward the rooftop.

REACH THE SUSPECT IN TIME.

Continue to follow Galloway after reaching the top. He stops and faces the direction of the bell tower—your destination. Run past him and quickly climb the ladder

to reach the top of the tower before the jumper leaps. If successful, you coax the jumper from the ledge and complete the case without incident. If you're too late, the jumper leaps to his death. You may recognize this guy as Cliff Harrison, from a DLC mission: "A Slip of the Tongue."

15: CANNED FISH

Objectives

* Subdue the suspects.

* Pursue the suspect.

* Apprehend the suspect.

Fail Conditions

* Phelps or Galloway die.

* Suspect escapes.

KGPL broadcasts to any available unit a citizen-reported suspicious activity at 111 South Alameda. Two male GTA suspects spotted with a delivery truck, which is reported as stolen.

TIME AVAILABLE: 19:00—06:30.

DRIVE TO THE CRIME SCENE.

When you arrive at the warehouse at 111 South Alameda , Frank Morgan is seen somehow connected to the illegal activities going down around the loading dock. The suspects spot the cops and a fight erupts.

SUBDUE THE SUSPECTS.

You and Galloway immediately engage two suspects. Let your partner deal with his battle while you work on knocking out your opponent. Just landing a few good punches puts a quick end to the fray. Once both suspects are down, Frank Morgan runs out of the warehouse and into a stolen truck.

PURSUE THE SUSPECT.

The next stage of this case involves you chasing the stolen truck (red vehicle icon on the mini-map). Do all you can to disable the truck. Your partner does very little to help, so stay with the fleeing vehicle as it veers left on 3rd and then takes another left through a narrow alleyway just beyond the BLA billboard on the left.

APPREHEND THE SUSPECT.

If you successfully follow the truck to the end of its programmed route, you end up watching it drop into the flood control channel, which renders the vehicle inoperable. Exit your vehicle and approach Frank to complete the arrest.

16: WOULD BE ROBBER

KGPL calls to any unit to assist in a citizen's report of a man with a gun on Grand between 4th and 5th. Suspect described as Hispanic, five foot six, and a hundred and forty pounds.

Objectives

* Pursue the robbery suspects.
* Subdue the hostage taker.
* Clear the roof of suspects.

Fail Conditions

* Phelps or Galloway die.
* Suspect escapes.
* Hostage is killed.

TIME AVAILABLE:
08:30—18:00.

DRIVE TO THE CRIME SCENE.

When you reach the crime scene on Grand between 4th and 5th ⑯, a shop owner helps a concerned

citizen that was shot while trying to stop a robbery. As the story is being told, the suspects are seen speeding away from the scene.

PURSUE THE ROBBERY SUSPECTS.

Follow the fleeing suspects closely as they take the first two immediate rights, and then the next left through an alley beside a hotel. Look for the street banner: "Keep L.A. Safe. Drive Safely" as a reminder to turn left into the alley. As you exit the alley, follow the suspects left down the next street. A block away, they stop at a gas station and take a hostage.

SUBDUE THE HOSTAGE TAKER.

The trick to completing this challenge is to not adjust your aim at all as you exit the cinematic lead-in. In the first instant of the challenge, the gunman puts his head into view to the right (your left) of the hostage's head. As soon as this happens, shoot.

CLEAR THE ROOF OF SUSPECTS.

With the hostage freed and the suspect dead, run to the right and find Galloway staring straight up a ladder to the gas station rooftop. Follow the last suspect up to the roof. You can then take cover behind the compressor to the left, or rush the armed suspect behind the furthest compressor and just run and gun him down.

17: RUNNING BATTLE

Objectives

* Pursue the suspect.
* Subdue the suspect.

Fail Conditions

* Phelps or Galloway die.
* Suspect escapes.

KGPL reports an armed burglary: 211 and shots fired. Officer needs help at 391 Broadway, Mallory's Café.

TIME AVAILABLE:
08:00—19:00.

DRIVE TO THE CRIME SCENE.

When you arrive at the armed robbery at Mallory's Café ⑰ the suspect inside is engaged in a gunfight with a patrolman who's covering behind his vehicle in the street. The patrolman makes a reckless move and gets shot as a result. Phelps demands that the suspect throw down his weapon and give up, but he just darts out of the store while laying down suppressing fire.

PURSUE THE SUSPECT.

Run after the armed suspect. He shoots back as he runs north on Broadway, ducking into the nearest alley on the right. You normally can't gain enough of a lead on the suspect to execute a warning shot in the alleyway, as

he quickly veers left around the corner at the end. So hold your fire and follow him out of the alley.

Keep approaching him as he begins to climb a pipe in an attempt to escape the rooftops. This is a particularly long pipe, but nearby obstructions make it

difficult to get a warning shot off. Follow the suspect up the pipe to the rooftop. Jump across the gap between buildings to your right and find the ladder on the second building wall to continue the pursuit.

SUBDUE THE SUSPECT.

Head to the back-right corner of the third rooftop. You'll see the suspect on the corner of the fourth rooftop. Try to gun him down as you cross the metal catwalk that connects these rooftops.

18: BANK JOB

KGPL reports an officer needs help at the Bank of America, 7th and Olive. 211 in progress and shots fired.

Objectives

* Subdue the armed robbery suspe[c]
* Investigate the vault.
* Clear the vault of suspects.

Fail Conditions

* Phelps or Galloway die.

TIME AVAILABLE:
08:00—16:00.

DRIVE TO THE CRIME SCENE.

A uniformed officer tells you there are half a dozen shooters at the scene ⑱. He believes they're real professionals. Witness says they bounced in, aced the guards, and went straight downstairs to the vault.

SUBDUE THE ARMED ROBBERY SUSPECTS

Begin the battle by remaining covered behind the police car where you begin the gun battle. Pop up and shoot the two gunmen behind the two vehicles directly across the street when it's safe to do so. Approach the trunk of the police car you are covering behind and take a more powerful weapon from the trunk.

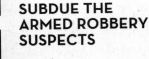

With your new firepower, approach and enter the front entrance to the bank. Take cover behind the right, unoccupied column or share the center counter for cover with your partner. Real cozy. He'll eventually find a new spot.

Three blips appear on the mini-map: two on the floor and one on the stairs to the right. Take out the highest suspect first as he poses the greatest threat to your cover. Next, take out the closest gunman on the floor. He's behind the next column on the left.

Move to the large marble bench on the left and use it for cover. This usually taunts the last gunman on this floor to show himself. He's armed with an assault rifle and can be spotted covering behind the entryway to the stairwell in the back. As soon as the gunman goes back to cover—this happens after he shoots—move up

and cover behind the next column on the left. This gives you a good shot at the gunman even while he's covered. Aim for the head.

INVESTIGATE THE VAULT.

Enter the back room labeled "Vault," where a uniformed police officer is waiting. Turn right and take the elevator to the lower level.

Make your move after he stops to reload. The angle is too great to shoot from cover, so step back, enter manual aim and shoot the crook. Aim for the head.

Run into the vault and charge to the right to take cover behind the desk. Do this quickly, as a gunman appears across the room using a similar desk for cover. Pop up and shoot him when the opportunity presents itself—the moment after he fires or stops to reload.

Now run to the opposite desk where the last guy dropped. Use that desk for cover from the final enemy, who is in the next aisle to the left. You can take this guy out as you did the last, safely from behind this desk.

CLEAR THE VAULT OF SUSPECTS.

On the lower vault floor, head toward the downed employee in the distance and find the open room to your left. Note that red blips appear on the mini-map as you head in this direction. Again, these are the enemies. Take cover beside the entryway and use the assault rifle to take out the gunman in the next room.

As you enter the next room, you'll notice the open vault door on your right. Use the left side of the open vault for cover from the gunman inside to the left.

CASE# UNASSIGNED

19: UNSUCCESSFUL HOLDUP

KGPL directs all units in the vicinity to a 211 and shots fired at 410 South Flower Street at Scott's Garage.

Objectives

* Pursue the suspects.
* Subdue the armed suspects.

Fail Conditions

* Phelps or Galloway die.
* Suspect escapes.

TIME AVAILABLE: 08:00—16:00.

DRIVE TO THE CRIME SCENE.

When you arrive at the scene at Scott's Garage ⑲, you witness a fight between Scott and the mob trying to collect protection money. Scott's had enough and begins firing on the armed suspects. They take off running on foot when they see you coming.

PURSUE THE SUSPECTS.

Follow the suspects around the large billboard and into the metal shack on the other side. Inside, Galloway shows you a ladder that provides access to the subway tunnels below. Climb down the ladder to continue the pursuit.

SUBDUE THE SUSPECTS.

Follow the hallway below around until you spot the two suspects at the end of a connecting hallway. Take cover behind the large crate where you discover the suspects. Pop up and shoot them when it's safe to do so. One man may escape before you have a chance to cap him. Continue through the tunnel to the end to find another ladder that leads down to the subway tunnel.

SUBWAY SHOWDOWN.

Enter the rail tunnel and allow the train to pass before you step on the tracks. Head left into the tunnel and prepare to run and gun down the remaining suspects covering behind metal objects between the tracks. Use the signal lights for cover while you shoot.

20: COP KILLER SHOT

All cars are called to a citizen's report of an officer in need of help. Shots fired and an officer is down at 6th and Lindley Place.

Objectives

* Clear the roof of armed suspects.

Fail Conditions

* Phelps or Galloway die.

TIME AVAILABLE: 08:00—16:00.

DRIVE TO THE CRIME SCENE.

When you arrive at Lindley Place ⑳, the officers on the scene are in a gun battle with two armed suspects

up high on a building. One of the cops catches a bullet. Another suggests someone scale the building to take out the armed suspects.

CLEAR THE ROOF OF ARMED SUSPECTS.

Begin by covering behind the police cruiser and shooting the lowest armed suspect from his perch on the balcony. The other gunman disappears from view as he heads further across the rooftop.

With the immediate threat gone, take a more powerful weapon from the trunk of the police car and follow Galloway to the back-right corner of the alley to find a climbable pipe. Scale it to a balcony, then climb the ladders to the rooftop.

Once you're up there, run forward and take cover behind the pile of bricks. The gunman begins taking shots at you from behind cover of the rooftop access structure. If he lives much longer, the suspect runs further across the rooftop. Use this opportunity to run to the north side of the rooftop structure.

Cover at the corner and peek around to find the gunman. He usually begins the return trip to his previous cover position while looking for you. Gun him down as he approaches.

CASE# UNASSIGNED

21: HONEY BOY

CASE UNLOCK

The Street Crime described in this section is unlocked during the Assigned Case, "The Silk Stocking Murder."

Objectives

* Subdue the suspect.

Fail Conditions

* Phelps or Galloway die.

KGPL reports shots fired and officer needs help with a 415 at 313 Bunker Hill Avenue.

TIME AVAILABLE:
08:00–16:00.
DRIVE TO THE CRIME SCENE.

When you arrive at 313 Bunker Hill Ave , you're thrown into the middle of a domestic disturbance.

An old couple that has just moved in together had a fight. He started chasing her around the yard with a 12-gauge shotgun.

SUBDUE THE SUSPECTS.

Use the picket fence for cover while trying to get the gunman inside his home in your sights. You have one opportunity to end the case quickly when he exposes himself in the beginning as he guns down an officer. If you miss that chance, there's a surefire way to take him by surprise.

Head around the back of the house and access the back porch through the unlocked door. Enter the house through the porch door and cautiously pass through the utility room via the next door on the left. From this doorway, you can spot the gunman in the living room. He's not expecting you. Shoot him. Case closed.

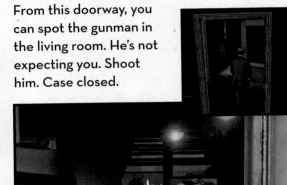

22: MISUNDERSTANDING

KGPL requests support for a citizen's report of a man with a gun at the intersection of Union and Rockwood Street.

Objectives
* Pursue the robbery suspect.
* Subdue the robbery suspect.

Fail Conditions
* Phelps or Galloway die.
* Suspect escapes.

CASE UNLOCKS
The Street Crimes described in this section are unlocked during the Assigned Case, "The Studio Secretary Murder."

TIME AVAILABLE: 08:00—16:00.

DRIVE TO THE CRIME SCENE.

When you reach the intersection of Union and Rockwood Street ㉒, you see a middle-aged Caucasian male holding an Asian man at gunpoint. The victim refuses to hand over what the robber demands and takes a bullet for his stubbornness. You are out of your car and chasing the robber almost as soon the victim's body hits the ground.

PURSUE THE ROBBERY SUSPECT.

Follow the robber as he runs into a backyard, through a privacy fence opening, and into the nearby alley heading right. If you lose sight of him, the pedestrians in the alley point in his direction. Cut through the backyards, following the robber to the next road.

The robber pauses when he reaches the driveway of the house across the street. He's armed, and he shot someone, so you can draw your weapon and try a warning shot here. If you miss, he runs into an open garage of a building behind this house, where again he pauses and gives you another opportunity to shoot.

SUBDUE THE ROBBERY SUSPECT.

If you chase the robber beyond the large, dark garage, he will turn and fire at you just before trying to escape the structure. Warning shot time is over. Gun him down quickly before you become another victim.

CASE# UNASSIGNED

23: THICKER THAN WATER

Objectives

* Pursue the suspects.
* Apprehend the suspects.

Fail Conditions

* Suspect escapes.

KGPL reports two 459 (burglary) suspects sighted in the vicinity of the trolley station on Lucas Avenue, between Court and Colton.

TIME AVAILABLE:
07:00—19:00.
DRIVE TO THE CRIME SCENE.

When you arrive at Lucas Avenue at Court and Colton 23, you witness an argument between a Bonnie & Clyde-like couple about whether or not they should have iced some folks they just robbed. When they spot you moving in on them, they flee in their hotrod and the chase begins.

PURSUE THE SUSPECTS.

Follow the vehicle out of the parking lot and through the alley across the street. Stay as close as possible so your partner can shoot out of the passenger window at the fleeing car's tires. To give your partner a decent shot, you must keep the vehicle in your

partner's field of view. So keep that car to the right of yours as much as possible.

The hotrod sticks to the alleyway until the robbers see the opportunity to cut through a construction site. Once they're through that winding course, the suspects head left on 1st Street, then make the first left and up an embankment at the end of the next intersection. Do your best to avoid hitting trees when performing this jump.

APPREHEND THE SUSPECTS.

After cutting a few corners and entering Lucas Ave, the suspects veer into an alley on the right. It's narrow and tough to navigate with its sharp right

angles. But if you've managed to follow them closely so far, you're doing well; the suspects reach the end of their run just beyond this alley as they collide head-on with a truck! Get out and make the arrest.

CASE# UNASSIGNED

24: KILLER BANDITS

KGPL reports an ambulance shooting, 943 South Broadway at Levine's Liquor Store.

CASE UNLOCKS
The Street Crimes described in this section are unlocked during the Assigned Case, "The Quarter Moon Murders."

Objectives
* Subdue the robbery suspects.

Fail Conditions
* Phelps or Galloway die.
* Suspect escapes.

TIME AVAILABLE: 08:00–16:00.

DRIVE TO THE CRIME SCENE.

When you get to Levine's Liquor Store ㉔, you find the assistant shopkeeper shot dead on the ground behind

the counter. Two robbers entered the store and the employee went for the shotgun under the counter. He missed.

They didn't. Now the suspects are fleeing on foot. During the cinematic, the two robbery suspects are spotted in an alley near the scene of the crime.

SUBDUE THE ROBBERY SUSPECTS.

From the start, you find yourself covered up against the corner of a building. You're looking down the alley at one suspect near a dumpster, who's ready to return fire; the other is fleeing deeper into the alley, attempting to make a vehicular escape.

It's pretty much impossible to gun down the running man before he enters the truck, so concentrate all your firepower on the closest suspect until he's dead.

Once the second suspect enters the distant truck, begin aiming at the driver's head and shooting repeatedly. Use an automatic aim (first shot from cover) to quickly find the driver in the truck, then continue shooting until he has also bit the dust.

25: BOWLING LANE ROBBERY

Objectives

* Subdue the armed suspects.
* Subdue the remaining suspect.
* Subdue the hostage taker.

Fail Conditions

* Phelps or Galloway die.
* Suspect escapes.
* Hostage dies.

KGPL reports a 211 (armed robbery) in progress at 9th and Grand at Rawling's Bowling Alley.

TIME AVAILABLE: 08:00–16:00.

DRIVE TO THE CRIME SCENE.

When you arrive on the scene at Rawling's Bowling Alley ㉕, an armed suspect carrying a shotgun is seen clearing customers out of the bowling alley.

SUBDUE THE ARMED SUSPECTS.

You begin this mission covered behind your patrol vehicle as the shotgun-toting suspect you saw in the opening cinematic comes running out the front door. Gun him down, take his shotgun, and then cover outside the entrance.

Look for the enemies by spotting red blips on the mini-map. Swing out from cover and shoot the gunman near the bowling lanes, inside the doorway and just to the right. Release your cover stance and enter manual aim. While aiming, slowly enter the bowling alley as you face the shoe counter, inside and to the left. There are two gunmen in this location. If you're quick enough, you can gun down both men and avoid a hostage situation.

SUBDUE THE REMAINING SUSPECT.

If the man behind the counter lives, he'll run down a connecting hallway. When control returns to you, run and leap over the counter to chase him. A cinematic shows the fleeing gunman take a hostage in the pin setting room.

SUBDUE THE HOSTAGE TAKER.

To defeat the suspect without harming the hostage, do not adjust your aim after the cinematic lead-in. In the first instant of the challenge, the gunman puts his head into view

to the right (your left) of the hostage's head. As soon as this happens, shoot. The gunman goes down.

VICE

CASE# UNASSIGNED

26: COMMIES

ASE UNLOCKS

he Street Crimes described
n this section are unlocked
ring the Assigned Case,
"The Black Caesar."

KGPL reports a 211 (armed robbery) in progress and shots fired at the corner of Hollywood and Highland at Hollywood First National Bank. The 211 suspects have taken several hostages.

Objectives

* Subdue the hostage taker.

* Subdue the armed suspects.

Fail Conditions

* Phelps or Earle die.

* Hostages are injured or killed.

TIME AVAILABLE: 08:00–16:00.

DRIVE TO THE CRIME SCENE.

When you arrive on the scene at Hollywood First National Bank ㉖, a gunman is holding a hostage at the main entrance. Three cops are lying on the sidewalk and street. The reporting officer tells you three guys tried to knock the place over and got jumped. Now they've got a half dozen patrons and staff for insurance: two inside covering the hostages, plus the charmer at the front door. He won't negotiate and he'll kill the hostage if they don't put him down.

SUBDUE THE HOSTAGE TAKER.

You begin the case crouched down and covered behind your patrol car. From cover, swing out and auto-aim, then fire on the hostage taker. With the suspect down, the remaining hostages flee the building, leaving the remaining gunmen inside with no insurance. Take a more powerful weapon out of the trunk of the patrol car you were covered behind.

SUBDUE THE ARMED SUSPECTS.

Move up to the entrance of the bank and cover along

the left side exterior column. Gun down the armed suspect behind the teller counter. After dropping that gunman, wait where you are until the last gunman creeps into view from the left interior. Then swing out from cover and shoot him to complete the case.

CASE# UNASSIGNED

27: FATAL PLUNGE

KGPL reports a 415 (disturbance) at the corner of Central Ave and 7th.

Objectives

* Reach the roof.
* Apprehend the suspect.

Fail Conditions

* Phelps or Earle die.
* Suspect is allowed to escape.

TIME AVAILABLE: 08:00—16:00.

DRIVE TO THE CRIME SCENE.

When you arrive on the scene at the corner of Central and 7th ㉗, you witness a rooftop altercation. Two men fight over a woman. The struggle escalates and gets dangerously close to the edge of the roof. Finally, the new lover is pushed over the ledge and falls to his death right in front of the LAPD officers gathered below.

REACH THE ROOF.

To get to the rooftop, scale the pipe near your starting position, then climb the ladder on the wall to the right when you reach the top. This takes you to the rooftop where the fight occurred. Once there, Dudley Lynch (bartender at Ray's Café from "A Marriage Made in Heaven") and his love interest (Shannon, also from the

same case) comfort each other. When Dudley sees you cresting the rooftop, he throws Shannon aside and takes off running.

APPREHEND THE SUSPECT.

Follow Dudley off the rooftop by sliding down the ladder to the left. As you descend, the suspect enters a white pickup truck. Run after the truck to the street; your partner will drive up and open the door of your police car and the vehicle chase begins.

There's only one outcome and to reach this you must follow the truck to the end of the line. You can smash and bump the vehicle all you want, but it will

do no good; it just keeps going until the inevitable happens.

So instead of trying to ram the vehicle, which often causes you to either wipe out or miss a sharp turn, just concentrate on following the suspect's every move very closely. If you lose sight of him for a second, look for the red blip on the mini-map to help orient your vehicle to get him back into view.

Dudley cuts through alleys and train yards in an attempt to lose you. In the second train yard, veer right to avoid being hit by an oncoming train. Also make sure you're on the correct side of it to continue the chase without obstruction; Dudley makes a sharp right to reach Santa Fe just after this incident.

The suspect then veers right into the final train yard and tries to make a break for the flood control channel, but is stopped by a speeding train. Follow the carnage to make the arrest and end the case.

28: AGAINST THE ODDS

KGPL request you look for the detective at the scene of a possible 484 (theft) at the bookmakers at Sunset and Ivar.

Objectives

* Find an incognito hiding place.
* Tail the suspect.
* Subdue the armed suspects.

Fail Conditions

* Phelps or Roy Earle die.
* You leave area.
* Suspect is allowed to escape.
* Suspect spots Phelps while being tailed.
* Suspect is killed before meeting his boss

TIME AVAILABLE: 08:00—16:00.

DRIVE TO THE CRIME SCENE.

When you arrive at the bookmakers ㉘, the detective on the scene reveals that a bagman named Rampley

is going to put a mint on some horse running in the fifth. He says they don't care about Rampley so much as they want his boss. Your job is to get Rampley to lead you to the big guy.

FIND AN INCOGNITO HIDING PLACE.

Notice the empty table with a newspaper. Approach it and press the indicated button to sit down and go incognito—
Phelps holds the paper high to conceal his identity.

TAIL THE SUSPECT.

Wait there until you see Rampley enter and lay down a grand on Cavalcade in the fifth. When the suspect leaves the building, get up from the chair and walk to the doorway. Rampley is indicated as a red blip on the mini-map. From the doorway, you can see him crossing the street, heading west; he's the guy in the black suit and black hat.

As soon as he rounds the next corner (past the green building), run across the street and cover against the corner of the building to keep your eye on Rampley as he continues west on the sidewalk.

Rampley stops at the next alley entrance to the left, then strolls into the alley after looking back your way a couple of times. When Rampley enters the alley, move up and cover behind the blue dumpster at the alley entrance. He walks past a man wiping down his pickup truck. Do not advance to the truck; remain behind the dumpster. Rampley will look back multiple times and moving to the truck is risky and unnecessary.

Remain behind the dumpster as Rampley approaches the right corner in the alley. When he disappears around the next corner, run up to the same corner. This triggers a cinematic where Rampley meets his boss about the race bet. Phelps busts up the party and guns are drawn.

SUBDUE THE SUSPECTS.

Rampley takes cover around the corner of the building on the right while the boss quickly takes cover behind his vehicle, making it impossible to gun him down before seeking cover for yourself. You have two choices: the blue dumpster on your left or the telephone booth on your right.

Concentrate your attack on the boss as he makes himself visible from behind his vehicle. Once he's dead, move slowly around the corner while aiming to reveal as much of Rampley as necessary to get in a shot. As soon as you spot him, gun him down before he repositions to get a better shot at you.

CASE# UNASSIGNED

29: DAYLIGHT ROBBERY

Objectives

* Pursue the suspect.
* Subdue the suspect.

Fail Conditions

* Phelps or Roy Earle die.
* You leave the area.
* Suspect dies.

KGPL reports a 211 in progress at Westlake Pest Control at 3rd and Union.

TIME AVAILABLE: 08:00–16:00.

DRIVE TO THE CRIME SCENE.

When you arrive at the pest control store ㉙, the robber is seen running out of the building, through the back lot and hurdling over a short concrete wall.

PURSUE THE SUSPECT.

You are given the opportunity to use your gun in this chase, since the robber was armed and dangerous. Chase him over the short concrete wall behind Westlake Pest Control. Do not attempt to shoot the

suspect or you'll fail the mission. A warning shot is acceptable.

Veer left through a yard and hurdle over a chain link fence. By now the suspect has turned right around a privacy fence—still no warning shot available. Veer right through another backyard and you'll spot him turning left, around a gray two-story house.

Follow the suspect as he cuts the corners of two blocks at a small intersection. Soon he steers between a dark gray house and a short brick wall. The suspect crosses the backyard and hops two consecutive fences to enter a nearby back yard.

SUBDUE THE SUSPECT.

If you've chased him this long without being able to fire a warning shot, then the suspect runs directly into a pedestrian, which puts an end to his escape. Now you can catch up to him and begin a fistfight. Your partner grabs him from behind, allowing one good punch to the gut that ends the case quickly.

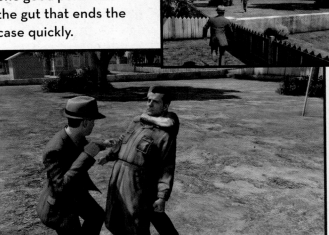

30: THE BLUE LINE

KGPL reports that an officer needs assistance on the grounds of 1825 North Highland Avenue. Multiple suspects must be taken in custody. Suspects are armed and dangerous.

Objectives
* Subdue the robbery suspects.

Fail Conditions
* Phelps or Earle die.

TIME AVAILABLE: 08:00–16:00.

DRIVE TO THE CRIME SCENE.

When you arrive on the scene ③⓪, the reporting officer explains that the bank robbers who hit The Citizens National Trust and Savings last month are cornered at the end of the police-secured street.

SUBDUE THE ROBBERY SUSPECTS.

You begin this mission covered behind the front of a patrol cruiser with five hostile enemies gunning for you on the other side. Check their positions on the mini-map.

Pop up and shoot the gunman you saw in the opening cinematic behind the pickup truck. He is now the furthest enemy on the right. Grab a Thompson from the trunk of the patrol vehicle, then run left for the building framework where your support team fights.

Take cover behind the tall stack of wooden posts and pop out from around cover to shoot the gunman due north, covering behind a pallet of large bricks. With him down, proceed forward to cover behind the plywood pile or the same stack of bricks the last enemy was hiding behind.

From the left side of your cover, swing out and shoot the gunman to the north, covering behind the pickup truck parked near the red house. There are now two targets remaining.

Move up and cover at the right corner of the red house's side porch. Swing out and shoot the gunman on the right side of the house—he's covering near some large wooden crates. Spot the next closest gunman in the back yard near a shed. He can easily be gunned down from this same location. One enemy remaining.

Pick up the dropped assault rifle from the gunman lying near the crates and approach the garage shelter in the back yard. The remaining gunman appears from between vehicles and jumps into the one facing you. Try to take him out before he enters the vehicle. If you miss, shoot him while he sits in the driver's seat. Continue firing on him until he wrecks. If he survives, he'll jump out and attack after colliding with a police car. If this happens, shoot him before he goes for a gun.

31: ZOOT SUIT RIOT

KGPL reports a 459 at 539 South Los Angeles Street at the Valor Tobacco Company.

CASE UNLOCKS

The Street Crimes described in this section are unlocked during the Assigned Case, "The Set Up."

Objectives

* Subdue the armed robbery suspects

Fail Conditions

* Phelps or Earle die.
* Suspect escapes.
* Citizen injured.

TIME AVAILABLE:
19:00—07:00.
DRIVE TO THE CRIME SCENE.

When you arrive at Valor Tobacco Company ㉛, a uniformed security guard asks you to move along, emphasizing that you're on private property. When you announce "LAPD" and state there was a burglary report, the guard tries to explain that the thugs in the nice suits are actually nightshift workers. The bad guys sense this conversation is not going well and one pulls a gun. That's when the violence begins.

SUBDUE THE ARMED ROBBERY SUSPECTS.

You're left vulnerable with no cover at the beginning of this challenge. Dart to the right to take cover behind the blue dumpster in the alleyway. Two enemies appear on the mini-map. Earl takes care of the first threat (the only one exposed and the guy who started the shootout).

The remaining gunman guards the entrance to the warehouse to your right. Roy pushes forward to find cover ahead.

Follow the right wall to the corner, then pop out and shoot the gunman near the entrance. If you miss, he'll run into the warehouse and join four other shooters. Note that one is up on a higher level (the red icon on the mini-map has an up arrow).

Enter the dark warehouse and cover behind the first stack of boxes. Move to the left side, then swing out and shoot the gunman on the left side of the lower warehouse.

You should also see the second shooter on the left, toward the back of the room. Move in that direction and cover behind the row of slot machines to get a better angle on him.

From the slot machines, you should be able to spot two of the three gunmen remaining on this first floor of the warehouse. Use cover and gun them down carefully. The shooter on the top floor begins firing during this stage of the battle. When you return the favor, an additional guard arrives from the left on the lower floor. Your partner usually advances further inside at this point.

Hold your position on the row of slot machines and move from the left edge to the right edge to find an enemy moving out of cover. Eventually, they both make that mistake and pay for it. Proceed to the top floor and eliminate the remaining gunman to complete the case.

CASE# UNASSIGNED

32: THE BADGER GAME

KGPL reports a 484 at 3155 West Fourth Street.

Objectives

* Pursue the suspect.

* Apprehend the suspect.

Fail Conditions

* Phelps or Earle die.

* Suspect flees.

TIME AVAILABLE: 19:00—07:00.

DRIVE TO THE CRIME SCENE.

When you arrive at the scene ③②, the victim explains to the reporting officer how some punks just jumped him while he was minding his own business. He directs everyone's attention to the nearby alley where they were last seen. After creating this false diversion, the victim/conman steals the nearby police cruiser!

PURSUE THE SUSPECT.

The suspect has a considerable lead on you by the time you enter the nearest vehicle and begin the chase. Watch the red car icon on the mini-map to

locate the fleeing vehicle, speeding west on 4th.

He veers right into the nearest alley to the right.

Avoid the hard corner posts on the fence near the alley entrance. Also watch out for the garbage truck that pulls in from the right at the first intersection.

The suspect swerves out of the alley and turns left on 6th, then takes an immediate right on Shatto Pl. He turns right at the next intersection at Wilshire Blvd, then quickly turns left into an alley. He cuts through the back lot and drives through a crumbled area in a wall and jumps down to a small residential street.

The suspect then turns left on 7th, drives on the sidewalk for a while, cuts right into another open alley, and crosses the next street before smashing through a construction yard barrier.

APPREHEND THE SUSPECT.

Follow him through the construction yard until he crashes into a large concrete foundation, then hop out of your vehicle and make the arrest. To beat this mission, you simply must keep up with the suspect and follow him to his own demise.

CASE# UNASSIGNED

33: CAMERA OBSCURA

KGPL calls attention to any unit about a citizen report of suspicious activity on a trolley car on Fountain Ave. The responding unit needs to see a woman about the 288 suspect (lewd conduct) on the Angeleno Heights trolley currently stopped near Fountain and Bronson.

Objectives

* Pursue the suspect.
* Apprehend the suspect.

Fail Conditions

* Phelps or Earle die.
* Suspect escapes.

TIME AVAILABLE:
19:00–07:00.

DRIVE TO THE CRIME SCENE.

When you arrive at Fountain Ave ㉝, you find two women on a park bench recovering from a lewd act on the trolley. A pervert with a camera was taking

indecent photos of one of them. She quickly identifies him, as he's caught in the act harassing another innocent passerby on the next corner.

PURSUE THE SUSPECT.

The suspect then jumps into his vehicle and flees. Chase the pervert as he takes the first left, heading north on Cole St. He cuts a corner and veers left on Ivar Ave. You can either follow him through the park

benches or take a less risky route by driving legally through the intersection.

He turns left on Sunset just long enough to veer right through a diner parking lot to reach Cahuenga Blvd. He drives on this road for a city block, then he veers left into a large parking lot. From there, he veers right around the first row of buildings.

The reckless suspect proceeds down Selma Ave and takes a sharp left through a courtyard after passing Seward St. He jumps a row of steps and continues through the Crossroads of the World, turning right onto Sunset Blvd.

APPREHEND THE SUSPECT.

Next, he swerves right on Orange Drive. The suspect is struck by another vehicle and is then subsequently hit by a speeding trolley car as he attempts

to cross Hollywood Blvd. Now pinned between the two vehicles, he has nowhere to run. Jump out of the vehicle and approach him to make the arrest.

CASE# UNASSIGNED

34: SECRET KEEPERS

ASE UNLOCKS

he Street Crimes described in this
ection are unlocked during the
ssigned Case, "Manifest Destiny."

KGPL wants you to report to the security guard that apprehended a suspect at the Southern California Auto Club at 6201 Santa Monica Blvd.

Objectives

* Locate the suspicious individual.

* Pursue the suspect.

* Apprehend the suspect.

Fail Conditions

* Phelps or Earle die.

* Commie is allowed to escape.

* Commie is killed.

TIME AVAILABLE: 08:30—17:40.

DRIVE TO THE CRIME SCENE.

When you arrive at the auto club ㉞, the apprehended suspect turns out to be a reporter that's been doing a feature for The Examiner. The patron he was following is a suspected communist under investigation by the feds. The reporter says he's in the back parking lot.

LOCATE THE SUSPICIOUS INDIVIDUAL.

The suspect does not appear on the mini-map until you exit the building. Once outside, enter the first possible right into a driveway that leads to the auto club's rear parking lot. The suspect is spotted as he gets into his nice vehicle and drives off. Enter the nearest available ride—a Delahaye 135MS Cabriolet—to give chase. If you have not yet unlocked this hidden vehicle, it's unlocked now!

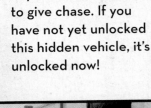

PURSUE THE SUSPECT.

Follow the suspect closely as he peels out of the lot. Pursue him through several alleyways and twists and turns.

The suspect takes a sharp right onto Afton Place. After a few blocks, he follows it up with a sharp left onto Gower. A block further and he speeds right onto El Centro, quickly followed by a left veer through a parking lot behind the Palladium (looks like an airplane hangar).

APPREHEND THE SUSPECT.

The suspect continues to race through a few parking lots until he smashes into the side of a building on Vine St. Get out of your vehicle and approach him to make the arrest.

35: BAD DATE

Objectives

* Investigate the crime scene.
* Pursue the suspect.
* Subdue the suspect.

Fail Conditions

* Phelps or Earle die.
* You leave the area.

KGPL requests you meet the officers reporting a 187 (homicide) in the alleyway at Union and 7th. The suspect is still at large.

TIME AVAILABLE: 21:00—05:00.

DRIVE TO THE CRIME SCENE.

When you arrive at scene of the homicide ㉟, the reporting officer says the dead lady was last seen falling out of a bar with some goon. He got fresh, she got shy, he got angry. Witness has him in his late forties, six foot, light shirt, dark trousers. The body is still warm so the suspect must be close by.

INVESTIGATE THE CRIME SCENE.

Examine the body to discover a clue that indicates the murderer's location. You can check out both arms and the head (where the clue is hidden). Move the victim's head as far as you can to the right to inspect the wound on the left side: Blunt force trauma.

Next, examine the bloodstain on the ground where Earle is hovering. The bloody footprints show the suspect heading up to the rooftop. Climb the gutter on the back wall to reach the rooftop and find the suspect climbing another ladder to a higher level.

PURSUE THE SUSPECT.

Follow him up and search the rooftop until you find the hiding suspect to initiate a fistfight.

APPREHEND THE SUSPECT.

Your opponent is tough, so dodge as many attacks as possible and always follow a successful dodge with a follow-up punch. The suspect is likely to hit the ground a few times before he becomes dazed enough for a successful grapple attack. Every time he falls, attempt to make the arrest to curtail the battle.

ARSON

36: ACCIDENT PRONE

KGPL requests you meet the reporting officer at the scene of a hit-and-run felony at the intersection of 6th and Alvarado.

Objectives

* Locate the hit and run suspect.

* Subdue the hit and run suspect.

Fail Conditions

* Phelps or Biggs die.

* You leave the area.

TIME AVAILABLE:
19:00—07:00.

DRIVE TO THE CRIME SCENE.

When you arrive at this hit-and-run crime scene at Fancy Shoes 36 on Beverly and Heliotrope, the reporting officer says it should be easy to find the offender; he left his car behind and hoofed it! Before the cinematic ends, a witness says he saw the guy run into a nearby alley.

LOCATE THE HIT AND RUN SUSPECT.

Run forward and veer left into the first alley. The hiding suspect is in the first clearing, down the

exterior stair well, behind the red transfer trailer. Find him, then subdue him!

SUBDUE THE HIT AND RUN SUSPECT.

Your partner is likely to assist in this fistfight. Dodge attacks and throw punches until you're prompted to perform a grapple attack, then do this to finish him off and make the arrest.

37: PAPER SACK HOLDUP

KGPL reports a 211 at the Bank of Arcadia at 253 Main Street.

Objectives

* Pursue the suspects.
* Apprehend the suspects.

Fail Conditions

* Phelps or Biggs die.
* Suspect escapes.

TIME AVAILABLE: 19:00—07:00.

DRIVE TO THE CRIME SCENE.

When you arrive at the bank at 253 Main Street ③⑦ , an officer reports that two guys made off with

about 10 grand in a paper sack. The drunken bum claims he witnessed the robbers' escape and points to the nearby parking lot.

PURSUE THE SUSPECTS.

After the cinematic, you and your partner run to the nearby parking lot to find the robbers breaking into a Cadillac. You commandeer a nearby Voisin C7, which can more than hold its own against the suspects' car.

The robbers begin their escape by speeding out of the parking lot and heading south on Spring St. They immediately veer right into another parking lot to try to lose you in a nearby alley.

Stay close so your partner can take his shots. Drive directly behind the fleeing vehicle. Don't try to get beside the suspect; the alleyways are too narrow.

Out of the first set of alleyways, the robbers turn right onto 4th St and remain there just long enough to cut into the next alley on the right. When they exit

this alley, you have a great chance to slam into the left side of their vehicle as they turn sharply to the left onto Olive.

APPREHEND THE SUSPECTS.

This collision opportunity arises again as they snake to the right, then to the left, through

the next two intersections. These three back-to-back opportunities are usually more than enough to allow you to stop the vehicle and make your arrest. If not, you can follow them off the embankment on 4th Street, jumping over Flower St. Upon landing, all sorts of vital car parts are lost, along with any chance for them to escape. Make the arrest.

38: CAFÉ HOLDUP

KGPL radios your 211 at Boos Brothers Café at 522 South Hill Street.

Objectives

* Subdue the robbery suspects.
* Subdue the hostage taker.

Fail Conditions

* Phelps, Biggs, or the hostage dies.
* You leave the area.

TIME AVAILABLE: 08:00—18:00.

DRIVE TO THE CRIME SCENE.

When you arrive at the café 38, you find an employee lying near the entrance, suffering from an apparent gun wound. Seconds later, you hear the suspects in the back parking lot through the opened back door. One of them points a gun at an employee and gives them five seconds to hand over the money. Subdue this thug before he shoots the hostage.

SUBDUE THE HOSTAGE TAKER.

Don't worry about the well-being of the customers in the holdup. You have a clear shot at the hostage-taker through the back door. Shoot him. The other suspects scramble after your kill shot. You have only five seconds to take the gunman down and rescue the hostage.

SUBDUE THE ROBBERY SUSPECTS.

As you run out the back door to take cover behind the line of nearby crates, a single vehicle pulls up and brings the support of one additional gunman (now a total of three enemies).

When the opportunity arises, pop up from cover and shoot the enemy to the far right, covering behind a dumpster. Then do the same to the gunman to the left, behind the blue dumpster. With the biggest threat out of the way, concentrate your fire on the gunman behind the vehicle. That's a wrap—forget the ambulance; order body bags.

39: BUS STOP SHOOTING

KGPL requests you meet the officer at the Greyhound Bus Station at Beverly and Union.

Objectives

* Subdue the armed robbery suspects.
* Pursue the remaining suspect.
* Apprehend the remaining suspect.

Fail Conditions

* Phelps or Biggs die.
* Suspects escape.
* Civilian dies.
* You leave the area.

TIME AVAILABLE: 08:00—16:00.

SUBDUE THE ARMED ROBBERY SUSPECTS.

When you arrive at the bus depot 39, the officer at the scene says the stickup boys lost their heads and a girl got shot. He explains that time is of the essence. There are still people inside.

PURSUE THE REMAINING SUSPECT.

You begin the case crouched down behind a police cruiser. Take a more powerful weapon from the trunk, then run for cover behind the bus depot entrance. Three suspects appear on the mini-map; one of them is visible inside the building when standing near the entrance. Gun him down!

Next, move up to the inside left wall and work your way up to the corner to get a visual of the next gunman in the seating area. Pop

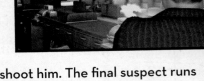

out from cover and shoot him. The final suspect runs into the bus parking lot in the back. Pursue him.

APPREHEND THE REMAINING SUSPECT.

A support vehicle pulls up outside. You now have two gunmen to deal with in the back lot. Do as the hiding suspects do and use the buses for cover as you search. Swing out and shoot the suspects from cover.

40: HOT PROPERTY

KGPL requests any unit in the vicinity respond to a citizen's report of a 459 (burglary) in progress at 38 North Catalina.

Objectives

* Pursue the suspect.
* Apprehend the suspect.

Fail Conditions

* Phelps or Earle die.
* Suspect escapes.
* You leave the area.

Stay close to the side of his vehicle to give your partner a shot opportunity at the pickup's tires.

Just through the Oakwood intersection, the suspects veers right through a residential alley, turns left around the first house, and uses the driveway to reach Rosewood where he then turns left. You can choose not to follow him as he takes this route around the house. Instead, try to remain on the same road and join him again as he cuts through the nearby diner parking lot.

TIME AVAILABLE: 08:00—16:00.

DRIVE TO THE CRIME SCENE.

When you arrive at 38 North Catalina Street **40**, you discover a burglary attempt in progress. A medium build, middle-aged, white male is trying to break and

enter into a residential home. When he spots you approaching, he takes off running and quickly enters his pickup truck to escape.

PURSUE THE SUSPECT.

The chase begins with the suspect heading north on Catalina. He veers slightly right through the first intersection to cut through a parking lot ahead, then enters an alleyway to the left.

APPREHEND THE SUSPECT.

After circling the corner house, he cuts right through the Joe's diner lot, steers around the place, and turns left on Mariposa. At this point he usually collides with a large delivery truck. Jump out of your vehicle and make the arrest.

OUTFITS

RANK	XP NEEDED	ACCUMULATED XP AMOUNT	UNLOCKS
3	20	(35)	SWORD OF JUSTICE OUTFIT
8	45	(210)	SUNSET STRIP OUTFIT
13	70	(510)	THE OUTSIDER OUTFIT
18	95	(1035)	HAWKSHAW OUTFIT

1

THE OUTSIDER

OUTFIT NUMBER: 1

UNLOCKED: Rank 13

DESCRIPTION: Don't believe everything you read in the papers.

2

CHICAGO LIGHTNING

OUTFIT NUMBER: 2

UNLOCKED: Sign up to the Rockstar Social Club

DESCRIPTION: Shoot straighter with the Thompson and the Shotgun.

3

SWORD OF JUSTICE

OUTFIT NUMBER: 3

UNLOCKED: Rank 3

DESCRIPTION: The City of Angels is much more dangerous by night.

GOLDEN BOY

OUTFIT NUMBER: 4

UNLOCKED: At the start of the Traffic Desk

DESCRIPTION: Get yourself two suits and get them pressed.

THE BRODERICK

OUTFIT NUMBER: 7

UNLOCKED: Downloadable Content

DESCRIPTION: Hit harder and take more punches before going down.

HAWKSHAW

OUTFIT NUMBER: 5

UNLOCKED: Rank 18

DESCRIPTION: Take an extra dose of damage and stay standing.

THE SHARPSHOOTER

OUTFIT NUMBER: 8

UNLOCKED: Downloadable Content

DESCRIPTION: Shoot straighter with the Garand and the Colt .45.

SUNSET STRIP

OUTFIT NUMBER: 6

UNLOCKED: Rank 8

DESCRIPTION: Best worn while rubbing shoulders with movie stars.

BUTTON MAN

OUTFIT NUMBER: 9

UNLOCKED: Collect all DLC Hidden Shields.

DESCRIPTION: Carry extra ammo for all weapons, just in case.

LANDMARKS

There are 30 hidden Landmarks around the city. Driving close to any of these adds it to the map. There's an Achievement/Trophy for discovering them all. Selecting a Landmark from the Main Map screen brings up an image of the location, as well as some historical information about the site.

100% COMPLETION

Finding all 30
Landmarks counts as 3%
toward 100% completion
of the game.

ACHIEVEMENT &
TROPHY

Finding all 30
Landmarks also earns
you the Star Map
Achievement/Trophy.

1 GRAUMAN'S THEATER

The result of a partnership between showman Sid Grauman and backer C.E. Toberman, Grauman's Chinese Theater opened with the premiere of Cecil B. DeMille's "The King of Kings" and has been hosting gala ceremonies ever since.

2 HOTEL ROOSEVELT

The Hollywood Roosevelt was built in 1927 at a cost of $2.5 million. Its "Blossom Room" hosted the first ever Academy Awards ceremony on May 19, 1929, where "Wings," a silent film about fighter pilots in WWI, won the inaugural award for Best Picture.

3 MAX FACTOR BUILDING

Max Factor acquired this building in 1928, and renovated it with the help of theater architect S. Charles Lee. The remodeled studio included four special, color coordinated makeup rooms, one each for blondes, redheads, brunettes, and "brownettes."

4 MUSSO & FRANK

Musso & Frank Grill opened in 1919. Though frequented by Hollywood stars, it's better known as the haunt of screenwriters. Raymond Chandler spent time at the bar, as did his hero Philip Marlowe in the 1939 novel "The Big Sleep."

5 CROSSROADS TO THE WORLD

Ella Crawford, widow of murdered underworld boss Charlie Crawford, funded the construction of this lavish outdoor shopping mall in 1936. It is designed to look like an ocean liner, and the 30-foot tower is topped with a revolving world globe.

6 BROWN DERBY

The original Brown Derby on Wilshire Boulevard was opened in 1926 by Robert Cobb and Herbert Somborn. There are many theories about the building's appearance, including Somborn being told "if you know anything about food, you can sell it out of a hat."

7 BULLOCKS WILSHIRE

John and Donald Parkinson designed an art-deco monument to house this upmarket department store, which opened in 1929. The 241-foot tower was paneled with green-tinted copper. Notable customers included Greta Garbo, John Wayne, and Clark Gable.

8 LA COUNTY ART MUSEUM

This site hosted racing and gambling until 1909, when concerned citizens had it recreated as a "cultural center." The museum kept fine art, while the rose garden hid wonders such as a sphere-within-a sphere celestial model, or "armillary sphere."

9 WESTLAKE TAR PITS

Father Juan Crespi wrote of Los Volcanoes da Brea in 1769. By 1901, archaeological specimens were emerging, including the skeleton of a human female in 1914. Trauma to her skull suggests that she may have been LA's first recorded Homicide.

10 PARK PLAZA

Built in 1925, architect Claud Beelman designed the Park Plaza as a lodge for the Benevolent and Protective Order of Elks. A passage of scripture is carved above the entranceway, and sculpted angels look down from the façade.

⑪ MACARTHUR PARK (WESTLAKE PARK)

Westlake Park was established in 1863, with the idea of beautifying the city and providing a "democratic" space that would be available to people from all walks of life. On May 7, 1942, the park took the name of General Douglas MacArthur.

⑫ THE GOOD SAMARITAN HOSPITAL

In 1885, Sister Mary Wood opened a care facility with just nine beds. Briefly known as the Los Angeles Hospital and Home for Invalids, the center was renamed when a good Samaritan donated funding for new property and larger quarters.

⑬ THE MAYFAIR HOTEL

The Mayfair was built in 1926, and its architecture and styling are typical of the roaring '20s—glass etchings, brass fixtures, and grand columns in its lobby. Raymond Chandler lived at the Mayfair briefly before he found success as an author.

⑭ INTOLERANCE SET

The Great Wall of Babylon set was built for D.W. Griffiths' silent epic "Intolerance." More than 3,000 extras paraded past the altar and throne, beneath eight giant plaster elephants. The film—the most expensive ever produced at the time—flopped at the box office.

⑮ CHRIST CROWN OF THORNS

Built in 1858, Christ Crown of Thorns was a Gothic Revival masterpiece, but fell into disrepair after a tree collapsed the roof in the storm of September 1939. A work of leadlight rises above the abandoned altar, depicting the crucifixion and a weeping Virgin.

16 CHINATOWN

The first so-called "China City" was built by American filmmakers, fitted out as a movie set complete with a miniature "Great Wall." It burned down in 1939, and construction of New Chinatown was coordinated and financed by the Chinese American Association.

17 EL PUEBLO DE LOS ANGELES

The El Pueblo de Los Angeles monument marks the spot where the city of Los Angels was founded. A site was chosen by missionary Father Juan Crespi, and a settlement party of just 11 families established the pueblo (town) on September 4, 1781.

18 UNION STATION

Designed in part by John and Donald Parkinson, Union Station was opened in 1939, and cost 11 million dollars to build. Its grand tile and marble waiting room and outdoor garden patios have led to it being called the "Last of the Great Railway Stations."

19 CIVIC SQUARE (HALL OF RECORDS)

The distinctive twin Gothic towers of the Hall of Records rise above a domed skylight some 50 feet across. The glasswork depicts a mountain cave overgrown with plants and wildflowers, and a waterfall chandelier hangs over the lobby.

20 ANGEL'S FLIGHT

The Los Angeles Incline Railway was built in 1901, earning the title of "world's shortest railroad." Renamed "Angel's Flight" in 1912.

21 BRADBURY BUILDING

The Bradbury was commissioned by Lewis L. Bradbury. It is most remarkable for its interior—a sky lit Victorian court with cage elevators, marble staircases, and ornate ironwork railings, all inspired by the futurist writings of Edward Bellamy.

22 LA PUBLIC LIBRARY

Bertram Grosvenor Goodhue drew on Ancient Egypt to create his high temple-like Central Library. The building is roofed over with a mosaic pyramid and a sculptured torch-bearing hand stands at the apex, representing the scientific "Light of Learning."

23 PERSHING SQUARE

LA's most famous architect, John Parkinson, redesigned this site in 1910, adding a grand fountain supported by concrete cherubs. In 1918, the park was renamed after General John J. Pershing, and it played host to recruitment rallies throughout WWII.

24 RKO THEATRE

The Hillstreet Theatre opened in March 1922. When a high-level merger created the Radio-Keith-Orpheum Picture Company in 1928, it was renamed the RKO Theatre. It seated nearly 3,000 and hosted live vaudeville shows, as well as film.

25 LOS ANGELES EXAMINER

This building, opened in 1914, served as headquarters for the Los Angeles Examiner. On January 15, 1947, the Examiner was first to break the story of a young woman found butchered in Leimert Park—an Examiner reporter christened her "the Black Dahlia."

26 MAIN ST TERMINAL

Also known as the Pacific Electric Building, the Huntington Building, or simply 6th and Main, this rail and bus terminal was completed in 1905. For more than four decades, the nine-story structure was regarded as the largest west of the Mississippi.

27 LA COLD STORAGE CO.

The Los Angeles Cold Storage Company built its first ice production plant in 1895. Feeding the growing city meant keeping produce fresh, and the six-story 4th Street warehouse was constructed, with more than a million cubic feet of freezer space.

28 4TH STREET VIADUCT

Built in 1931, the 4th Street Bridge replaced the last remaining wooden bridge over the LA River. It exhibits a range of architectural styles, from Beaux Arts in its four concrete towers to Gothic Revival in its porticos, lighting standards, and railings.

29 6TH STREET VIADUCT

The 6th Street Viaduct was the last of LA's grand river bridges to be built, connecting the Downtown and Boyle Heights areas when it opened in 1932. Two thirds of a mile long, its twin steel arch design comes from the Classical Moderne School of architecture.

30 NATIONAL BISCUIT COMPANY

Edmond Jacques Eckel was commissioned by the National Biscuit Company to design their New Cracker Bakery in 1924. The building was completed the following year, standing seven stories tall and coming in at a cost of two million dollars.

GOLDEN FILM REELS

There are 50 Golden Film Reels hidden throughout the city, and each one is labeled with an actual noir movie title from the era. For example, "Sunset Boulevard" is a 1950s American film noir directed and co-written by Billy Wilder, staring William Holden and Gloria Swanson. This section of the guide provides precise locations for all 50 reels.

To help you on your quest, set a custom destination for each of the areas we have marked on our map. Doing this will direct you toward the location via the mini-map. Using a trip skip is the quickest way to reach your waypoint, so keep your partner with you.

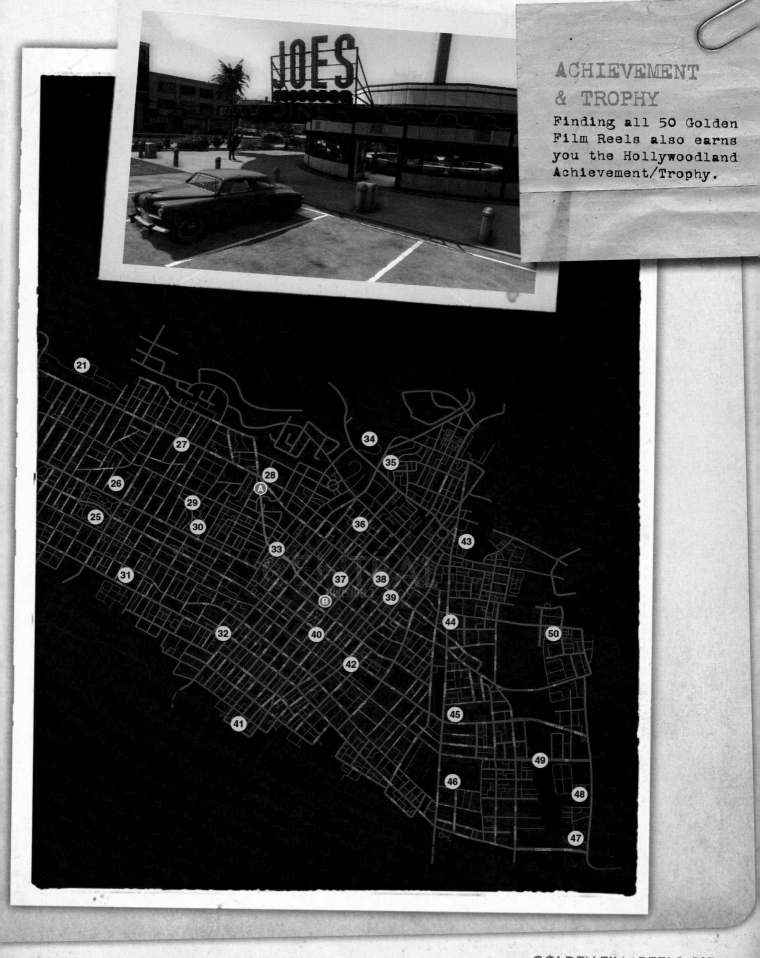

① THE BIG SLEEP

In Hollywood, under a small water tower at the west end of Hollywood Blvd, where the trolley tracks loop for a turnaround.

② THE LETTER

Just north of the Crossroads of the World in Hollywood. From Selma Ave, climb the first set of stairs on your left to reach the hidden film reel on the second level townhouse porch.

③ BRUTE FORCE

In Hollywood, just above the first "l" in "Hollywood" on the in-game map. Find the short dead-end road west from Schrader Blvd. The film reel is on the sidewalk between the end of the short residential road and a public football field.

④ NIGHTMARE ALLEY

Find the two-story shopping area, just north of Franklin Ave in Hollywood, near the Ivar Ave intersection. Enter the alley on the west side of the shops. The film reel is at the end of a narrow walkway and beside some dumpsters. Look below the captain character on the Capt'n Saltee potato chip billboard.

⑤ WHERE THE SIDEWALK ENDS

On the ground behind the large column at the entrance to The Palladium theater on Sunset Blvd, between Vine St and El Centro Ave. Currently on the marquee: The Big Sleep and The Lady From Shanghai.

6 GILDA

Behind the Circle K gas station in Hollywood at the intersection of Cahuenga Blvd and De Longpre Ave. Look on the ground, between two large palm trees

7 IN A LONELY PLACE

Find the Hawaii Mini Golf course on El Centro Ave in south Hollywood. The film reel is on the eighth tee.

8 ODD MAN OUT

On the back porch of this turquoise bungalow in the neighborhood off of St Andrews Pl (located at the end of the "d" in "Hollywood" on the in-game map).

9 THE NIGHT OF THE HUNTER

Find the south entrance into the Hillside Motel's courtyard. Then look on the ground in the northeast corner of the motel's pool.

10 THE SPIRAL STAIRCASE

In a small park beside Samuel's Delicatessen, off of Santa Monica Blvd in Hollywood. Look in the grass near a birdbath.

11 THE WOMAN IN THE WINDOW

In a subdivision off of Lemongrove and Wilton Pl. Look on a picnic table in a central courtyard amongst some "modern" homes with blue, orange, or green trim.

12 SUNSET BOULEVARD

In a courtyard on Melrose Ave. Look on the ground by a tree in front of a small strip shop.

13 THE NARROW MARGIN

Find the brown stucco mansion with a red tile roof on the corner, then enter the driveway from the east side. The reel is on the ground by a garden fountain behind the detached garage.

14 WHITE HEAT

On the second floor walkway of a two-story apartment building between Mariposa and Alexandria Avenues. To reach the walkway, climb the set of stairs on the south side of the two-tone green building.

15 CROSSFIRE

Find the Southwestern Motors filling station on the corner of Melrose and Heliotrope Drive. Head between the station and the adjacent All Purpose Mechanical Repairs garage to approach the outer wall of the LA Speedway where a transfer trailer is parked. The film reel is in front of a side door.

16 M

On the ground next to a see-saw in the small backyard of a white, one-story home. Look for the nearby two-story green house (it's much easier to spot) in the neighborhoods between Clinton St and Rosewood Ave.

17 THIEVES' HIGHWAY

On the counter of Joe's Drive-In Diner on Maplewood Ave. The reel is beside the register, near the main entrance.

18 THE KILLERS

In the northwest corner of the construction house at the corner of 1st St and the main southern entrance into the Elysian Fields housing development (an unnamed street).

19 THE LADY FROM SHANGHAI

On the pitcher's mound of a baseball field in Wilshire.

20 THE THIRD MAN

Find the park on Hoover St in Wilshire, then follow the ascending dirt path at the north end of the park to reach the overlook. Find the reel on the ground between the first tree and the row of park benches.

21 SHADOW OF A DOUBT

Inside the small hangar at the Wilshire airport.

22 LAURA

On the edge of a picnic table in a small Wilshire children's park.

23 THE SET-UP

Find the beige two-story house with blue trim in the neighborhood between Berendo St and New Hampshire Ave, just south of 6th St. The film reel is on the back porch.

24 THE KILLING

Find the large cathedral (First Congregational Church) on the corner of 6th St and Hoover St. The film reel is on the covered walkway on the west side of the church.

25 NIGHT AND THE CITY

In the MacArthur Park pond, on the island/gazebo. The water is only knee deep, so just wade through to reach the reel.

26 THE BIG CLOCK

On the front porch of the white house (address 131) found on the winding unnamed street between Grand View St and Alvarado St in Wilshire.

27 THE NAKED CITY

Find the two-story building on the corner of Bonnie Brae St and Beverly Blvd. This large sky blue house with dark green trim is hard to miss. The film reel is on the lower, wrap-around porch on the east side of the building.

28 THIS GUN FOR HIRE

On the wooden scaffold in a construction area. Use a car to smash through one of the entry gates.

29 SWEET SMELL OF SUCCESS

Under a shelter at the base of a deep building foundation; a construction project in a residential backyard.

30 RIFIFI

On the front porch of a modest aqua/turquoise home on the corner.

(31) MURDER, MY SWEET

In an underground parking shelter. Find the stairs in a courtyard area between stores within the borders of Burlington and Beacon Avenues, and 9th and 8th Streets. Head down the stairs to the lower level and find the film reel next the tree in the middle.

(32) THE BIG CARNIVAL

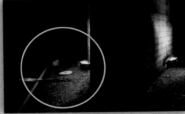

On the back porch of a two-story gray house near the corner of Figueroa and 9th street. The back of the house faces a small public parking lot with an attendant in a booth.

(33) MILDRED PIERCE

This is the hardest film reel to find. When you go to the location of the map icon, you find yourself standing in the middle of a stretch of 4th Street with no film reel in sight. That's because it's under your feet. Enter one of two train tunnel entrances a few blocks away to the northwest (A) or southeast (B). Midway through, you'll find the reel at a fork in the path.

(34) KEY LARGO

On the side porch of Ira's ranch house from "A Different Kind of War."

(35) LEAVE HER TO HEAVEN

Enter the abandoned public pool from the east entrance, then follow the path to the right and around the building. This leads to a small yard, which can be seen through the fence from the street. The film reel is on the ground in this yard.

36 THE MALTESE FALCON

On the ground in the fenced lot behind Bakers, off of Grand Ave.

37 THE BIG HEAT

At the top of the world's shortest railroad. The top is a block northwest from Angel's Flight on 3rd St in Central.

38 ANGELS WITH DIRTY FACES

Go to the construction site on the corner of Spring and 2nd Street. The reel is on a wire spool table inside a small shelter on the raised scaffold platform that surrounds the site. Find the ladder to reach the upper tier under the platform on Spring Street. Climb to the top of the ladder and enter the shelter to the left to claim the reel.

39 STRANGERS ON A TRAIN

Find the Bell Systems Depot building at the end of a large corner parking lot (with a guard booth) on the corner of Main Street and 2nd St. Enter the half-wall walkway near the guard booth and follow it to the Bell Systems building. The reel is on the covered walkway.

40 TOUCH OF EVIL

On the rooftop of the Los Angeles Theater on Broadway. Run around the block to the alley on 6th St that leads to the back of the theater. Look for the LA Theater marquee on the back wall near some stairs. Climb the pole in the corner (to the right of the marquee), then ascend the ladders to the rooftop. The reel is toward the front of the theater.

㊶ OUT OF THE PAST

On the ground, in the middle of the large, shadowy interior of the trolley station.

㊷ THE ASPHALT JUNGLE

On the walkway where tracks converge, at the end of the shelters on the train platform.

㊸ PICKUP ON SOUTH STREET

Inside Union Station, on the gift shop counter on the right.

㊹ HOUSE OF BAMBOO

Enter the Western Iron Works factory by driving through the parking barricade arm on the south side. Continue into the factory, then climb up the catwalk stairs on the left in the rear of the building. At the top, turn right to find the film reel.

㊺ SCARLET STREET

On the ground in an alley nook off of Palmetto St.

46 DETOUR

On the tracks between two unhitched railcars, by a train terminal shelter near Bay St.

47 NOTORIOUS

On the floor, inside an open office inside a lumber warehouse. From the easternmost road in LA, follow the dirt path to the warehouse, then enter through the southern opening and find the office on the right.

48 DOUBLE INDEMNITY

Follow the easternmost street in LA north from Olympic Blvd to reach a military base on your left. Crash the gates in a car, then drive behind the first large building on your left. Follow the sidewalk around to the fork, then continue to the right. The film reel is on a table in what appears to be an outdoor military firing range.

49 BODY AND SOUL

Hidden on the lower level of the 7th Street bridge. Drive down into the flood control channel below the bridge, then find the stairwell inside one of the bridge supports on the west side of the channel. Follow the stairs up to the first level. Just past the vagrants, you'll find the film reel on the right, along the north edge of the bridge.

50 GUN CRAZY

At the eastern end of 1st St in Central LA, follow the trolley rails as they veer right off the street and come to loop around a small water tower (adjacent to a much larger water tower behind a brick wall). The reel is on the ground, in the shadow of the small water tower.

NEWSPAPERS

There are a total of 13 newspapers that can be found in crime scene areas around LA. Each one also reveals another segment of "the story behind the headlines" that adds detail to the unraveling mystery. Collected newspapers are tracked in the case logs on the desk in the Cases menu where you replay past missions or enter Free Roam mode.

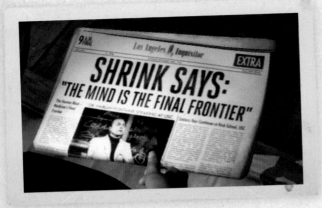

NEWSPAPER (1)

HEADLINE: "SHRINK SAYS: The Mind Is The Final Frontier"
DESK: Patrol
CASE: "Upon Reflection"

DESCRIPTION

In the alley of the first crime scene, on a crate along the right wall before you reach the bloody door. Pick up the paper and press the button indicated onscreen to trigger a cinematic sequence that reveals more story details.

NEWSPAPER (2)

HEADLINE: ALIENIST FONTAINE. Provides Help To Troubled Vets
DESK: Traffic
CASE: "The Driver's Seat"

DESCRIPTION

On the Black's Residence dining room table in "The Driver's Seat." Headline provides another important piece of background information.

NEWSPAPER (3)

HEADLINE: SHRINK TO THE STARS. Promises Mental Breakthrough
DESK: Traffic
CASE: "A Marriage Made In Heaven"

DESCRIPTION

In Ray's Café, on the bar in front of Dudley Lynch. Once again, you get a snippet of interaction between Dr. Harlan J. Fontaine and Courtney Sheldon, the USC medical student.

NEWSPAPER (4)

HEADLINE: DOPE FLOODS STREETS. Cops Chase War Surplus Contraband
DESK: Traffic
CASE: "The Fallen Idol"

DESCRIPTION

On the workbench in the storage alley of Silver Screen Props. Examining the story behind the headline triggers the scene of a meeting between Courtney Sheldon, the young medical student at USC, and the infamous mob boss Mickey Cohen.

NEWSPAPER (5)

HEADLINE: FAMILY BURNT TO DEATH. Cops Say House Fire Deaths Are Suspicious
DESK: Homicide
CASE: "The Red Lipstick Murder"

DESCRIPTION

Just inside the front door of the Henry Residence, on the floor. Once again Harlan Fontaine plays a prominent role as he discusses a house fire with a very disturbed man calling from a payphone.

NEWSPAPER (6)

HEADLINE: MISSING MORPHINE. Cops Say: Goons Fighting Dope War
DESK: Homicide
CASE: "The White Shoe Slaying"

DESCRIPTION

Inside Stuart Ackerman's shack at the Hobo Camp. In the cinematic, Courtney Sheldon, the medical student we've seen earlier, pleads for help from Jack Kelso, his platoon sergeant during the war and now an insurance investigator.

NEWSPAPER (7)

HEADLINE: MICKEY COHEN. Heir Apparent To Bugsy Siegel
DESK: Vice
CASE: "The Black Caesar"

DESCRIPTION

On the desk directly across from the one with the ledger in the Ramez Removals warehouse. The story behind the headlines fills in another important part of the backstory.

NEWSPAPER (8)

HEADLINE: ALIENIST FONTAINE. Working Selflessly To Help The Infirm
DESK: Vice
CASE: "The Set Up"

DESCRIPTION

On the training table in the American Legion Stadium. Cinematic shows another meeting between Dr. Fontaine and Courtney Sheldon, the medical student at USC.

NEWSPAPER ⑨

HEADLINE: LAPD VICE SCANDAL. Could Go All The Way To The Top
DESK: Vice
CASE: "Manifest Destiny"

DESCRIPTION

In the shootout alley at Haskell's Finest men's Wear, near the first fallen shooter. It triggers a peek behind the scenes at some of the city's most powerful men, including the mayor, the district attorney, and the police chief. The Vice squad's Chief Detective also makes an appearance.

NEWSPAPER ⑩

HEADLINE: HOUSING DEVELOPMENT BURNS.
Ex Servicemen Irate As GI Houses Razed
DESK: Arson
CASE: "A Walk in Elysian Fields"

DESCRIPTION

At the Morelli house fire, in the right corner of the front lawn, near the end of the privacy fence. You learn a little bit more about the persons responsible for these fires.

NEWSPAPER ⑪

HEADLINE: SUBURBAN REDEVELOPMENT.
Fund Promises 10,000 New Homes
DESK: Arson
CASE: "A Polite Invitation"

DESCRIPTION

On Leland Monroe's desk when you raid his mansion and have him on the floor bleeding. Headline reveals an argument between Sheldon and Fontaine that ends in murder.

NEWSPAPER ⑫

HEADLINE: CRUSADE AGAINST CORRUPTION.
Petersen Pledges To Clean Up LAPD
DESK: Arson
CASE: "A Different Kind of War"

DESCRIPTION

At Rapid Exterminators. It's on the front counter in "A Different Kind of War." The cinematic reveals the event when Cole loses an old war buddy.

NEWSPAPER ⑬

HEADLINE: "THE FACE OF PROGRESS"
Says Mayor Of Developer Leland Monroe
DESK: Arson
CASE: "A Different Kind of War"

DESCRIPTION

On Harlan Fontaine's desk at the crime scene in Dr. Fontaine's Surgery center. Important story details are revealed in a conversation between Fontaine and Monroe.

HIDDEN VEHICLES

There are 15 rare Bonus Vehicles hidden in specific locations around the city. These are unique rides and do not appear in the general vehicle population; they can only be found behind the blue garage doors marked **Angel City Security**.

These garages gradually appear on the map in three groups of five as your rank increases. Each garage reveal happens at Rank 3 (35 XP), Rank 10 (315 XP) and Rank 15 (665 XP). This chapter provides vehicle specs and locations in the order they appear in the Showroom.

100% COMPLETION

There are a total of 9
vehicles in the game.
The 15 hidden Bonus
Vehicles are part of
this total. Collectir
all 95 vehicles adds
15% toward 100%
completion of the ga

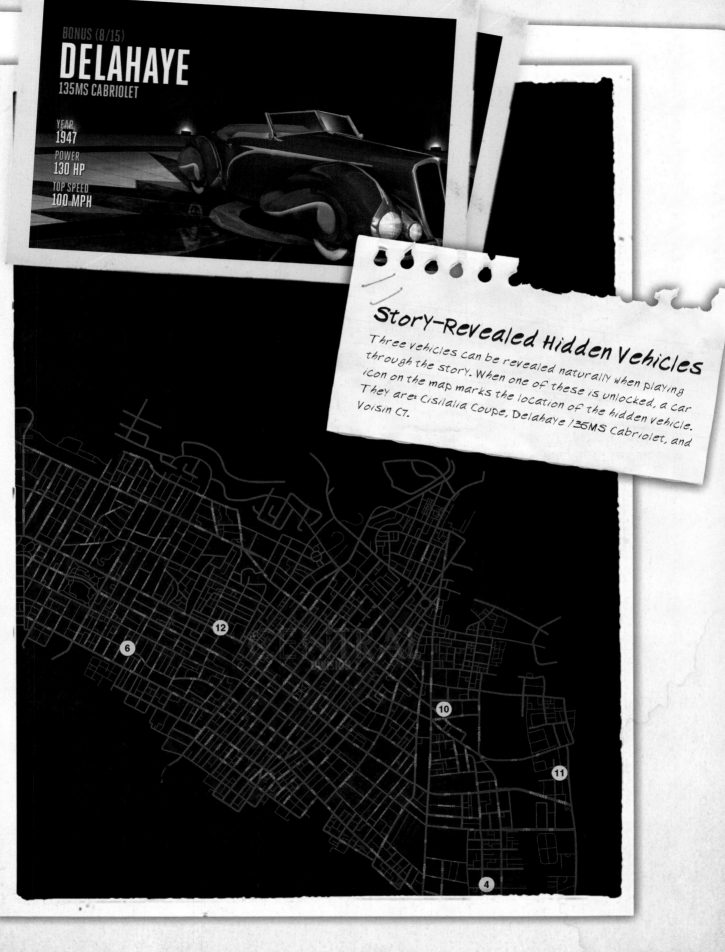

BONUS (8/15)
DELAHAYE
135MS CABRIOLET

YEAR
1947

POWER
130 HP

TOP SPEED
100 MPH

Story-Revealed Hidden Vehicles

Three vehicles can be revealed naturally when playing through the story. When one of these is unlocked, a car icon on the map marks the location of the hidden vehicle. They are: Cisilalia Coupe, Delahaye 135MS Cabriolet, and Voisin C7.

1 CADILLAC TOWN CAR

Showroom Number	1/15	Power	135 HP
Year	1936	Top Speed	93 MPH

In Hollywood, in the garage of the Alaco station on the corner of Bronson Ave and Fountain Ave.

2 CHRYSLER WOODY

Showroom Number	2/15	Power	135 HP
Year	1946	Top Speed	96 MPH

In a residential garage, at the end of a long alley just west of where 7th and Vermont Ave meet in Wilshire. The door is on the side of the garage facing the house.

3 CISILALIA COUPE

Showroom Number	3/15	Power	69 HP
Year	1939	Top Speed	109 MPH

In the Wilshire Division 7, hidden behind the Angel City Security garage door of an Alaco station on the corner of Vermont Ave and Melrose Ave. Use the unlocked door adjacent to the garage door to enter the facility and take the vehicle. This is also the vehicle presented to you during "The Studio Secretary Murder" when you chase James Tiernan out the back of Rawling's Bowling Alley.

4 CORD 810 SOFTTOP

Showroom Number	4/15	Power	170 HP
Year	1936	Top Speed	130 MPH

Find the old two-story building on Mateo Street pictured here. The hidden vehicle is in a sublevel, behind the building at the bottom of a sloped driveway. Enter the garage through the adjacent door with the golden knob. You can also find one of these during the Street Crime "Hotel Bandits." It's presented as a nice chase vehicle selection.

5 DAVIS DELUXE

Showroom Number	5/15	Power	60 HP
Year	1948	Top Speed	100 MPH

Inside a residential garage on the border of Hollywood and Wilshire, near Melrose Ave between Wilton Place and Western Ave. Use the side door with the golden knob to enter the garage.

6 DELAGE D8 120

Showroom Number	6/15	Power	120 HP
Year	1937	Top Speed	110 MPH

Find the L-shaped alleyway between Beacon Ave and Union Ave at the southwest side of Central. The car is hidden inside a garage in this alleyway, behind Meisner's Hardware Store. It can be accessed via a side street off Union Avenue, located at the bottom of the 13-story building.

7 DELAGE D8 120 S POUTOUT AERO-CO

Showroom Number	7/15	Power	120 HP
Year	1937	Top Speed	110 MPH

In a residential garage in east Hollywood. Look for a gray building with white trim that belongs to a nice mansion with matching colors. Located on the corner of Normandie Ave and Lemongrove Ave.

8 DELAHAYE 135MS CABRIOLET

Showroom Number	8/15	Power	130 HP
Year	1947	Top Speed	100 MPH

Adjacent to the shopping area where you find the fourth Film Reel. This plush home has an attached garage. A pair of short but full willow trees beside the driveway obscure your view of the garage door, baring the **Angel City Security** logo. The vehicle inside is also the one used in the Unassigned Case "Secret Keepers." To access it here, head to the back parking lot of the Automobile Club of Southern California, where the case sequence is triggered.

9 DUESENBERG WALKER COUPE

Showroom Number	9/15	Power	265 HP
Year	1934	Top Speed	140 MPH

On the corner of Santa Monica Blvd and El Centro Ave in Hollywood. Enter a garage behind the Automobile Club of Southern California

10 PHANTOM CORSAIR

Showroom Number	10/15	Power	190 HP
Year	1938	Top Speed	115 MPH

Inside the Alaco station, on the corner of 3rd Street and Traction Avenue in Central LA.

11 STOUT SCARAB

Showroom Number	11/15	Power	85 HP
Year	1936	Top Speed	75 MPH

Look for a five-story, rectangular, gray building with an **Angel City Security** garage to the east of the Los Angeles River, between 4th Street and Whittler Blvd. This vehicle is in the garage in the back of the building, under a small tin roof.

12 TALBOT GS26

Showroom Number	12/15	Power	190 HP
Year	1948	Top Speed	125 MPH

Hidden inside an Alaco station in Central LA, on the corner of 6th Street and Bixel St.

13 TUCKER TORPEDO

Showroom Number	13/15	Power	166 HP
Year	1948	Top Speed	120 MPH

Hidden in a small brick garage that's wedged between two buildings in Wilshire, on the corner of Oakwood Ave and Western Ave. The garage is tough to find from the road; you must access the back parking lot to reach the garage door.

14 VOISIN C7

Showroom Number	14/15	Power	93 HP
Year	1938	Top Speed	89 MPH

In an Alaco station in Hollywood on the corner where La Brea and Sunset Blvd meet. You can also find it in the Hall of Records parking lot during "The Quarter Moon Murders." You drive this car to chase the fleeing suspect in the Street Crime "Paper Sack Holdup."

15 FORD H BOY

Showroom Number	15/15	Power	130 HP
Year	1932	Top Speed	115 MPH

Inside a Wilshire Alaco station, on the corner of Beverly Blvd and Kingsley Dr.

This compelling app features a unique, interactive street map of 1947 Los Angeles. It's an entertaining and indispensible resource for tracking your progress as you uncover the secrets of L.A. Noire. Locate and acquire all of the following collectibles with this essential digital companion—for iPhone and iPad:

- **50 Golden Film Reels**
- **30 Landmarks**
- **15 Hidden Vehicles**
- **20 Shields—a DLC Exclusive**

Download the BradyGames Official L.A. Noire App from the iTunes App Store today!

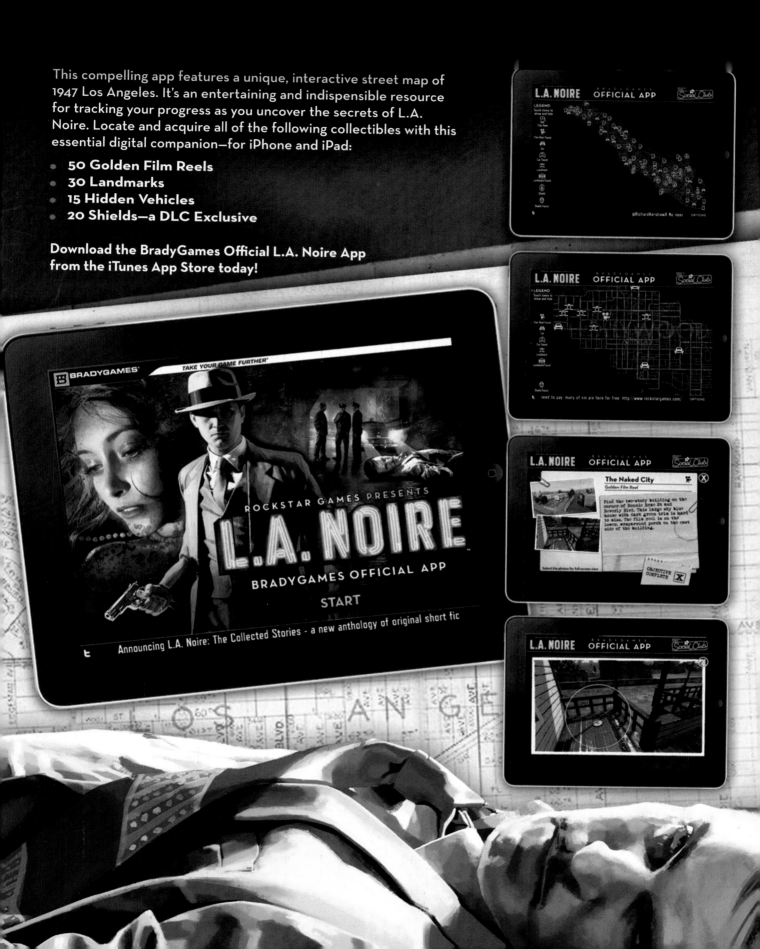

ROCKSTAR GAMES PRESENTS

L.A. NOIRE

SIGNATURE SERIES GUIDE
By Tim Bogenn & Rick Barba

DK/BradyGames, a division of Penguin Group (USA) Inc.
800 East 96th Street, 3rd Floor
Indianapolis, IN 46240

ISBN 10: 0-7440-1254-6
ISBN 13 EAN: 9-7807440-1254-5

Printing Code: The rightmost double-digit number is the year of the book's printing; the rightmost single-digit number is the number of the book's printing. For example, 11-1 shows that the first printing of the book occurred in 2011.

14 13 12 11   4 3 2 1

Printed in the USA.

ACKNOWLEDGEMENTS

All of us at BradyGames would like to thank Sam and Dan Houser, along with the entire Rockstar team in New York. Special thanks to Mark Adamson and Ramon Stokes for their outstanding support and cooperation throughout this entire project.

BRADYGAMES STAFF

PUBLISHER
Mike Degler

DIGITAL AND TRADE PUBLISHER
Brian Saliba

EDITOR-IN-CHIEF
H. Leigh Davis

LICENSING MANAGER
Christian Sumner

OPERATIONS MANAGER
Stacey Beheler

CREDITS

SENIOR DEVELOPMENT EDITOR
David B. Bartley

BOOK DESIGNER
Tim Amrhein

PRODUCTION DESIGNER
Tracy Wehmeyer

DIGITAL SUPPORT
Tim Cox

TRANSLATIONS
Chris Hausermann